$6.00
15

The Bedside Guardian 39

The BEDSIDE Guardian

A selection from
The **Guardian**

1989 ~ 90

Edited by

NICHOLAS DE JONGH

With an introduction by

JEREMY ISAACS

Cartoons by

STEVE BELL

CLARA VULLIAMY

&

MARK HADDON

FOURTH ESTATE • LONDON

First published in Great Britain by
Fourth Estate Limited
289 Westbourne Grove
London W11 2QA

Copyright © 1990 by Guardian Newspapers Ltd

British Library Cataloguing in Publication Data
The Bedside Guardian – 39
1. English essays – Periodicals
082'.05 PR1361

ISBN 1-870180-07-0

All rights reserved. No part of this publication may be reproduced, transmitted or stored in a retrieval system, in any form or by any means, without permission in writing from Fourth Estate Limited.

Typeset in Garamond by
York House Typographic Ltd, London W7
Printed and bound by Clays Ltd, Bungay

CONTENTS

EDITOR'S NOTE

THIS year's *Bedside Guardian*, number 39 in the annual series which is even longer running and certainly more worthwhile than Agatha Christie's murder play *The Mousetrap*, looks a touch different and is a touch different. After many years of publication by the old publishing house of Collins, which was recently absorbed into Rupert Murdoch's international maw, we have changed horses and set ourselves up with the young and independent publishers Fourth Estate, which is not only publishing the *Bedside Guardian*, but a series of *Guardian* books under its imprint as well.

Fourth Estate has given us a new design which still allows the essential bedside frame to be displayed. Last year I gave the book a facelift, arranging the pieces chronologically, with the writer's name and date of original publication printed before rather than after the article. The idea was to make the book more suitable for reading straight through from beginning to end and to give it more of the feel of the original newspaper. A selection of photographs by *Guardian* photographers were also included for the first time.

These changes were popular and have been retained. This year we have also included biographical notes on the contributors, on the grounds that readers may wish to know a little more about the journalists who are employed by or write regularly for the *Guardian*. The faces behind the bylines turn out to be a solidly conventional lot – save perhaps for a few like our India correspondent, Derek Brown, whose early career details read like an exotic and sensational spoof, but are, I am assured, authentic.

The pieces selected for this book are regularly chosen as a result of appeals by its editor for submissions and his own independent culling process. As the *Bedside*'s editor for two years, I have been persistently importuned by people whose moral purpose was to make it between hard covers. It has been a pleasure to comply, though not, on occasion, to refuse. No more of all that.

Bedside editors, I believe, should be treated like bed linen and changed regularly, thereby ensuring that not too many of the same people and the same sort of things end up on these sheets. But I hope I leave the *Bedside* still looking what it has so long been – bedworthy.

Nicholas de Jongh

INTRODUCTION

PILLARS of society become columns in the *News of the World*. Today's newspapers wrap tomorrow's fish and chips. Can journalism ever last?

I doubt there are enough fish in the sea to be wrapped in today's newspapers. It is not just that, at this end of the market, there are more of them around than there used to be, but some of them bulk larger and larger year by year – never mind the quality, feel the weight. Newsboys and newsgirls nowadays heft these massive tomes, fleshed out with magazines and tabloid supplements, along the avenue and up the stairs. Once read or whipped through, encased now in thin black plastic, or squared into bundles bound in string, yesterday's hot news is off in bulk to the recycling depot. Who can possibly remember what any of last year's lot said?

Yet some of it will last, and deserves to. Auden on Yeats, forgiving him and his opinions:

> Time, that with this strange excuse,
> Pardons Kipling and his views,
> And will pardon Paul Claudel,
> Pardons him for writing well.

It is not the fact that sticks in the memory, but the word that preserves it. Faced with an ampler plethora of print year by year, the reader chooses quality. Good writing sells good newspapers. Not mannered elegance, mind you; the conscious essayist's day has passed, at least for me. It is the reporter, with alert eye and retentive ear, who can arrest the passing scene best for us, and give it meaning. Capturing just a fraction of that changing scene is the reporter's trick, and a hard trick at that, as A.J. Liebling noted. But when it is achieved, newspapers more than hold their own, though by no means easily, against the eyes and ears of radio and television.

The *Guardian* has always had writers I have enjoyed reading. It still does, and should bind them to its bosom, with the hoops that really matter: ample space, bold display, gentle subbing.

And what a year they have had to write about. 1992 nothing, 1990 has turned out to be the year that has changed our lives. Berlin, Moscow, Prague and Bucharest succeed each other on the foreign editor's assignment slips. Tiananmen stemmed the flow of things in China, and turned our perceptions of what was happening there. Even Albania has got into the act. And, in South Africa, Nelson Mandela walked free. Compared to these, poll tax, riot and all, looms small, and questions of leadership at home seem only light relief. Useful, then, to have the right man or woman on hand. In these page writers such as Ian Black, inside the intifada, Bill Webb on Prague and the writers' part in events and in bringing them about, Angella Johnson in South Africa – that was a week that was – more than justify their assignments, and their preservation now between hard covers.

Not much of a year for jokes, though Andrew Rawnsley and Nancy Banks-Smith keep their ends up. The Cameroons had something to celebrate; so did the Guildford Four. Ian Gow, making the first televised speech in Parliament, made good jokes at his own expense. He has not lived to see them memorialised here. Aids claimed its victims; Ian Charleson played a great Hamlet. Here Richard Eyre nobly sings him to his rest.

Before next year's great events and little surprises are all over us, it is good to look back and be reminded of what has passed, but need not altogether fade.

JEREMY ISAACS
August 1990

The Bedside Guardian 39

THE GREEN NINETIES – WITH CONDOMS

Owen Bowcott
19 June 1989

Beneath the pyramid-shaped main stage the crowds stamped and swayed in the full heat of the day to the rhythm of African drumbeats.

Stewards passed forward cups of water to the parched. Occasionally the crowd passed back over their heads the limp, sprawling bodies of those who had fainted.

A police helicopter circled far above the Glastonbury Festival. At moments the sweet scent of cannabis wafted through the air.

But there were other intoxicating substances – not least the spirit of ecological triumphalism. 'This is the end of the grey eighties,' Derek Wall, one of the Green Party's three national speakers, enthused into the microphone.

'If you thought the sixties were good, you will find them a pale imitation of what the nineties will be. We have trashed the Democrats, we have given Maggie and Neil a shock. This is where the green nineties start.'

Sunday was the festival's African music day. Free Mandela and Freedom, the crowd chanted in unison with the plainsong group, Amubutie.

Police officers – the first year they had been invited on to the 500-acre site – patrolled the fields. Occasionally they danced, self-consciously, for a short time.

On the greenfield site, in the calmer, higher fields, a band of American-Indians from Quebec was practising a ritual dance on neatly patterned piles of beans, red lentils and corn.

In the Speakers' Forum a woman, in a headscarf and skirt, was addressing the subject of Sex and Relationships in the Age of Aquarius. 'Men of my age, in their forties, often open the door for me,' she told listeners. 'It's a gesture left over from the age of patriarchy.'

Back on the valley floor throngs of pedestrians kicked up the dust from dry tracks. A troop of Hare Krishna devotees passed by chanting with fixed smiles on their faces. There were cries of 'Acid', 'Afghan Hash' and 'Speed' as drugs dealers operated besides the busiest paths.

Altogether police arrested about 300 people for drugs offences during the three-day festival. The police helicopter picked one man from the site suffering from a heart attack and flew him to hospital at Taunton.

Just beyond the perimeter fence groups of full-time travellers had settled in a field intended for car parking. In the narrow country lanes, teams of police with hired tow trucks were removing vehicles from verges and embankments. By Sunday morning their tally had reached 512 cars and vans.

A local farmer sat at the entrance to his field selling one-gallon flagons of home-brewed scrumpy. 'It's six per cent proof,' the farmer claimed. He proffered a trial glass. It tasted deceptively smooth. Another customer grinned. 'There's brain damage for you,' she said.

'Sometimes at night people are completely lost and can't find the way back to their tents so we put them up,' said Penny Mellor of Festival Welfare Services, operating out of a farmyard barn.

'There are always a few people with drug overdoses or relationship breakdowns. But we are also giving away lots of condoms. We have all sorts of types for people to choose from.'

ACADEME NINETIES – WITH CHAMPAGNE

John Vidal
21 June 1989

At 3.30am the bright young things are momentarily wilting. In the half light of the long hot coming morning the bra straps of Academe are showing and the dickie bows droop. A cavalry officer, scarlet of tunic and red of face, is getting shirty; down by the river the punts still glide with their loads of snogging couples, but a girl sobs in the grass and small groups huddle round glowing braziers, exhausted shapes by exhausted bottles. Good morning Trinity College, Cambridge.

It's the lull before reveille. Within the hour the great quadrangle is buzzing purposefully again. Kilts swing g'day, hired ball gowns rustle their goodbyes. There's a mist above the meadow and steam rising from the disco.

A hot-air balloon is there and miraculously gone. In the mock casino, which the can-can dancers have long since deserted and where breakfast (croissants and yoghurt) is being served, a Fellow leans to his young companion at the bar and says he has a picture of Tolstoy in his rooms, 'because as he got older he became more energetic and crazy'. Exactly. Champagne under the arm, they teeter off as the old honeyed stones light up around them.

Trinity wears its erudition lightly for the May Ball. Two thousand two hundred go to play all night or as long as they can remain half-conscious in tight social uniform. For many the aim is just to stay until the survivors' photograph – a six o'clock snap of the detritus. Look, mum, I was there.

Clare balls may have a reputation for being sweet and couply, Jesus for getting closed down by environmental health officers at 2am, but Trinity – to be precise the First and Third Trinity Boat Club May Ball – is the real games locker, full of toys and trifles for growing-up souls, lavishly conceived, lushly appointed and set in Cambridge's most exalted college where the tally of Nobel prizes exceeds all of France's.

So it's bubbly and Southern Comfort *gratis* and everything round the theme of America, probably because so many other colleges had this year chosen the French Revolution. In the manicured fields, a dozen students have spent hours building a Tiananmen Square Liberty lookalike. Poor Liberty. She's atrophied and frumpy, wears a grotesque Stars and Stripes, and her crown's upside down. One don reckons it's an entry for the £250 Rouse Ball mathematics prize under the title of Chaotic Behaviour of Nonlinear Pyramidical Systems.

Back in the Great Court, under severe portraits of distinguished old boys (Newton, Macaulay, Tennyson, Byron *et al.* – but no Anthony Blunt or Prince Charles) a trad band warms up. But real, throbbing life is in the largest of the many tents, where couples feverishly battle with their clothes to keep up with the nine fine bands. Jazz, jive, Irish, folk and Caribbean combos play elsewhere, apprentice jugglers, unicyclists and fire eaters – two each from Queens' and Trinity – parade around.

In 10 hours, £200,000 goes up in fireworks and frivolities and there are only half-serious accusations of profligacy from the guests. 'Too much, too much,' cries a third year from Magdalene – but she's referring to her partner's advances by the riverside.

The river, though, does give unrivalled views of the gate-crashers, beaching their punts and clambering out. If you must crash Trinity don't do what one fool did yesterday morning, which was to break into the Master's chambers and try to sneak through. The Master, it seems, was there and the police were called.

And don't try climbing over the roofs. It's not worth it. But what is? A one-night advanced course in establishment potty training – guaranteed preparation for all British social functions – does not come cheap.

Besides, the benefits are incalculable; the story goes that Domesday has come and the dons of Trinity have drifted into the Great Court to meet their maker. Montagu Butler, the then Master, is pushed forward to greet him. 'Perhaps I may most fittingly voice Your welcome,' he says, 'since You are Yourself, in a sense, a Trinity Man.'

AMERICA SWITCHES BACK TO THE FIFTIES

Martin Walker
21 June 1989

There is a curious nostalgia in America these days for the 1950s, for its fashions and furnishings, its pruderies and primness, and for some of the mental furniture of the period. There are thoughtful editorials about an age of innocence before the sixties came along to spoil it, and for a time when the Cold War might have been blowing a blizzard, but Americans were still sure they could win, and that even after a nuclear war there would be enough of them around to enjoy the victory.

The fifties was the decade when people could talk of 'the American century' without embarrassment, when American politicians and diplomats slid easily into assumptions of moral superiority over the enfeebled old European powers with their anachronistic colonial wars in Algeria and Cyprus, and when the US economy still accounted for about 40 per cent of the global economic activity. No wonder so many Americans look back with longing.

There are instructive parallels to be drawn between then and now. Years of arms race and hostility had given way to a thaw as the reforming Mr Khrushchev denounced Stalin's crimes and promised a new liberalism. Now, the Thirty Years War of US domestic politics appears to be over, or at least to be shifting into a different and rather familiar phase. The Kennedy-induced Passions of the Sixties, Nixon's Betrayals of the Seventies, Reagan's Crusades of the Eighties, all seem to be giving way to the genial bi-partisanship of George Bush (although his Bad Cops at the Republican National Committee keep up the old vendettas).

After three decades of obsession with the occupant of the White House, America's political classes have turned their attention to the affairs and the sleaze of Congress, just as they did in the 1950s when the Eisenhower Presidency seemed too boring to inspire headlines.

All this is fairly harmless musing, rather like an intelligent party game, so long as no one takes it seriously, or seeks to push the joke too far. Enter *The American Spectator*, a magazine which I have learned to relish for the literacy of its writing, and the breezy extremism of its conservative opinions, and the occasionally skewed shafts of its supposedly comic writers.

When its jokes do come off, they can profoundly increase the gaiety of nations. Consider one recent stunt, when its editor, Mr R. Emmett Tyrrell, concocted a postcard of the famous memorial Mount Rushmore, with its monumental carvings of Presidents George Washington, Jefferson, Lincoln and Teddy Roosevelt, and inserted a bust of Ronald Reagan on a small space in the middle. He handed this doctored postcard, not originally intended for publication, to the then President Reagan at a party. Everyone chortled, spiffing wheeze, have another glass . . .

But then the jape took off. Other conservatives, who lack Mr Tyrrell's taste and his wit, took the matter seriously. Funds are being raised and geologists have been despatched to the mountain to assess whether the Old Thespian man indeed be hewn from the living rock, or whether a specially carved nose and thrusting jaw could somehow be bolted to the cliff-face, just below a patch of reddish vegetation which the faithful deem heaven-sent to be Mr Reagan's hair.

And now another of the jests in Mr Tyrrell's magazine seems poised to assume a life of its own, and cavort around the fevered imagination of the American Right like a Frankenstein on heat. The latest issue plunges us once more into the comforting dust of the fifties attic: Eisenhower on the golf course; ponytails and Davy Crockett coonskin hats; interstate highways snaking across the land; Sony and Honda unheard of.

Then the author of the latest Modest Proposal, one P.J. O'Rourke, who has made a career of bringing beer-belly sensitivity to the Preppy magazines, gleefully plunges the needle into the outrage vein by demanding a return to the fifties in tooth and claw, and bringing back McCarthyism.

The list of enemies; the Un-American Activities Committee; the chilling rhythm of that monosyllabic probe 'Are you now or have you ever been . . . '; the friendships and marriages tested and the careers and lives blown apart by a Congressional subpoena: O'Rourke evokes it all. And he has a jolly wallow in memory's swamp, playfully running through a McCarthyite hit list of roastable Reds for the 1990s, ranging from eco-friendly Meryl Streep to the editorial staff of the *New York Review of Books*.

No doubt it would be wiser to dismiss this as a joke in bad taste, except that I was recently reading through the small print of Britain's new, improved Official Secrets Act, and my flesh is still creeping. For the past four years or more, ever since it became plain that Mikhail Gorbachev was seriously intent on reforming and liberalising the Soviet system, I have had a recurrent nightmare. This is not something that wakes me up screaming, but it does sometimes keep me awake and brooding.

It is a harmless enough vision, a simple graph with two lines on it. The first line is human rights and liberties in Britain, which started out at the top of the graph, and the second line is for the same rights in the Soviet Union, which started out at the bottom.

During those past three years, the Soviet line on my graph was inching steadily upwards. It jumped with the release of Dr Sakharov, with the amnesty for political prisoners, and is now moving strongly towards the British line, which was drifting steadily, depressingly down. There was the union-bashing at GCHQ and the Miners' Strike, the otiose *Spycatcher* business, and now with the new Official Secrets legislation the British line has taken a plunge downwards.

My fascination with the possibility that these two lines might actually one day intersect, or even cross, is now being joined by a new concern about the thrust of events in America, and the dangers of self-delusion.

So I too have been playing this game of historical parallels to come up with a simulacrum, or perhaps a precursor, of the Bush era. Where else have we seen this triumphalist approach to the rest of the world, based on the conviction that history was marching on our side?

Where else have we seen a policy of detente graciously followed, on the grounds that the Cold War was over because the other side was faltering?

Where else have we seen trade deficits and budget deficits and economic decline all steepening, while the political leaders blithely insist that all is going splendidly?

Where else have we seen life expectancy start to fall, largely because of growing despair and deepening drug abuse among the lower classes?

Where else have we seen a mounting public disillusion with a political system that is seen to be corrupt, run by politicians who almost never lose office?

The sobering answer, however much it may offend the new McCarthyites, is the hollow empire of Leonid Brezhnev's Soviet Union.

PRAISE THE LORD AND PASS THE BALLS

Frank Keating
24 June 1989

Whither the Wimbledon we knew and loved to hate? Where have all the young brats gone? Gone to Sunday school every one.

Messrs Connors and McEnroe are here again, sure, but now only as geriatric talismans to remind us of the long ago when – you canNOT be serious – a simple game of tennis could readily degenerate into, well, the very pits of the world.

Michael Chang, the 17-year-old Californian and the new champion of France, is the pale, frail, gentle standard-bearer of the new breed. Oh, yeah. Him and whose army? God's, as a matter of fact.

A new sporting movement has been taking over the locker rooms of America. Cynics call it the 'Jocks for Jesus' brigade. It is gathering ground, less flamboyantly but just as diligently, in Britain, too. They are athletes prepared to speak up in the name of the Lord – to offer up their successes, and failures, to Christ, He who gave them their cross-court backhand return in the first place.

Chang looks an unlikely prophet and missionary. He is shy, thin, and managed and 'minded' by his Mom, Betty, who doles out the pocket money. At tennis, as Paris showed us, he has the patience and the feathery touch of a champion swordsman, and the stamina, heart and grit of a fighting terrier. He has not long been a committed Christian.

His parents are both research chemists who settled in the United States via Canton and Taiwan. Michael was born in 1972, in Hoboken, New Jersey, birthplace too of another devoted public missionary, Francis Albert Sinatra.

Michael was still in his cot when Jimmy Connors had his first tantrum on Centre Court. His other minder, apart from Mom, is Brian Gottfried, the US pro who was at the other side of the net, of course, when McEnroe made his pong about the pits. So everything sort of ties in together. No wonder Michael has turned to God.

When he won so dramatically in Paris, he stood on the victory rostrum, a tiny waif with a massive cheque – and a microphone. He thanked everyone, as is the custom, then added: 'And thank you to the Lord Jesus Christ, without whom I would be nothing.' He then told the packed amphitheatre, the smartest turnout in world tennis: 'And please pray for the people of China.'

Gerald Williams, the BBC tennis correspondent, was there, and deeply moved. 'I'm glad I wasn't "on mike". It was so touching I would have been lost for words.

'It was remarkably brave of Michael in the first place, mentioning Our Lord, Jesus. Because he's so well aware how all the jaundiced cynics in sport have been trying so desperately and cruelly to undermine the other young American tennis star, Andre Agassi, for being such a publicly committed and devout Christian. They try to say that Agassi's committed Christianity proves he's the ultimate phoney.'

The winner's speech in Paris also heartened the Reverend Drew Wingfield-Digby, a former first-class cricketer and now the full-time director of the British Christians in Sport movement. 'Sport, at last,' he says, 'is waking up to the idea that the Christian ministry is now a totally acceptable thing.

'Michael Chang's courage at standing up to be counted was gloried in by all of us. Mind you, in Britain our ministry, culturally, has a more modified way of expressing our devotion and commitment.'

Williams, an affable and expert courtside summariser with the O-O specs and the ears that out-Tobyjug Julian Wilson's, is on the executive committee of Christians in Sport, and has had to suffer derision himself over the years.

'Sport just can't seem to cope with people being high-profile Christians. It scares sport. The cynics feel you're putting yourself up as some sort of higher being, blessed supernaturally by Christ. In fact that's totally false and hogwash, for any true Christian by definition puts himself up as a "lower being". We know we're humble, human sinners. But humility disturbs sports people, doesn't it? So they attack Christian sportsmen as being weirdos or cranks or something.'

But Wingfield-Digby, determined, devoted man of goodness and a highly infectious giggle, and the zeal of the likes of Williams, can put out quite a few teams of accomplished sportsmen committed to Christ: the footballers Glenn Hoddle and Garth Crooks, for instance; the hurdler-soldier Kriss Akabusi; county cricketers like Roland Butcher, Graham Cowdrey, Mark Frost, Duncan Martindale and Vic Marks; at golf, Bernhard Langer and Larry Nelson; rowing, Martin Cross . . . all happy to offer up their talent to the Lord.

How, though, did he square Christianity with the obvious 'hostility' of competition? I tried him on I Corinthians 9:24: In a race only one of the runners wins a prize; run then, in such a way as to win the prize. And even I Timothy 4:7: Exercise thyself rather unto godliness; for bodily exercise profiteth little.

He laughs: 'Hebrews, chapter 12, is my favourite text. I paraphrase: "Run with perseverance and patience the race that God has set out before you." That is the crucial thing for sportsmen at any level of accomplishment, isn't it? Participation in, and celebration of, a God-given thing, which after all is what a game is, isn't it?'

But do Christians in Sport pray to win? Graham Cowdrey, for example, lists in the Cricketer's Who's Who his habit of 'Saying a prayer at the top of the pavilion steps every time before I go out to bat'.

Wingfield-Digby chortles on: 'It's not just the winning or losing that's remotely important in this context. When someone like Michael Chang nobly gets up in public and says, "Jesus helped me win," he's not invested himself with supernatural "coaching" – in fact he's just setting himself up to be rubbished by you blokes, if the truth was told. No, the committed Christian knows only too well – think of Gethsemane and the Cross – that losers are just as important as winners.

'The point of Christianity in sport is that, sure, you can want to win, indeed you play to win,but you can also cope with losing and you must give thanks for that, too.'

Gerald Williams has seen more than 30 Wimbledon finals. His favourite remains the first one to be played on a Sunday – after a downpour on the Saturday, in 1972. Smith v. Nastase. The epic. Stan, of course, was a devout Christian.

Williams remembers it well. 'Stan was woken first thing in the morning at his hotel by a call from an outraged English vicar berating him, fire and brimstone stuff, for agreeing to play on the Sabbath. He gave him a really hard time.

'Stan is such a solid Christian that he was more than disturbed by the call. He was really shaken. He thought it through and, of course, decided he could handle it, God would understand.' God did, too – and must have enjoyed the glorious five-setter as much as anyone. Especially as His man won.

Williams, for all his devotion to tennis and Wimbledon, is also disturbed by the All England Club's recent knee-scrape to US television, which is why the final is now held on a Sunday. 'It means I have to be at Wimbledon well before 10 o'clock. It might be the Wimbledon final, but I tell you what, quite honestly, I'd much rather be praying to the Lord in my church on a Sunday than watching a Wimbledon final. '

But another victory for Master Chang a fortnight tomorrow would be more than a slight – and very Christian –

compensation. Praise the Lord and pass the new balls, please.

BRIEF HISTORY OF HARD TIMES

Ellen Walton
9 August 1989

Nearly a quarter of a century ago, a young woman student committed her future to a 23-year-old scientist just setting out on his career. He had already been diagnosed as suffering from a muscle-wasting disease.

'We did not know what the future would hold,' says Jane Hawking. Doctors held out little hope for the young physicist she married.

Today, the world knows her husband as Professor Stephen Hawking, the scientist who has succeeded in extending the limits of the human mind in space from the prison of a severely crippled body.

Professor Hawking can only speak through a computer using an artificial voice, but his ideas have reached out to people worldwide. His book, *A Brief History Of Time* (Bantam Press), has been a best-seller for more than a year.

'This year has been the crowning glory of all Stephen's achievements,' says Jane Hawking. The Hawkings were just celebrating his honorary degree from Cambridge University, a rare accolade for one of its own dons, when the announcement came that the Queen had made Professor Hawking a Companion of Honour.

Over the years honours have come from all over the world. But when Jane Hawking is asked if she can share in her husband's triumph she feels she has to say no. 'I am not a scientist,' she says.

But that does not make her triumph any the less, for without her Professor Hawking's success would not have been possible. Before their marriage, Stephen, depressed by his illness, was working only half-heartedly. 'Without the help that Jane has given I would not have been able to carry on, nor have the will to do so,' he said when success began to come.

Four years ago, Jane Hawking was at his bedside when he was hovering between life and death from a critical attack of pneumonia. Once again she tried to give him the will to live.

'The future looked very, very bleak,' she recalls. 'We didn't know how we were going to be able to survive – or if he was going to survive. It was my decision for him to have a tracheotomy. But I have sometimes thought – what have I done? What sort of life have I let him in for?'

For 20 years Jane Hawking had coped single-handedly at home, looking after a severely disabled husband – Professor Hawking has motor neurone disease – and bringing up their three children. 'There were days when I felt sometimes I could not go on because I didn't know how to cope. I have been desperate for a home help but they have never been forthcoming from the authorities.'

It became clear that Stephen would need round-the-clock nursing. Jane was absolutely determined that her husband, who had spent weeks in intensive care, should come home to live with his family. It was the only way he could continue his work as a physicist.

But the National Health Service offered only care in a residential home. Otherwise it was a case of only seven hours' nursing help a week in the Hawkings' own home plus a couple of hours' help with bathing. 'There was absolutely no way we could finance nursing at home,' says Jane Hawking.

She turned to America for help. Her husband's fame brought from an American foundation the £50,000 a year needed to make it possible for Stephen Hawking to return home and finish the book that has become an international best-seller.

Today, some British charities contribute to the cost of his care – though one or two have suggested pulling out now that the book is a success. Jane Hawking, who pays tribute to the quality of his hospital care, is bitter that a health service to which her husband has contributed a great deal in taxes should not provide nursing at home. She is hoping to start a campaign for people in a similar predicament to her husband, to get the NHS to fund complete home nursing.

And she is battling not just for Stephen. She is very conscious of the fact that if he had been an unknown physics teacher he would now be languishing in a residential home. 'Think of the waste of talent,' she says.

So much of Jane Hawking's energies have inevitably had to go into looking after her husband that she acknowledges there has been a real problem in establishing an identity of her own.

'When I married him I knew there was not going to be the possibility of my having a career, that our household could only accommodate one career and that had to be Stephen's. Nevertheless, I have to say I found it very difficult and very frustrating in those early years. I felt myself very much the household drudge and Stephen was getting all the glittering prizes.'

After their marriage in 1965 Jane completed her degree in Spanish at London University and the couple decided they should not wait before starting a family.

Robert, now 22, and Lucy, 18, were born in the next few

years. The couple were living in Cambridge, where Stephen had embarked on research. Within a few years of their marriage he was in a wheelchair. He could neither help with nor play with the children. 'I think that has been very hard for Stephen,' says Jane.

'I absolutely adored my children and would not have wanted to farm them out to anybody else, but Cambridge is a jolly difficult place to live if your only identity is as the mother of small children. The pressure is on you to make your way academically,' she says.

So she embarked on a PhD in medieval languages. 'It wasn't a very happy experience. When I was working I thought I should be playing with the children, and when I was playing with the children I thought I should be working.' Tim, now 10, was born after she finished the PhD.

So in many ways, she has had to be both mother and father to her children. Even the hours she spent as a schoolgirl on the cricket pitch of St Albans High School, alternately bored to tears and terrified of the cricket ball, were to have their value.

'I have been the one who has to teach my two boys how to play cricket – and I can get them out!

'I think inevitably you get to realise there is some sort of pattern. I would not like to put it in any philosophical terms but I have to say that at times things have looked absolutely dire for us and then something has come out of those crises.'

She cites the time in 1985 when Stephen came home from hospital, too weak and ill to work on his original research. Unexpectedly a new computer for the disabled arrived from America with a complete word programme for Stephen to try out. 'Someone had heard of his plight.'

He found he could operate it with a small hand movement. 'It was the ideal situation. He needed to learn to use the computer and the book needed revising.'

A Brief History Of Time, has been much praised for being lucid and concise. 'You think very carefully about what you are going to say when time is of the essence,' says Jane Hawking.

She is convinced that it was his illness which helped Professor Hawking to scale the heights of success. 'He had to work to be able to support me. Then he discovered he had an almost obsessive interest in this branch of physics he had gone into. But he had to work very hard to develop his powers of memory so that he could grasp the enormous maths equations and hold them in his head.

'But then his condition enabled him to develop his mental capacity further than anybody else because it was totally unrealistic to expect any physical help from him in the home or with the children. And he put his time to best advantage. It wouldn't necessarily have happened if things had been different.'

Today, she has work of her own which she loves. She has a part-time job teaching French and Spanish to sixth formers. 'It is fulfilling a part of me that I feel has been suppressed for a long time and the marvellous thing is that it is totally compatible with what goes on at home.'

This has been an exciting and enjoyable year for the Hawkings. 'I am just terribly happy for Stephen because so much seems to have fallen into place,' says Jane. 'I think he is very happy about it.'

The various honours are icing on the cake. 'I wouldn't say that is what makes all the blackness worthwhile. I don't think I am ever going to reconcile in my mind the swings of the pendulum we have experienced – from the depths of a black hole to the heights of all the glittering prizes.

'I think for me the satisfaction is a sense of fulfilment that we have been able to remain a united family, that the children are absolutely superb and that Stephen is still able to live at home and do his work.'

MANN'S EGO

Desmond Christy
18 August 1989

Thomas Mann And His Family
by Marcel Reich-Ranicki (Collins)

On August 2, 1914, Kafka wrote in his diary: 'Germany declared war on Russia. Swimming lesson in the afternoon.' A hard entry to match? Not if you are Thomas Mann. Exiled in California from Hitler's Germany, he wrote, on August 6, 1945: 'Went to Westwood to buy white shoes and coloured shirts. – First raid on Japan with bombs utilizing the energy of the split atom (uranium).'

Maybe only with hindsight does this entry seem so funny and so awful, but even if Thomas Mann knew how terrible atom bombs were, the entry might have read the same. Thomas Mann's ego was a Big Bertha of an ego compared to the under-developed little fire-crackers that fizzled around him and which sometimes were extinguished altogether. His was the full-blown ego of a full-blown genius. As Marcel Reich-Ranicki puts it, you have to go back to Goethe to find another such beast. But just as Goethe the God turned out, when a new unbewitched generation of young writers started attacking him, to be more human and therefore a little closer to the rest of us, so it is time to dislodge Thomas Mann from his pedestal.

Who better to give this work to than Marcel Reich-Ranicki? In West Germany, partly in admiration and partly in mockery, he is known as the Pope of literary criticism, and – not just because he was born in Poland – more of a Pope John-Paul II than some Vatican Council liberal. As a Jew he might have died when the Warsaw ghetto was herded towards the extermination camps but he escaped and was protected by a brave man who was forever losing his nerve and asking Reich-Ranicki to find another hiding place. Our author kept translating the German papers for him and telling him stories from his great hoard of yarns and thus, like Scheherazade, he survived to tell the tale. And to become a prominent Communist, to rethink that allegiance and thus to be disgraced in the eyes of the Polish state and, eventually, to become the highly respected literary critic of *Die Zeit*, which is based in Hamburg, and to edit the literary section of the *Frankfurter Allgemeine Zeitung*, which treats culture as seriously as the British treat cricket. This book is principally made up of some of the essays he wrote in *Die Zeit* and the *FAZ*.

It has long been Reich-Ranicki's view that Thomas Mann needed to be 'demonumentalised' and, with the gradual release of Mann's diaries, starting 20 years after his death, that has been made easier. If we believe the Pabst, Thomas Mann, after a lifetime spent playing the embodiment of German culture, has arranged an autopsy, let the mask of dignity slip to reveal the human weakness and the feet of clay.

What do we learn? Thomas Mann wore silk underpants (but he changed back to cotton), suffered from constipation, recalcitrant bowels, a tendency to diarrhoea, had an irritated bladder, lots of colds, lived in fear of losing his mind, got terribly agitated when he read reviews of his work, had terrible tremblings and heart palpitations. Less trivially, we learn a bit more about his homosexuality. He claims this was a love like any other, but Reich-Ranicki doubts whether it was consummated like any other love. Most of all we learn about the sheer size of Thomas Mann's ego. The rest of the world, including his children, never seemed to be important.

Mann was always writing letters to people telling them how good their novels were. It was no doubt a pleasure to receive them – unless you lived long enough to discover in his diaries what he really thought. He could write to his son Klaus that his novel *Mephisto* 'gave me great pleasure. It is light-footed and amusing, brilliant, in fact, often very funny and stylistically very delicate and clean.' As Reich-Ranicki says: 'there are good things to be said about *Mephisto*' (and an awful lot of bad things, too) 'but "stylistically delicate and clean" it most certainly is not.'

You cannot accuse Reich-Ranicki, though he is the foremost fan of Thomas Mann's work, of shirking the work of showing us the unattractively human side of his hero. Yet most of us would be less forgiving of Mann's politics – however unreasonably – than Reich-Ranicki, preferring perhaps to side with Klaus. 'It was the immature and unstable Klaus Mann who in 1933, when Hitler established his dictatorship, was not fooled for one moment, who, unlike too many émigré writers, did not harbour the slightest illusions.'

This is also a book about the Mann family, but though the talent of Thomas Mann completely dwarfs brother Heinrich and his children, most of our sympathy may be with them. Huge claims have been made for Heinrich Mann's fiction, especially in East Germany, but who reads him now? Reich-Ranicki's chapters on Heinrich do not so much deal the death blow to his reputation as put another row of nails in his coffin. It is a merciless but, alas, judicious display of what Reich-Ranicki can do when he feels the need to cut a reputation down to size.

His account of Klaus Mann's tragic career is kinder and,

as always, the quotations he uses are perfectly chosen. Klaus Mann was trebly afflicted: 'He was homosexual. He was a drug addict. He was the son of Thomas Mann.' It is hard to say which was the worst of these afflictions. Of his homosexuality he wrote: 'One cannot serve this Eros without becoming a stranger in society as it is today; one cannot commit oneself to this form of love without incurring a mortal wound.'

Worse, perhaps, he loved his sister Erika, that amazing character who was a brilliant cabaret artiste, at home in journalism, creative writing, the cinema and the theatre. When she came back to Germany after the war she was in an American army uniform and is said to have been 'as beautiful as a war goddess and as domineering as an Amazon'. She was also married for a time to Gustaf Gründgens (thinly disguised in Klaus Mann's novel *Mephisto*).

If Erika might seem to overburden one family with talent, she is not the end of it. Still writing is Golo Mann, one of West Germany's most brilliant and independent-minded historians. His achievement is all the more impressive when you consider how grim his childhood was. It may seem strange that Golo Mann can offer so gentle a judgement of the industrialists who financed Hitler as the following: 'It is not as easy to emigrate with steel mills as it is with the manuscript of a novel.' But this is the same Mann who, Reich-Ranicki tells us, wrote of Heine: 'Closest to the truth are those who deal lightly with it because they know it is inexhaustible.'

There is a sense of this in Reich-Ranicki too. You look in vain here for any big, interesting theorising about Thomas Mann's work, perhaps because this collection of journalism is not the place. In the end you grow a little weary of what sometimes reads like a rather superior account of the Royal Family of German culture. But let's hope that this book, so well translated by Ralph Manheim, precedes other collections of Reich-Ranicki's essays.

NO TRUST IN NUDITY

Paul Brown
24 August 1989

Nude bodies on a Dorset beach have forced a vote of 1,780,672 National Trust members.

Believing bequests to the trust are being used for what is termed 'trendy purposes', 10 members have asked it to ban nudity as 'contrary to the spirit of the trust'.

But the trust has been advised that it cannot stop people taking off their clothes on its property.

Instead, it has put up notices warning visitors that 'nudists may be seen beyond this point'.

Corfe Castle Estate, in Dorset, was bequeathed to the trust in 1985, along with three miles of beach at Studland Bay used by naturists.

Under pressure from the anti-naturist lobby, the trust put up warning notices. But a spokeswoman for its council, Miss Emma O'Reilly, said: 'We have more complaints about noisy radios and dogs.'

Of 1,200 people interviewed on the beach, 11 per cent objected to litter, 13 per cent to dogs, and only 2 per cent to the nudes. Some 16 per cent said they had come specifically to take their clothes off.

Miss O'Reilly said: 'We try to be fair. Simple nudity is not a problem if people take their clothes off in secluded bits of our properties where they can be private. In any event we have been told we cannot get a by-law to stop it, so we tolerate it. We are not a moral arbiter.'

Mr Rowland Hitchcott, the proposer of the resolution, said: 'Nudist areas effectively restrict access to these areas for certain groups – such as families, youth groups and individuals – who wish to avoid them. This is contrary to the spirit of the trust.'

Mr Ernest Stanley, controller of the Naturist Foundation, said nude bathing was for families.

'It is only voyeurs, male exhibitionists and parties of homosexuals who make a thundering nuisance of themselves that give rise to misgivings in ordinary decent people.'

Mr Hitchcott's resolution before the November annual meeting is likely to get a large majority. He claims the wording would force a nudity ban. The trust disagrees, but recommends members vote for it. Thereafter, the council says, nudists can carry on as before.

PARADISE LUST

Peter Lennon
26 August 1989

When the French sit down to dine in a restaurant they talk about culinary experiences. When the English sit down to dinner in France they reminisce about being sick. Or about sex.

At the table next to us in a restaurant near Le Touquet, one of the favoured staging posts for the English in pursuit of new game in the Pas de Calais – cheap real estate – two middle-aged couples sat down to *hors d'oeuvres* of *escargots* and *confit de canard*. In the small smoke-beamed *auberge* they spoke loudly and confidently.

The younger woman said to her husband in a complaining voice: 'Well, how would you like to have spent the night curled around a toilet basin?'

'How dreadful for you, Cynthia,' the elder woman said, her tone distant with indifference.

'Jack was sick too,' the woman countered, indicating the cool lady's husband.

Jack ducked his bald head over the dish: 'I found myself drinking a bottle of claret virtually alone,' he explained.

His wife gave him a silent stare.

The elder of the couples, Jack and his commanding wife, were apparently toying with the idea of swapping Malaysia for Le Touquet, although they had complaints about coachloads of visitors arriving at the golf course and a problem with the new, surly dark chap who had replaced their usual caddy.

When the waiters served the *fricassée de volaille de Licques à la compote d'oignon*, the second man poked his plate and said: 'You realise it's not just the listeria. The shells of free-range eggs are so thin they also absorb poisonous metals.'

'You know the story of . . . er . . . ' Jack began.

'You won't remember again,' his wife told him confidently.

'Casanova,' he remembered, pleased. He leaned greedily across the table and said: 'I often wondered how he did not get more women into trouble; it was because he would have five dozen oysters first which are, er . . . '

'Aphrodisiacs is the word, Jack,' said the other man.

'Aphrodisiacs. But they also contain a metal which renders the semen, you know . . . '

'Really?' the younger woman exclaimed.

Jack avoided his wife's eye.

The younger lady then recalled a night when she visited Jack's rubber plantation. 'The service is so good and the

Burmese girls are so accommodating and so lovely. Did you have a massage that night, Jack?'

Jack evaded the question.

'They *are* pretty little things,' his wife commented. Her voice, like a steel comb, raked the words mercilessly.

The English, desirous of establishing a profitable base, first laid siege to Calais in 1346. The stained-glass window over the main staircase of Calais Town Hall commemorates their departure. A little prematurely, it appears.

The English in all shapes and sizes have for the past 18 months been swarming into the area from Calais by Le Touquet to Berck-Plage, and inland along the valley of the River Canche, whose deceptive dreaminess conceals a tendency to be profligate with its waters. Come winter new home buyers may have to have their dinner rowed into their picturesque home.

Abandoning a country where a house costs a lifetime's income, the English have become inflamed by stories of tidy *firmettes* with a generous portion of land going for less than a one-room studio in London.

Le Touquet was always an English resort, with its pony club, 38 tennis courts, golf course and discreet casino. But now the British appear intent on owning it outright. According to *Libération* they have bought the casino and the golf course, and British restaurateurs are buying up châteaux to convert into luxury hotels with tennis courts. There are at least three new high-rise luxury *appartement* blocks under construction in Le Touquet; they have reassuring names, such as Cambridge and Wimbledon. At Etaples, the railway station serving the area, 'Way out' is on an equal footing with '*Sortie*'.

Despite the Mayor of Honfleur (further along the coast by Le Havre) making a name for himself crying out that the English invasion will kill French towns, turning them into museums alive only in the summer, the French in the Pas de Calais are being very accommodating with the new arrivals.

Heavy industry and mining in northern France have been running down for some years, bringing unemployment to around 20 per cent. Work on the Channel Tunnel and the line for the TGV high-speed train has already reduced the unemployment figure appreciably. One source of prosperity is that the industries associated with the Tunnel, finding land unavailable in Kent, are shouldering their way into the Pas de Calais and setting up there.

At the Mairie, the deputy mayor, Michel Sajot, told me there was no animosity towards the invaders. (It helps that many of the *firmettes* for sale had little market attraction before the English became interested.) M. Sajot is concerned with a port through which a little over three million 'travellers and excursionists' passed in 1972, a figure which rose to nearly nine million last year.

But in Calais, redeemed by the Tunnel, the attitude is more than just placid anticipation of lucrative fall-out.

The attitudes of the British and the French to the Tunnel are so opposite you would imagine the exits were in different hemispheres. The French are astonished by the reactions of the English, which they see as ranging from deep scepticism to genteel rowdyism.

But with all the opponents of the Tunnel in Calais now converted to ardent supporters – according to the local *Voix du Nord* – the French are whipping themselves up into orchestrated joy. This has been expressed notably by launching a Tunnel wine, a full-bodied Chinon symbolising the attachment of France to England. They chose a Chinon because this was the area favoured by the Plantagenets when they reigned over Britain and France.

On September 16, a general meeting of Calais Parent – Teacher Associations passed a resolution urging that an experiment in teaching English in three nursery schools should be extended to all the nursery schools in the region. 'Calais will soon be a bilingual town,' they declared.

'It is true the English do not have a very good reputation in France at the moment – because of the football fanatics,' *Libération's* correspondent in the region, Florence Deltombe-Traullé, told me. 'But the people who are the most anxious are the English in Le Touquet who are afraid their refined community will be diluted by all those vulgar English coming in by the Tunnel.'

Le Touquet is the luxury end of the market. But estate agents report a daily stream of English, young, old, yuppie or modest tradesmen, pouring in looking for bargains. This is the result of sophisticated co-operation between British and French estate agents advertising property in both countries.

The plan is to have a second home in France, which they all hope to get for a snip before the Chunnel is completed and then, when England becomes permanently moored to the Continent by the Tunnel, settle down to become continentals with a base in England or flog the property for a fortune in 1993.

But house buyers will find that whatever bargains existed a year ago are no longer for the having. The French quickly caught the British disease of property inflation. The estate agents are becoming positively alarmed by the success of their marketing technique.

'The message to take back', Mlle Véronique Libbrecht of the Somaprim Agency in Le Touquet told me, 'is that there are no houses or apartments going for £40,000–£50,000. Any going at that price need extensive and costly reconstruction.'

Somaprim has already decided on its prices strategy for two years hence: flats which cost £70,000 this year will be at least £98,000 in 1991.

At La Madeleine near Montreuil-sur-Mer, where Jean Valjean became Mayor before being flushed out by Javet, I met two English ladies with a mission to purchase a property for a friend in Zimbabwe 'in case there was trouble'.

They were staying at an hotel, the Auberge de la Grenouillère on the banks of the Canche. La Grenouillère was founded by an English woman, Miss Hahn, in the twenties. In the *livre d'honneur* there was an entry from a briskit Englishman: 'We have motored here from Le Touquet and enjoyed a pleasant dinner. We are now going sand yachting.' It was dated July 18, 1939.

La Grenouillère is the kind of place that fulfils all the South-East Englanders' dream of England with French advantages. On the banks of the Canche beside a wood, it has the tame, damp charm of Kent and the luxury of France.

La Grenouillère has only four bedrooms. The chef and his wife, M. and Mme Gauthier, deciding that they are more restaurateurs than hoteliers, close hotel and restaurant on Tuesdays and Wednesdays. In theory you can have a gourmet meal (one star in the Michelin) for under £20. But one look at the menu and the wine list and prudence is generally undermined.

One of the ladies from Norfolk would only identify herself discreetly as being 'connected with the medical profession', her friend said she 'did nothing'. They made La Grenouillère their last stop after a wearying seven days' house-hunting. Disillusionment already weighed down their spirits.

'What we have seen has been pretty cruddy so far,' the medical lady said. 'The buildings are flimsy. Most of the places we saw were all clay lump, wattle and daub; the plumbing primitive, the upright beams wormeaten. The English steaming over here are in for a shock. The French are not stupid, you know, they know how to charge. If you found a house for £50,000 you would probably have to spend as much again to make it habitable.'

I told them about the Canche and its wayward waters. 'We noticed many of the houses had these pretty little moats around them!' they said, alarmed.

There are other hazards buying property in France. The French *notaire* will not, as a British solicitor will, conduct a search for you; you are buying with invisible risks. And a minority worry: the French won't allow you to leave all your property to the cats' home – children are considered to have precedence over eccentricity.

'Will you be using the Tunnel?' I asked. 'With fire, terrorists, rats and rabies?' the medical lady said. 'Certainly not!'

France may have an attraction for the British beyond that of an apparently advantageous property market. When you arrive at Calais, take the train along by Boulogne to Etaples, the stop for Le Touquet, and on to Berck-Plage: at every stage in tabac, café, hotel or toilet there is a dreamlike tidiness. There is no garbage strewn about, not even fast-food refuse to any extent at the railway station; the second-class carriages are polished and clean, the bins unchoked; everywhere shops are clean, doors fit, there is no woebegone trail of fixtures that don't fit; graffiti is not a feature of the area.

There is an eerie abnormality to this country which functions in an orderly, quiet, clean manner, but without any inhibiting sense of being in an over-regimented society as you might have in Germany.

There is also something vaguely familiar about the order and the cleanliness: Britain used to be like this.

As we came out of the hoverport at Dover to board our coach, a quiet weekday at half-past six, there was only a small group in the half-deserted lounge. But like some pushy minority political party, determined to have representation wherever 50 people may gather, there were four lurching lager louts with great packages of beer.

A scuffle broke out between a couple of them and the police. As we watched from the coach a youth began to thrash around among the police. Two of them got him to the ground, handcuffed him and, with difficulty, folded the writhing figure into the back of a police car. A moment later a foot shot over the back seat and appeared through the driver's window.

The youth's mate turned on a police sergeant and made gestures which seemed to express a desire to stick his finger up the sergeant's left nostril, his own nose and mouth working furiously. This one was also flung to the ground, handcuffed and folded with difficulty into another police car.

A moment later a leg stuck out through a side window of the second police car.

As the coach pulled away a shoe and bare ankle signalled from each police car.

'Welcome to Great Britain,' announced the driver.

GRATEFUL DEAD – LIVE

Mike Oldfield
14 September 1989

He's standing in the central reservation of the main drag in Berkeley, California. He's in his mid-twenties, wearing T-shirt, jeans and highway-dusty trainers. Over his shoulders is slung a battered rucksack and tattered sleeping bag. He's holding up his right index finger, pad outwards, and in his left hand is a square of cardboard on which is scrawled: 'From NJ. Need to shake them bones.'

The finger indicates that he wants one ticket; the sign is a line from the Grateful Dead's 'Throwing Stones'. This guy has travelled 3,000 miles for a Dead concert. *And he doesn't even have a ticket*.

The road weaves upwards through the mixed architectural beauties of the spacious Berkeley university campus, Palladian splendour crossed with East German concrete ugly. By the time it reaches the entrance to the Greek Theatre it's obvious that the man with the finger is not alone. Milling happily and gently around are a couple of thousand people, at least half with a finger up and signs that read: 'Buffalo . . . hey now! . . . Chicago . . . I need a miracle . . . Pittsburgh.' They all want to buy. But no one's selling.

That's hardly surprising. The Dead are playing three nights at the Greek, an outdoor amphitheatre with a capacity of around 7,000, at a time when they're usually doing 100,000-seat stadia.

Despite the crowds, it's as peaceful as Sunday afternoon. Across the road a bunch of cops sit on the boots of cars and laugh at private jokes. So the fans are blocking the pavement? They'll all move along when the music starts to a nearby car park where the whole show will be relayed over speakers: hey, now – this is California on a balmy summer's evening and everything's cool . . .

Walking inside the Greek is like falling into a paintbox. Milling in the pit, standing on the steeply banked stone seats, lounging on the grass, is a human oil-and-water light show. Blues and greens and pinks and purples and reds and yellows merge and blur into a sea of colour. Everyone's moving and, with a swish of floor-dusting skirt and a nod of bandana, greeting each other with bounteous hugs and kisses: there are no strangers at a Dead concert. Not so much an audience, more a tribal gathering. A little too alert and prosperous to be mistaken for hippies, they're close enough to the image of the Summer Of Love to qualify as Beautiful People.

In marked contrast to rock custom and practice, where greedy hands rifle the linings of fans' pockets for stray change, the Dead let their fans do most of their merchandising. This provides an income for the thousands who dedicate their lives to joining the long, strange trip that is the Dead's career, an uninterrupted line stretching back to 1966.

Their current status is as one of the Top Five bands in the US and the only one that makes an annual commitment to tour extensively. They amble on stage, no introduction, no fanfare, dressed as though they've come direct from chopping firewood in their backyards. Grey beards and spectacles, bald patches and pullovers, this band is aggressively middle-aged.

But – tup-ta-ta-tup-ta-KRUNG! – music is their elixir of youth! From the first drumbeat, the entire audience dances. The Greek Theatre seethes and shakes and stays that way until the Dead stop playing hours later. The band are merely musicians. The audience is the show.

They came to dance: that's a precise but fair summary of San Francisco's contribution to the history of rock. If you were going to San Francisco in the sixties, you needed more than flowers in your hair; you needed your dancing shoes.

The music scene that led to West Coast/San Francisco/acid rock was set up in 1965–6 to break the mould of a passive audience who sat back and waited to be entertained; but in San Francisco audiences entertained themselves. In these circumstances the deification of the musician simply didn't happen in San Francisco.

Still, musicians were drawn magnetically to San Francisco in the late sixties. And when the Haight-Ashbury hashdream became a smacked-out nightmare and the wilted flower children drifted home, many musicians stuck around.

A surprising number still exist. The Jefferson Airplane have re-formed for an album and tour 17 years after they split into a host of – mostly San Francisco-based – offshoots. Big Brother and the Holding Company lost Janis Joplin before she lost herself and are now performing with an impressive new girl singer. Country Joe is solo and Barry 'The Fish' Melton has a band.

Half-forgotten names jump out of the club ads in local papers . . . Hey, can that be the Daily Flash? Or is it just a bunch of post-punks who've hit on the same name?

From the Paul Butterfield Blues Band (whose debut LP in 1966 is probably still the finest white blues album ever) is guitarist Elvin Bishop. He has a band on the thriving club circuit. The old keyboards player Mark Naftalin has a weekly gig in a bar on Fisherman's Wharf. Harpist Butterfield and his extraordinarily gifted lead guitarist Mike Bloomfield haven't, alas, made it, but Bloomfield's ambitious rock-soul experiment, the Electric Flag, lives on with co-founder Nick Gravenites.

As well as their hangers-on, San Francisco bands have had their casualties. None was more keenly felt than the death this year of John Cipollina, the quintessential Bay Area musician. His band, Quicksilver, were turning down offers of stardom back in '66 and after its dissolution he obstinately remained no more than a musician.

No stretch limos for him. He strolled into the bars and small clubs with his amp and speaker in hand, guitar slung over his shoulder, and performed with maybe a dozen different bands.

Forget Woodstock – just an ill-fated East Coast attempt to steal the spirit of the West that this year was pummelled back into the American consciousness by cynical commercial forces: San Francisco has never been a nostalgia trip and it isn't one today.

Young musicians are neither dominated by the older generation nor cowed by tradition. Old and new coexist peacefully, mutually supportive, each needing the other to survive.

In the Paradise Lounge former Green On Red member Chris Cavacas is jingle-jangling through a set of new songs with his own band. Across the street at Slim's an unbilled Boz Scaggs – whose guitar propelled the early Steve Miller Band before he lost himself in superslick seventies soul – is pumping out Texas jump blues with a ten-piece band. 'Linda Lou', 'Ooh Poo Pah Doo', '634-5789', 'T-Bone Shuffle' . . . they pour out with scarcely a pause to wipe away the sweat. Even when Robert Cray steps up to take over Scaggs's guitar and drip achingly sweet pearls of blues on 'Goin' Down Slow', nobody stops to gawk. They came to dance, not gawp.

Despite their propulsion on to a national stage, the Grateful Dead strictly maintain the San Francisco tradition. They play dance music.

Occasionally guitarist Bob Weir will cock a pose in ironic parody of rock star macho, but most of the audience is too busy to notice. The rest of the band – Jerry Garcia (lead guitar), Brent Mydland (keyboards), Phil Lesh (bass), Bill Kreutzman (drums/percussion) and Mickey Hart (drums/percussion) – barely move at all except to wander offstage between numbers for purposes unknown. None of them speaks to the audience. There are no song introductions.

At the Greek they've got a computerised lighting rig set up so half the beams are aimed at the audience. Night creeps in and the low clouds roll back from the Berkeley clocktower. In the distance a freighter lazily ducks under the amber glow of the Oakland Bay Bridge. In the foreground the audience has become a bubbling cauldron of colour, swirling abstract shapes of light, a fusion of sound and vision in human form.

But the band played on. And on. And on. Three nights. Two sets per night, with a half-hour break between each set. A full three hours of music every night.

And they never played the same song twice. All songs have equal value and appear in no fixed order. No distinctions made between old and new, cover versions or originals, Dead songs or material from solo albums. And they perform them in a totally unique fashion, having over the years abandoned traditional rock structures. They have two drummers who don't play together; a bassist who plays lead lines; a keyboard player who will switch from funky Jimmy Smith organ to flourishes of delicate Keith Jarrett piano. Nominally they have a lead and a rhythm guitarist, but who can tell them apart?

'Not Fade Away' chant the Dead, and the lights swivel out to bathe the audience in blue and purple velvet richness. The audience picks up the beat as a handclap and chants the title-line too. Then the musicians are gone.

When the lights eventually came up, a familiar figure was bobbing and weaving in a private dance of ecstasy. On his back a cardboard sign: 'Bus riders wanted to New Jersey and points East.' Hey now! He found his miracle and he shook them bones!

VERDI: THE SURREAL THING

Tom Sutcliffe
16 September 1989

A bit of booing and a lot of cheering greeted David Alden's new ENO production of *A Masked Ball* at the Coliseum.

The booing, I guess, came from that diminishing element which can't accept the prevailing ENO house style – for Alden's provoking, energised, intensely expressive surrealism is in line with stagings by Graham Vick, Richard Jones, Tim Albery, David Pountney, Nicholas Hytner and David Freeman, however different each producer's signature may be.

The principle at work is by now familiar, even conventional – that operas are not simple costume dramas where characters just happen to sing rather than speak, but psycho-historical mysteries whose resonances and implications (submerged in music) invite daringly imaginative amplification and experimental synthesis into the imagery and philosophy of life and art today.

The antis say this is against the composer's intentions, but I can't imagine any composer who would rather be buried in a museum than dominating current theatrical life.

Verdi's opera was based on the 1792 assassination of the theatre-obsessed (and homosexual) Swedish king Gustavus III. Due to Neapolitan censorship sensitive about the shooting of a monarch, Verdi eventually relocated it in Boston a century earlier, but recent productions have restored the original plot.

Gustavus, who faces a conspiracy of would-be assassins, is fixated on Amelia, wife of his Prime Minister Anckarstroem, and though neither knows the other's feelings she is in love with him.

She turns to a palm-reader for help in shaking off the emotion, and is directed to pick a herb under a gallows at midnight. The king, overhearing her assignation, meets her and shares a moment of blissful romance before her husband arrives – prompting Amelia to mask her face in a veil – to warn of an ambush by assassins. The king swaps clothes with the minister and escapes. But the conspirators insist on seeing who the lady is, and as a result Anckarstroem, finding himself betrayed, joins the conspiracy and shoots Gustavus.

Alden's designer, as with *Mazeppa* and *Simon Boccanegra*, is David Fielding. The central concept is Gustavus's self-dramatisation, his inadequacy for the role of monarch and romantic sense of doom. Arthur Davies as Gustavus (a charmingly elegant Edward VIII kind of figure given to Nextish casual clothes and disguises) emerges during the overture through the red plush curtains behind the ornate gold neo-classical picture-frame leaning against the proscenium.

He glares longingly, desperately at the audience, an introspective Hamlet figure, obsessed with fate and death and time running out. He leans a giant hourglass against the gold frame. On the left, against a rising hillock covered in skulls, a death mask is spotlit.

When the curtain goes up Oscar, Gustavus's intimate (a travesty role brilliantly sung by a chain-smoking conspiratorial Lesley Garrett disguised in a red wig, goatee beard, trilby and specs) is playing with a chandelier at floor level, swinging it like a pendulum and dancing with it wearing angel-of-death wings.

Fielding's designs throughout have an arresting clarity and grandeur, using simple colours, defining adaptable and tellingly dramatic spaces, and providing a sequence of memorable images. Most striking is the ballroom itself, dominated by a huge horseman of the apocalypse. The production is lit with extraordinary expressiveness by Wolfgang Gobbel from the Berlin Schaubühne, working here for the first time, a frequent collaborator of Peter Stein and Luc Bondy.

From the second seance scene on, where Gustavus (disguised as a sailor) plays pranks and has his palm read, Fielding's designs get increasingly disturbed and manic.

Linda Finnie sings Madame Arvidson gloriously, creating of her a Tippett-like Madame Sosostris – genuinely tranced and ambiguous, stripping down to her petticoat (as Janice Cairns's Amelia also does) at moments of emotional revelation.

Alden's major skill, though, has been to tease out the disparate threads of a complex narrative in which Verdi frequently presents three or four different points of view on stage simultaneously about what is actually happening – which the old-fashioned period costume staging of this opera never manages. Everything Alden shows is rooted in Verdi's dramatic requirements, nothing is extraneous – or inexplicable when you actually think about it. The result is thrillingly exciting and gripping. However sweetly Arthur Davies sometimes sings, neither he nor Cairns has quite the heroic measure of these roles – the great duet is not the climactic thrill it can be. But the staging expresses a lot of what the voices can't. The conspirators, with their black coach carrying Madame Arvidson in a silver-lamé ballgown, present a studied ferocity that dangerously matches the morbid wit of the music.

Once you start exploring the imaginative world of Verdi's opera, with its remarkably fertile and memorable music, here very sensitively played by the ENO orchestra and conducted with confident fervour and commitment by Mark Elder, you realise how difficult it is to express it all on stage.

Alden's highly charged, grippingly emotional account of the opera as seen through the central character of Gustavus is so full of expressive and effectively theatrical ideas that one must surely see it more than once to get the measure of it.

DEATH ON REQUEST

Christina Koning
21 September 1989

London Fields, by Martin Amis (Johnathan Cape)

This book is a cheat. A con-trick. From start to finish, all 470 pages of it, it's an elaborate tease. A whodunnit without a motive. A meditation on the way the world ends which turns out to be just another metaphor for the writing of fiction.

Like Roth's Nathan Zuckerman stretched out on his playmat, Martin Amis is obsessed with the act of writing. Or not writing. Of course, he's obsessed with a lot of other things, too: nuclear weapons, ecological disaster, sex, love, death. But even these are grist to his mill. Even these become metaphors for writing.

Amis's well-publicised opposition to nuclear weapons (exemplified in his last collection of short stories, *Einstein's Monsters*) has given rise to a lot of speculation about new directions in his fiction, but on the evidence of this novel these are yet to be explored.

London Fields comes on as a novel of ideas about the post-Einsteinian world, but in fact it's the same mix as before: baroque (and savagely funny) low-life episodes alternating with lyrical descriptions of the moronic inferno. Stripped of its superficial concern with millennial anxieties, it's the usual boy-meets-girl (or, in this instance, girl-meets-boy) stuff, given a sardonic twist. Set in London in 1999 (although it could be any time now or in the near future, so little do the events of history impinge on the action) during some unspecified nuclear and/or ecological crisis, the novel deals with the efforts of a young woman, Nicola Six, to liaise with her murderer at a certain time and place known to her in advance. All that is left in doubt is the identity of the killer: will it be yobbish Keith Talent, petty criminal, 'cheat' and darts fanatic, or Guy Clinch, rich, good-looking and hopelessly ineffectual? The opening scenes establish the scenario (she knows where and when but not who); the rest of the book plots the trajectory of Nicola's – and the century's – journey towards annihilation.

Despite attempts to establish her as a real person (the reader is invited to accompany her not only into the bedroom but also into the lavatory, to discover the truth of Jonathan Swift's horrified realisation about Caelia for himself) Nicola remains an automaton, a beautiful puppet with a nice line in black lingerie and literary criticism, whose death can arouse no terror or pity because it is a foregone conclusion.

Nicola, like her creator, is a bit of a tease. As part of her strategy for systematically humiliating both men in order to provoke one of them – Keith or Guy – to murder, she cons Guy out of a large amount of money, on the pretext of helping her childhood friend 'Enola Gay' to escape from war-torn Cambodia. Simultaneously, she works him up into a frenzy of lust, in what must be the most interrupted coitus in literature. Since neither she nor the reader knows which of her two admirers will be the one to administer the *coup de grâce*, Nicola is obliged to practise similar tactics on the luckless Keith, satisfying his craving for pornographic videos and flattery just enough to keep him coming back for more.

More than once in the course of the book Amis's unease at the deterministic nature of his fable betrays itself. Nicola's king-sized deathwish ('Begging for it. Praying for it') is stated, never explained. Instead, Amis takes refuge in that familiar device for disowning authorial responsibility, the writer as a character. Samson Young, his Bellovian *alter ego* (Jewish, American, with a bad case of writer's block) is the fall guy left with the messy business of disentangling motives and attributing blame, while the real author gets on with the enjoyable part of the job: describing the set-pieces; doing the police in different voices.

It has to be said that what Amis does well, he does better than anyone else you can think of. The set-piece scenes, like the darts match in the Marquis of Edenberry, or the conversations between Guy and Keith in the Black Cross, the seedy West London pub which is the characters' main rendezvous, are realised with all Amis's considerable powers of comic invention. It is in his evocation of the smells and tastes of poverty – the texture of poverty – that the book is most effective, not in its ostensible concern with the horrors of global warfare.

If the Black Cross pub stands at the centre of the little universe whose four points are the dwellings of the four main characters (extremes of poverty and wealth conveyed with typical Amisian mirror-imagery in the contrast offered between crumbling council block and Georgian terrace) the figure of Keith Talent, latest incarnation of the John Self/Terry Service/Little Keith persona in Amis's *galère*, is the book's real centre. When set beside his alarming vitality, his fierce instinct for survival, the other characters seem insubstantial.

Keith dominates the action. In spite of his villainous propensities, his inarticulacy, his grotesque behaviour, he comes across as eminently human. Amis's sympathies seem most fully engaged when he is describing Keith's centre of operations: the pub, the congested streets (like something out of one of Philip K. Dick's wilder nightmares), the bedrooms of his various paramours and the hideously cramped flat where he lives with his wife and baby. The scenes involving Guy Clinch and his family – his bossy wife Hope and monstrous offspring Marmaduke mirroring Keith's downtrodden Kath and ethereal daughter Kim – are shadowy by comparison. Like Guy himself, you find yourself itching to get back to the wrecked streets and the fetid pub, where the action is.

This book is a con-trick. It leads you to expect one thing, and offers you another. It breaks its own rules of consistency and plausibility. It fails to integrate its supposed theme (the devaluation of human life by the imminence of universal death) at a structural or narratorial level. And yet it is a powerful book. Some of the best writing in it occurs in those passages which deal with what it feels like to live in a society whose technologies can no longer sustain it. Like his creation, Keith Talent, Amis's preoccupations are 'modern, modern, modern'; more than any other British writer of his generation he gets to grips with the post-modern condition.

MURDER IN THE CEYLONESE STYLE

Jasper Becker
26 September 1989

I had not expected to be faced with the horror so soon, but driving from the airport into Colombo we found the road was blocked on the bridge over the Kelani River. People had stopped their vehicles and a small crowd was gazing at the muddy monsoon waters swirling below.

'What are they looking at?' I asked idly, thinking that perhaps a ceremony was taking place. 'Bodies. They come here to see the corpses floating down the river,' said the friend who had picked me up. Every day the bodies float past, and on one day this week 50 were seen drifting together where an eddy in the river gathered them. At first I couldn't quite make out the objects floating in the water, but there were big black crows perched on them.

My friend said they were always youths, their faces slashed to prevent identification and their genitals often removed. People believe that the death squads remove them as evidence of the successful elimination of a JVP (People's Liberation Front) terrorist.

Bodies are found everywhere in Sri Lanka: on the beaches, along the roadsides, in the jungles, and in the towns. It is now customary in Sri Lanka to prevent recognition by burning the bodies with tyres, but others are thrown in the rivers as a warning to the living. Even the remains of those cremated are not left in peace and the ashes are sometimes found to have been stolen for voodoo rites – or so people say. There is a bizarre unreality to what the press reports. Side by side with an announcement that Dr Lakshmi de Silva is giving a lecture on Colonialism as a Catalyst in Drama, the papers carry brief stories such as 'Wattegama police found thirteen bodies of youths killed by unidentified gunmen near the bus depot at Pitiyadem, Wattegama, in Patha Dunban, last Monday. Police are investigating.'

The murderers are rarely caught, and many of the deaths are not reported at all. But, even according to the papers, the daily death toll is 50 or more. Last weekend 170 were said to have been killed in and around Kandy. Most people estimate that more than 10,000 people have died over the last ten months, making the undeclared civil war in Sri Lanka the world's bloodiest conflict. The world made such a fuss about Tiananmen Square, but how many died? A thousand out of a population of one billion. But here this has become Asia's new killing field and no one seems to notice, my friend said. The independence war in the north-east, where the Tamils first fought the Sri Lankan army and then the Indian peacekeeping force, has now paled into insignificance, even if the current ceasefire does not last. When the Indian troops leave, the civil war is certain to worsen as the Sri Lankan forces struggle to control the rival Tamil forces and the JVP. More people are said to have died than during the 1971 insurgency, when the newly elected government of Mrs Bandaranaike suppressed the JVP. The ringleaders were held in camps, indoctrinated, and then released in 1978. They included Rohana Jayawardene Witeweera, the Moscow-trained Communist whose father was paralysed after being beaten by members of former President Jayawardene's United National Party. Even now little is publicly known about the JVP, but it is among the last of the Communist insurgencies which have torn Asia apart since the war.

The JVP's aim is to paralyse a government it regards as hopelessly corrupt and replace it with a Marxist regime, although Sri Lanka officially remains a Socialist republic and for many years ran a nationalised economy. In the last month the JVP has forced schools, hospitals, factories, and tea plantations to close, bringing life almost to a standstill. When the JVP threatened to kill members of the families of security forces who refused to strike, the government abandoned all restraint. These families are now held in schools, and for every one of them who is nevertheless killed the army is shooting ten people. Who they are does not seem to matter, nor is it always clear who is doing the killings.

Death squads dressed in plain clothes round up anyone between fifteen and twenty-nine years old. An acquaintance was visiting a friend in Colombo when he was summoned to a neighbouring house by men with handkerchiefs over their mouths, pushed and beaten a little, and questioned. He feels he was meant to think they were JVP – and that if he had indicated any sympathies with the JVP cause he would have been killed.

Another acquaintance was on a bus which had stopped when the army arrived, ordered the passengers into trucks, and drove them to a camp in the jungle, where they were kept for days, fed one meal a day, and interrogated. Even among Sri Lanka's highly educated elite no one seems able to comprehend, let alone explain, the horror that has been unleashed. Some trace the problems back to the 1950s, when the government declared Sinhalese the only official language and sowed the seeds for inter-communal discontent. Others blame the decision to release 200 JVP leaders from prison in 1978, or Jayawardene's decision to postpone a general election in 1982. Still others criticise his successor, President Premadasa, who is said to be ignorant and ruthless. Many believe India set out to destabilise Sri Lanka to bring it under its domination. But none of these causes provides answers to the barbarity taking place. In many ways it represents a failure of Western democracy and law to cope with the country's economic and ethnic divisions.

In Colombo I was shown around the new, beautiful building that houses the Supreme Court. The centre is supported by a black column on which the UN Declaration of Human Rights is chiselled in gold letters. It was built with Chinese help, and by a painful irony the ceremonial entrance is called Tiananmen Gate, because of the lions copied from those at the entrance to the Forbidden City. It is an impressive assertion of the country's ideals, and in keeping with Sri Lanka's record of building one of the best and widest-reaching educational and health systems in the Third World. But all this, together with the Supreme Court and its bewigged judges, has not been enough to prevent the bloodbath. Now the only question worth answering is: when will the killing stop?

THE RISE OF THE VERMIN

Helen Chappell
27 September 1989

The greenhouse effect really stings you when you open the door of the nursery to find 300 angry wasps buzzing around the baby's cot. That's when your voice rises a couple of octaves and you get on the phone to London pest controller Kim Edwards. 'In that case we found the wasps had eaten right through the ceiling into the baby's bedroom,' he reports laconically. 'We had to seal off the room and destroy about 2,000 wasps in a huge nest above it.'

These are halcyon days for wasps. Kim Edwards blames it on the unnaturally mild winter of 1988/9. In fact, he has already destroyed 20 wasp nests today and has between 15 and 20 such calls a day. 'It's an explosion,' he says. 'And that's not all. We're up 60 per cent on our workrate, bedbugs are well up and we're snowed under by calls about pigeons.'

Although people may feel insecure about their status in the sub-tropical, post-Fordian, free-market world of the nineties, vermin seem quite shameless in their self-confident glee. Rats, for instance, have taken to the luxury edifices of London's Docklands like sewage to water. Only the other day Kim was called up to rid a just-opened shopping mall and an entire block of new flats there of their unwanted furries.

'The developers haven't thought of pest-proofing their new buildings,' says Kim. 'A lot have cavity walls for the pipes and cables and once rats get inside them they run up and down and take over the whole place.'

Now the rats are coming up from the river and out of the drains. The most apocryphal of urban folk tales about monsters in the loo are beginning to sound sensible. It's Nosferatu and Temple of Doom time for any forlorn yuppies stranded out there among the cement mixers and teetering piles of trash. 'I could take you there at night and really show you rats,' mutters Kim darkly. You can't escape the horror by sticking to more traditionally posh venues for your meal out or dirty weekend, either. Bedbugs and fleas are on the march. 'We find them in the best hotels,' says Kim, 'as well as the big restaurant chains. You wouldn't believe it in this day and age, would you?'

Many hoteliers get Kim and his three workers to park their van out of sight, use the service entrances and wear unmarked overalls. They are often expected to work in the dead of night, for fear of starting a panic among the punters. Restaurants may be more blasé. While customers are dining on expense account lunches overhead, Kim will be downstairs poisoning rats in the kitchen. 'People are so unaware of this. The restaurants spend a lot of money every year on pest control, but they're still not free of vermin.' This is good news for N. A. W. Edwards & Co. Ltd, of course. Since Kim took over the family firm from school 14 years ago, business has never been so brisk. Pest victims pay anything from £25 to dispose of a wasps' nest to £20,000 to to de-roach an entire housing estate.

It pays to be discreet, however. Kim recognises a repertoire of euphemisms which customer and rat-catcher collude in employing. 'Big mice' are rats, 'doves' are pigeons and 'creepy-crawlies' are cockroaches but could also be Pharaoh ants (tiny, tropical insects which love hospitals and live on jam, blood, cat food and other high-protein gunk).

There is something about vermin which shows people at their worst – or most vulnerable – depending on how cynical you feel. One local borough called him out to fumigate a block of tenement flats infested by maggots breeding inside two dead greyhounds left to starve when their owner went into prison.

One lonely and eccentric lady in a mansion block insists upon feeding the cockroaches he comes to destroy. 'She puts bread and milk out for them. She calls them her pets. When we spray them with insecticide, she says: "You've murdered my animals".'

Kim loves his work, but even he becomes concerned by the bizarre variety and scale of the demands on his services. He feels a sense of mission. No bait in the capital's sewers, he complains, no street-sweepers to clear the litter – it's a false economy. He's had 2,000 calls to terminate rodents alone over the last three months. He's working round the clock, seven days a week. His vision is getting apocalyptic. 'Everyone agrees the cities are getting filthier and filthier,' he says, 'but until rats are running down the high street, will they do anything about it? And is that time very far away?'

PARTING THOUGHTS

Jonathan Steele
27 September 1989

Lev has never had it so good in Moscow. Since Gorbachev came in, things have looked up enormously. For one thing, ordinary people can get licences to operate a small business. So Lev gave up his job at an institute, and started to use his battered Zhiguli as a taxi. The licence costs him 60 roubles a month, which is less than he earns in an average day. Another change is that he can talk freely, say what he thinks and become friendly with foreigners without any fear.

But all this is not enough, Lev says, presenting me with a paradox. He has decided to emigrate. Along with all the other improvements, the prospects for Jews to leave the Soviet Union are also better than ever. He is leaving while the door remains open. This summer he, his wife and their baby went to Southern Russia, where his elderly parents live. The family conference discussed and debated for many hours, and then decided they would go. 'My parents have had very tough lives. I want to be able to give them some comfort in their old age,' he explained.

Lev has always been something of an internationalist. He is an enthusiast for Esperanto. He believes that an 'international lingua franca' will encourage human contact. But the daily queuing, the slog for food and basic necessities, and the hours at the wheel give him little time. 'In spite of all the changes here, it's hard to have any broader ideas, or entertain any notions of improving the world when you're trying to feed a perpetually hungry family.'

Twice a day Lev stops his taxi beside the US Embassy and registers his name on the unofficial list of those who want to leave. Most are Armenians or Jews, but there is an increasing number of Russians. As with so many aspects of life here, money talks. Just to get inside the embassy there are two queues. The 'live' queue consists of people living in Moscow. For every hundred people on the list there is a self-appointed marshal who maintains the roll-call. If you do not turn up every morning and evening, they ruthlessly strike you off.

The 'live' queue has about a thousand names. The last man on it will get inside the embassy in about five months' time. There he will hand in his application and discuss his case with a consular official. (Because of the pressure of work the Americans then take 10 months to clear it.)

The 'dead' queue, which has some 13,000 names, is made up of people from outside Moscow. They come up to Moscow, give in their names but only come back when the marshals phone them and tell them their time is near. It is a lucrative business for the marshals. The 'live' queue is hard to manipulate since everyone in the street is watching like a hawk. The 'dead' list is another matter. It is padded with non-existent names, so if you slip the marshal the right tip, he can put you high up the queue.

Sometimes fights break out between the 'dead' and 'live' queue people. There is an unofficial pact that every day 40 dead and 10 live get into the embassy. But there is always suspicion of queue-jumping. Last week a joyful Lev announced that he had moved from 567 on the live queue to 219. A friend on 219 got impatient and paid a marshal 500 roubles to go to the top of the dead queue. Lev took his place.

He is still nagged with doubts about the decision to emigrate. Presumably they will pursue him to the airport, and long after he arrives in the United States. 'You're a journalist. You're doing something serious. You're telling people in Britain what's going on here,' Lev told me the other day. 'Maybe you think that leaving here now is escapism. I feel that too. That's what has held me back for so long.' The advent of glasnost has broken the old certainties and caused a psychological and intellectual crisis for Lev and his friends. 'You may not believe it, but in Brezhnev's time people still had more faith in the system.

The ideological pressure from the propaganda machine had its effect. We knew less then, both about this country and the outside world.'

Another impulse to go is fear of instability. Pessimism has always been a strong element in Russian life. Many Russian Jews suffer from a double dose. He says there were rumours of imminent anti-Semitic pogroms a few weeks ago. His wife's parents were so worried that they came to stay the night. Lev finds it hard to explain what prompts such fears. 'It's not that I think Russians will suddenly turn on the Jews as scapegoats. But there's a climate of instability everywhere – the violence in Fergana, in Uzbekistan, Sumgait and the Caucasus. Will it spread? Who knows?'

In cooler moments, he accepts that perestroika is irreversible. 'I don't think Tiananmen Square could happen here. The political reforms have gone too far. The Congress of People's Deputies is a safety valve. For 70 years this country was moving towards something unknown. Perhaps now we are moving towards normal standards of civilisation and a better standard of living. I believe the capitalist and socialist systems will converge, although our government has rejected this for years.'

Just in case it does not happen, Lev wants to watch developments in the Soviet Union from the tranquillity he hopes to find in the US. Over there he is likely to run across people in the professional Moscow-watching community who are less well-disposed towards the Soviet Union and even more pessimistic. Doomsday speculation has a long pedigree in the US, fed partly by Cold War stereotypes and partly by the fact that many of the watchers are themselves long-time émigrés who need the subconscious reinforcement of feeling they made the right choice.

Squeezed between these camps, those of us who feel

that reform in the Soviet Union will muddle its way forward without major violence or repression are in an exposed minority. We can take comfort from some crumbs. US Sovietologists failed to predict Gorbachev or that change would come so far so fast. Why should one believe their speculations now? Surely it is better to analyse in detail the kaleidoscope of changes going on today than indulge in glib long-range predictions.

In Russia pessimism has a long and justified pedigree. All but a handful of Russians have been powerless spectators all their lives. Under Gorbachev the perspective has changed; a pluralistic society is emerging but the fact of powerlessness still remains uppermost for most people. Hence the anxiety which Lev and his family feel. Around them they see rising crime. The television shows pictures of apparently pervasive ethnic violence. There is loose talk of a Russian backlash, and even civil war. Meanwhile, the ruling apparatus is still in charge. Why should people who have never seen political conflict resolved by peaceful and democratic means believe it can ever happen?

Westerners have no such alibi. We know it can. Every day that perestroika lasts gives more and more Soviet citizens a taste of power, a sense of making a contribution to a society in flux. Which is why I continue to argue with Lev that things will gradually improve. But I don't blame him for leaving.

FEELING THE EARTH MOVE

Matthew Engel
9 October 1989

It was a strange sensation but not, in itself, an unpleasant one. The horror came much later. For 15 seconds the earth just shuddered.

It was like standing on the ground floor while heavy machinery started up in the basement or, this being California, experiencing a little choppiness in the Jacuzzi.

It was 5.04 and 46 seconds in the evening. The clock stopped in the studio at KGO Radio then and almost 24 hours later the clocks were still stopped throughout central San Francisco. So were the Jacuzzis, the videos and the electronic garage doors.

Hundreds of people were dead and thousands of lives shattered by individual tragedy. The millions who escaped face problems for which the world's most advanced society has no technological solution. The routine of Californian life has suddenly become elemental again.

A city block by the marina, in one of the most desirable parts of town, has vanished. Sombre firemen hopelessly poured water pumped from the bay on its charred remains.

Across the road, another apartment block has collapsed. The second floor is now the ground and the rest is nothing more than piles of bricks and planks. Other houses lean at strange angles and elegant driveways have become crazy paving.

The Big One has struck. The fear which every Californian carries in the back of the mind has been justified. But when dawn broke yesterday the most striking fact was not how much of San Francisco had gone, but how much was still there.

Houses in the rich districts of Pacifica and Russian Hill stood, solid, creamy and handsome in the morning light, as though nothing had happened.

When the earthquake struck I was standing unheroically in the press room deep in the concrete bowels of Candlestick Park waiting, like 60,000 others, for the third game of the Baseball World Series. In theory, it was a dreadful place to be caught in an earthquake, but it turned out there were many worse.

As at Hillsborough, it took a long time for people to realise that sport had been overtaken by a sterner reality.

Many spectators saw the stadium shimmy against the sky. When the shaking stopped, there was a nervous cheer. Only a few people knew what it meant: 'I've lived here all my life,' someone said, 'and that was big.'

Just how big only became clear as the news filtered through of the disaster at the Bay Bridge, symbol of the baseball series between San Francisco and Oakland, and on the Nimitz motorway. Meanwhile, the oblivious fans chanted: 'We want ball.'

There was no baseball. The crowd was sent away, not because there had been a tragedy, but because there was no electricity and therefore no floodlights and no television coverage. As people inched back into an evening rush hour that had turned into near-gridlock, the scale of events started to sink in.

From the viewpoint of Diamond Heights, the city stretched beneath us towards the stricken bridge. Dusk was falling but there was no light except from the headlamps of stranded cars and from police beacons flickering on the bridge. A long plume of black smoke hung over the Twin Peaks.

Central San Francisco had no power all through a long night. Without television, the radio came into its own.

Station KGO was knocked out for 45 minutes. Two of its broadcasting towers were down and the third operating at a fraction of its normal power. But when the station came back, it pushed out the stream of information, advice and reassurance that prevents society breaking down in these circumstances.

Announcers kept telling people to read the advice on page B9 of the phone book. They were supposed to do that before this happened: 'Before the next earthquake. Be prepared. Take the time NOW to read the following checklists.' But, when things are normal, who reads page B9 of a phone book and gets in a week's supply of water and powdered milk on the off chance? Throughout the state, people were frantically trying to remember where their gas taps were.

A KGO producer called in with the dreadful news from across the bay. 'The freeway has fallen on top of itself . . . An entire freeway collapsed like a sandwich.'

The first reports of mayhem in the darkened streets soon followed. A three-year-old girl whose father's car had been attacked by thugs was taken to hospital with her head cut open. 'There are some bad people in the streets of San Francisco tonight,' said the announcer. 'The warning is going out again. Stay off the streets of San Francisco.'

For those with nowhere to go except the streets, there was some relief. At the Moscone Centre, in the hall where Walter Mondale was nominated for President in 1984, the Red Cross took over from the Water Pollution Control Federation, which had been holding its annual convention.

A mixture of conventioneers from the Midwest, stranded commuters and down-and-outs sat around eating junk food, or trying to stretch out and sleep.

Market Street was full of people with nowhere to go, but then it always is. There was still no light and the dome of City Hall stood stark in the darkness, like St Paul's in wartime.

There was no noise, except for the sirens and whirring generators in the smarter hotels and office blocks. As dawn broke, there was the sound of a squadron of helicopters. When morning came, you could tell where the bad people had been. The windows were smashed at Radio Shack and the radios, televisions and computers had vanished with a completeness no mere earthquake could contrive. A sign advertising a Fall Clean-Up Sale swung listlessly in the breeze.

There was no logic in the pattern of damage. Occasionally the surface of the road was wrenched apart. Near the Radio Shack the walls at the Psychedelic Shop had been shaken to a crazy angle, appropriate to the business.

Normal business was being resumed. On the windscreens of parked cars were messages from an operator who knew there was no time to waste: 'Experience in earthquake repair/clean-up. Have truck – will move furnishings. Call Mike Kenny, MK Construction.'

THE CHAINS OF A NATION

John Gittings
11 October 1989

By daylight in Beijing, under the clear autumn sky, life seems normal enough to sit beneath the cypress trees in the Temple of Confucius and discuss the sage's relevance today.

Night-time is far less amenable to philosophical discourse. People stay indoors to avoid the unannounced martial law curfew. Those willing to talk to foreigners – and there are not many – keep their voices down, shut doors, and enquire nervously whether men from the Ministry for State Security are waiting outside.

Under the cypress trees one may even look for solutions. Confucius once said: 'The soft can overcome the hard.' It was the lesson he had learnt from Laozi, the master of the Dao (in a wholly apocryphal meeting in which, nevertheless, every Chinese believes).

It would be nice to think that the peaceful tradition of ordinary Chinese society, essentially Daoist in its avoidance of conflict, will prevail before too long over the stern authoritarianism which demands obedience to the new feudal lords of the Communist Party.

But night-time conversations bring a harsher reality. Though the people are comprehensively alienated from the regime, no one has the slightest idea how it can be budged without more bloodshed.

There is no Hungarian-type reference to some reformist grouping in the Party. The events of June – even party members assert – have 'opened our eyes' about that institution.

The next step, wherever it may lead, is more likely to be taken from within the ranks of the armed forces. The most hopeful suggestion is of a cleansing operation by young officers who are appalled by the bloodshed and nauseated by the corruption of their elders.

The conventional wisdom of foreign China-watchers is widely shared: Something is bound to happen after Deng Xiaoping dies, but it may not be very pleasant.

In the meantime, the alienated majority takes refuge in anecdotal humour and subtle contempt. For the foreign journalist, even the anecdotes cannot be reported straightforwardly. It is as if China has slipped back more than a decade to the time when every source or detail had to be protectively transposed.

So it must be with the tale (also involving Confucius) of the four-character message scratched on a door which recently brought in the secret police investigators: 'Ten years is not too late.' Every literate Chinese knows what

Confucius said. 'The superior person who intends revenge [on the wicked] will wait 10 years [to carry it out].'

But I had better not say what sort of door it was or where it was located, although it would improve the story.

There are plenty of anecdotes too about the self-critiques which many people have been required to write – some three times over at 3–4,000 characters a time – explaining what they did last May.

There are two ways of dealing with this: admit you went to Tiananmen but only as a bystander, or deny it altogether. If your workmates, including your bosses, also took part in the democracy movement, there is a good chance of a mutual cover-up.

At least one government office, heavily involved in the movement, has received a special bonus for supposedly not having participated. But the money was soon returned to its source, clawed back as a 'voluntary' purchase of government bonds.

This unpublicised campaign to take money out of circulation and reduce inflation was much more of a talking point than the generally ignored North Korean-style, National Day celebrations.

Offices, factories and other institutions are obliged to purchase a fixed quota, so that any employee who exercises his 'voluntary' right not to buy is merely increasing the burden on his colleagues.

It works out at anything between 65 and 110 per cent of a month's salary. One hundred yuan worth of bonds is repayable with an 83 yuan bonus at the end of three years – but only in four separate tranches extending another two years. No one is impressed by the bargain.

Those who joined the National Day celebrations did pick up some extra cash – between 10 and 15 yuan. But there are stories about workplaces asked for 50 participants who only managed to provide 10.

There have been endless obligatory meetings at the workplace to discuss the 'counter-revolutionary turmoil' of May–June.

Not everyone is cowed on these occasions. The cadres in charge (many of whom supported the democracy movement) have to clap loudly whenever Deng Xiaoping's name is mentioned – to smother the unfavourable comments.

But there is also a collective sense of self-preservation. After the massacre, the Central Philharmonic Orchestra decided to scrap Verdi's Requiem from its rehearsal schedule. No one from above had banned the performance, but it would have been only too clear who was being mourned.

People can, in a detached way, sum up their chances of attracting or escaping punishment. Those most at risk work for organisations directly under the control of the ultra-right (tinged with ultra-left) Beijing Party Committee. Elsewhere there is a good chance of being protected. College heads have shielded students by giving them sick certificates, hospital chiefs have altered records showing how their staff helped the demonstrators.

The purge is more intense among the ordinary working class of Beijing who most vigorously resisted the army. Opponents of the regime estimate that some 10,000 have been 'seized', of whom perhaps 4,000 were later released.

Many were picked up by the martial law forces (the police keep well in the background to avoid possible future reprisals, but provide the lists on which the army acts). There has been some slackening off in the activities of informers, who may receive up to 200 yuan for shopping a known 'counter-revolutionary element'.

There are many horrifying tales of random brutality and humiliating treatment. The parents of one innocent young man, released deaf in both ears after severe beating, are still seeking the right authority to whom to complain.

Artists and writers have been relatively free from persecution, both because the authorities are aware that they have friends abroad and because they were less influential in the democracy movement than the social scientists.

He Jingzhi, the Maoist poet who replaced the novelist Wang Meng as Minister of Culture, appears unprepared to conduct a ideological witch-hunt. His deputy, the actor Ying Ruocheng, has called on at least one liberal critic (the translator Yang Xianyi, who denounced the Li Peng regime in foreign radio and television interviews) with words of reassurance.

But the price for immunity has to be silence. No one is writing anything serious at all. One contributor to an English language journal felt obliged to explain that the article in question – an innocuous survey of folk art in south-east China – had been finished long before the events of May–June.

The memory of those events is almost too painful to discuss for many Beijingers. Previous conservative backlashes – the 1983 'anti-spiritual pollution' campaign and even the much tougher anti-bourgeois liberalism purge of 1987 – could be shrugged off as deviant currents against the main tide. Now the balance of power has been reversed by armed force. Older intellectuals, in particular, know they will be lucky to live long enough to see a new 'reversal of verdicts'.

Others still rage: What happened on June 4, they say, was a rape against the Chinese people and its essentially peaceful approach. They dissect in detail the military moves from the night of June 3 onwards.

The invading forces included units from half a dozen different armies, deliberately mixed to spread the blame. Even the notorious tanks and armoured personnel carriers comprised three separate divisions from three separate commands.

While the foreign news reports of imminent civil war within the army were far-fetched, several units certainly refused to fire against the people. Some abandoned their vehicles in the certain knowledge that they would then be immobilised or set on fire.

Even today, apparently, no one in the armed forces is keen to admit that his company shot innocent civilians down. The killing was always done by another unit. It seems, too, that no one actually gave an explicit command to open fire. According to one account, when the units attempting to advance into Tiananmen Square asked for more instructions as they met resistance, they were told that the orders were clear and that they should not ask again.

In the Temple of Confucius, the oldest cypress tree is invested with the peculiar property of distinguishing between good and bad ministers. If an unworthy servant of the emperor passed beneath, his hat would get caught in the branches. The problem in Beijing today is not how to detect those who are unfit to rule, but how to remove them from the throne.

JUSTICE IN THE DOCK

Leader
20 October 1989

Over fourteen years after the criminal justice system found the Guildford Four guilty, that system itself now stands, shamefaced and wriggling, in the dock. The Court of Appeal heard yesterday that police officers in the case had misled the court, altered notes of interviews, suppressed and fabricated much significant evidence. Three police officers were said to have concocted contemporaneous statements in which the defendants confessed to the crime. Drafts of the so-called interviews were discovered by Avon and Somerset police, who have been investigating the original police investigation. Two other police officers suppressed genuine interviews which the defendants had given. A full criminal investigation into the conduct of the Surrey police officers ('not only junior officers') who so grossly misdirected the court has now begun. Meanwhile, as the Director of Public Prosecutions signalled on Tuesday, all four defendants in the Guildford bomb trial had their convictions quashed yesterday. So far, so very late, so good.

But it is not just the conduct of the police which needs to be investigated. Even more disturbing evidence has emerged, as our crime correspondent has reported. The former Director of Public Prosecutions, Sir Norman Skelhorn, appears to have withheld crucial alibi evidence from defence lawyers at the 1975 trial of the Guildford Four. A key alibi witness for one of the four, whom the defence lawyers were unsuccessful in tracing, was found by police and interviewed. His evidence upheld the defendant's account; but the defendant was still prosecuted and that alibi evidence was never passed on to the defence. There could hardly be a more damning allegation. It suggests a prosecution system so committed to securing a conviction after a horrendous bombing that fundamental principles of justice were jettisoned, even by the men at the top. The first task of the judicial inquiry announced yesterday in the Commons by the Home Secretary will be to investigate this disturbing evidence. The second will be to examine the convictions of the seven people – including the McGuire family – convicted of producing bombs in a separate trial, but one begun purely by the confessions which the Surrey police obtained from the Guildford Four.

The most important question the inquiry will have to answer is whether it all could happen again. Three reforms have been introduced since the unlucky four were taken to Surrey police stations. First, the Police and Criminal Evidence Act has introduced greater accountability to the conditions under which suspects are held inside police stations, and tighter controls over police interrogations and the length of time suspects can be held before they must be brought before a court. Second, duty solicitor schemes have been introduced, so suspects held in police stations have a right of access to a lawyer. Third, and perhaps most pertinently in respect of the Guildford Four, who were bullied into making false confessions, all police interrogations will have to be tape-recorded by 1991. Yet, alas, *none of these reforms* applies to people suspected of letting off bombs, making bombs, or other terrorist activities. There are justifiable reasons why the police have more powers over a suspect terrorist than a suspect burglar; but there is no reason why all suspects should not have the same right to have their interrogations tape-recorded. Moreover, as the European Court of Human Rights has already ruled, some judicial control is needed over the police power to hold and interrogate suspect terrorists for seven days without charge. The Home Office has still not responded to this ruling.

Sir John May, the former Lord Justice who is to conduct the judicial inquiry, must also look at the rule which still allows convictions in England and Wales on the basis of uncorroborated confessions. The Guildford Four could not have been convicted in Scotland, where all confessions have to be backed with some other evidence –

forensic, circumstantial, or of identification. The only evidence in the Guildford case were the false confessions. Two former Law Lords, Scarman and Devlin, both want the law changed.

Meanwhile, the present leaders of the judiciary should recognise the role that the media have played in correcting this scandalous miscarriage of justice. The judges are too ready to dismiss genuine investigations by journalists. Better still, of course, would be a proper investigatory body for such miscarriages of justice, but the judges still resist such an initiative in the belief that it would erode the position of the Appeal Court. They, and all who profess to care about British justice, should reflect with humility and pain on the Guildford experience. Terrorism, of its nature, threatens the fabric of a democracy and its laws. Terrorism wins when that fabric is surreptitiously, degradingly, torn apart. The terrorists won fourteen years ago when the system failed; and they must not win again.

A CHAMPION FOR SOUTH AFRICA'S DEATH ROW

David Beresford
21 October 1989

The news came through on the South African wires shortly before 10am yesterday – three men had been hanged at Pretoria Central prison at dawn. Which wasn't bad for Shucks. He'd done better and he'd done worse. But to save two lives in one week is something worth doing in anyone's book. 'Shucks' is this country's 'execution monitor'.

Every week Shucks goes out to bat for those miserable people who live on South Africa's death row and uses every trick and talent he's got to try and save them.

It's a terrible job in more ways than one: terrible having to go and talk to those guys, knowing that next morning they're going to be corpses; terrible having to tell the families that the next morning their sons are going to be corpses and, above all, terrible because to the world they are nothing but corpses – you know, another three hanged in Pretoria yesterday . . . Forty-five have died so far this year on South Africa's gallows.

Shucks is not his real name, of course. It's Huggins Sefanyetso, but everyone knows him as Shucks. He's not sure where it came from, but it suits him.

'Cool, man, cool,' he's always saying, half listening to the telephone clutched to his ear, his other hand frantically scribbling instructions for a barrister or an announcement to the press. He looks a bit like Sammy Davis Jnr, with those quick, nervous and yet graceful movements.

He landed this terrible job almost by chance. Shucks had always wanted to be a lawyer and he did study law, at the University of the North – one of those 'bush colleges'. But his studies were disrupted by political unrest on the campus and he never got started again.

Instead he became an articled clerk and later was taken on by Lawyers for Human Rights, which was set up in 1979 by some of South Africa's top barristers. It's a noble organisation that tries to push black lawyers. They became closely involved in capital punishment last October, when they heard there was a man on death row who was about to be hanged although his lawyers had not got around to filing a petition for clemency to the President.

They decided to try for a stay of execution, on the grounds that the prisoner had not explored all legal remedies open to him. The director, Brian Currin, asked

Shucks to handle the application to the Supreme Court. He did and won the case and then another one, and so the process snowballed until Shucks found himself working full-time on the job.

The great scandal of the South African legal system is the inadequacy of legal representation. Legal aid is virtually non-existent, so the vast majority of people who appear in South Africa's courts – who are of course black and poor – are sent to jail without the privilege of a professional defence. In capital cases, however, *pro deo* lawyers are provided. The fees paid for such work are so pathetic that the briefs are usually picked up by newly qualified youngsters, or old hacks.

The accused, for their part, in capital cases are usually uneducated. They frequently think that their lawyers are acting for the state, rather than God. All of which gives rise to such circumstances as people being hanged without exhausting the appeals procedure.

Since he began the work Shucks must have saved more than 50 lives. The way he does it is to hang around Pretoria Central prison waiting to hear when notices of execution have been issued, giving a prisoner seven days until his death. Then he bangs off a request to the Justice Department for the dates when the prisoners' various appeals were dismissed.

If the reply shows that any of these lines of appeal has not been tried, Shucks hares off to the Supreme Court with a barrister to stop the execution on the October precedent.

Sometimes he uses other strategies, as in the case of Almond Nofomela, a security branch officer who had murdered a white farmer. Last Friday he received his notice and sent word to Shucks that he had a story to tell about political killings.

On Wednesday Shucks sent a young white barrister in

to hear the story. The barrister came back and said Nofomela had a long story about how he had not killed the farmer. Shucks was impatient – almost everyone on death row says they didn't do it – and he sent the barrister back.

Meanwhile, he was fighting for a second prisoner, Freddy Dreyer, a young Coloured killer. Dreyer had not filed a petition for clemency, so Shucks sent in another barrister to get his permission to go for a stay.

The lawyer came back, disconsolately, with a scrawled statement from Dreyer: 'I the undersigned, Freddy Dreyer, (23 years of age) declare hereunder that I am not prepared to make a petition for clemency to the State President, because I don't know about and I don't believe that I did commit the offence for which I find myself here. That's all. I have made peace with the Lord.'

Shucks had no more time for that case – Freddy had to be left to his God now – and he raced around to nearby chambers to see the barrister who had just got back from Nofomela. The barrister was looking shaken – the policeman had confessed to nine murders as a police 'hit man', including that of the civil rights lawyer Griffiths Mxenge.

The two men argued strategy. Shucks wanted to go for the jugular – a court application and press conference; the state couldn't afford to be seen to be covering up on the Mxenge killing. The barrister wanted to negotiate; the precedents for a stay on these grounds were dubious. Shucks conceded and the barrister went to see the Attorney-General.

The day before executions is always a frantic day for Shucks, and so it proved on Thursday. Nofomela was taking all his attention. Dreyer was a goner. There were three others due to be hanged – Harry Ncqobo, Khalewayo Gumede and Mfanozi Mthethwa – but there was no hope for them.

In mid-morning the wife of an ANC prisoner on death row wandered into Shucks's office and said she had managed to have a few words with Ncqobo while visiting her husband earlier; he had said that he had not heard from his lawyer since the last stay of execution. Shucks flicked through the papers littering his desk, looking for the Department of Justice briefing, which showed that all three men had their petitions rejected on specified dates. How could they have petitioned without being consulted? Frantically they start trying to locate the *pro deo* lawyers in the cases.

At 11.50 they get through to the Durban office of the lawyer who represented Ncqobo. He's out, but the secretary promises to fax the petition. At midday the fax comes through: the petition was no more than a rehearsal of the trial. At 12.55 the lawyer confirms he did not even send Ncqobo a copy. There's hurried debate in Shucks's office. He's also worried about Nofomela – there's still no word from the Attorney-General.

At 1.14pm they agree on a delicate call to the Durban barrister; they need an affidavit from him saying his client was inadequately represented.

By 3.25pm there is still no sign of the affidavit and they're getting frantic. It arrives at 3.45. The face of the LHR's assistant director, Lucretia Seafield, falls as she reads it. The thrust is that Ncqobo had a comprehensive defence. The co-director, Peter Mothle, is pulled in. He urges them to go for it.

Shucks has vanished – he's gone to Nofomela's barrister. At 4pm he's back triumphant. The Justice Minister has capitulated and Nofomela has his stay.

Now for Ncqobo. Shucks has set up a judge at home for a 6pm hearing. At 5.30pm they're packing to go when I ask Lucretia: what about the other two men? She looks bewildered. Ncqobo had said he did not think the other two men had heard from their lawyers either, I pointed out. Lucretia said she would check it.

The outcome was on the wires this morning: Dreyer, Gumede and Mthethwa are now corpses, so Ncqobo was saved. Had Gumede and Mthethwa seen their *pro deo* lawyers about their petitions? I could telephone Pretoria and ask Shucks. But I'm not going to. I just wish him good luck: he's already got six to bat for next week.

HANGING – 'A CRAFTSMAN'S JOB'

Dennis Barker
26 October 1989

Syd Dernley is a wizened elf of a northerner who, at 68, enters a room with a little skip, and enjoys his bowls and being treasurer of the Mansfield Conservative Club.

He is also the only surviving British public executioner, a man who regarded hanging as 'a craftsman's job' and still makes little jokes about it. It was he who, in 1950, helped hang Timothy Evans, found guilty of murdering his wife. Years later, Evans was found innocent, and became the first man in Britain to receive a posthumous free pardon.

Asked yesterday by the *People* profilist (whom he obligingly strapped, hooded and noosed with a real hangman's rope – it is a memorable experience) whether he had changed his mind about hanging after the Evans case, and now the Guildford Four, Dernley did not hesitate.

'No, it gives me no doubts at all about the efficiency of the death penalty and its deterrent effect. Had it been me that hanged the Guildford Four, I should have been rather distressed about it. But I would manage to save my peace of mind as I have done over the past 40 years.'

He expresses his unsullied belief strongly in his memoirs, *The Hangman's Tale*, out today (Robert Hale). Callous murderers who now laugh at judges' sentences did not do so when sentenced to death, says the man whose father was an insurance agent.

Dernley was born in Mansfield where, after reading an Edgar Wallace crime novel at the age of 11, he decided to be a hangman because even then he was fascinated by crime. Later, he says, when working for a colliery, 'I decided it would get me out of the rut for a day or two and perhaps let me meet the people I wanted to, such as detectives and major criminals. My wife was astounded at first, but when my mother-in-law heard I was hanging people, she was delighted.'

He describes the awesome silence in prison when an execution was imminent; but it is the little human details that cause the most unease: the chief hangman Pierrepoint basking in the adulation as he arrived to execute someone, and exploding when offered a ham and cress salad, which he took as a slight on his status; Pierrepoint lighting a cigar before he went into the execution and picking it up from the ashtray still alight when he returned to leave the corpse hanging for an hour; the chitchat and the jokes (Dernley's own about a 'well-endowed' male corpse was responsible, he thinks, for his unexplained sacking).

Dernley debunks the notion that there is a 'long walk to the gallows', or that the victim suffers much (eight seconds from being tapped on the shoulder in the cell to the actual drop was the expected standard, and Pierrepoint was discouraged when one took 15 seconds).

'Some people think I am a brutal sod, but I am only

stating facts,' said the man who will take an almost forgotten epoch of British history with him to his grave.

TWO-TIMING NIGEL

Andrew Rawnsley
27 October 1989

Friends last night reacted with shock and disbelief to the news that Nigel Lawson had thrown himself out of the Government, saying he couldn't go on any more. He was 57.

A woman was to blame. Colleagues of the late Chancellor of the Exchequer said he had been feeling acutely depressed for some weeks about his relationship with the woman next door, a headstrong blonde, who liked to dominate her men.

Once inseparable, the two of them had been growing steadily apart ever since Mr Lawson's discovery that she was seeing another man – Sir Alan Walters, an American professor who shared her extreme views about the European Monetary System.

When she refused to stop two-timing him, Mr Lawson could see no other way out. In a note left behind for the Prime Minister, Mr Lawson confessed he could see no other course but to leave this world 'without further ado'.

Earlier in the day there had been little clue to what was about to happen apart from Mr Lawson's unexpected absence from the Government front bench during Prime Minister's Question Time. From the despatch box, Mrs Thatcher had told MPs: 'I have always supported the Chancellor of the Exchequer', giving the impression that she and Mr Lawson were still as devoted to each other as ever. But less than three hours later a sombre announcement from Number Eleven Downing Street confirmed that Mr Lawson had breathed his last as Chancellor.

It fell to Sir Geoffrey Howe to break the news to MPs.

He first revealed that Mrs Thatcher had tried to talk Mr Lawson off the ledge. But, said Sir Geoffrey, 'The Prime Minister was unable to dissuade my Right Honourable Friend' from ending it all.

Sir Geoffrey then detailed the brisk round of Cabinet musical chairs – set to a *presto agitato* beat – to fill the yawning gap around the Cabinet table left by the Member for Blaby.

Tory MPs heard the news funereally, with faces which, in the circumstances, could only be called full of resignation. Opposition MPs heard the news jubilantly, with voices roaring at the rest of the Cabinet: 'Resign! Resign!'

Emotional scenes followed Sir Geoffrey's statement. In an upstairs committee room some Labour MPs hymned Mr Lawson away by singing 'The Red Flag', with the resonant line: 'It shrouded oft our martyred dead'.

The shadow Leader of the House, Frank Dobson, stricken with glee by the news, talked of 'the most profound economic and political crisis'. Eric Heffer, sobbing with delight, said 'the rat has got off the ship before it sinks'. Dennis Skinner, hardly able to wipe away the tears of joy, was almost rendered speechless.

Paddy Ashdown best caught the mood of all Opposition MPs, and not a few Tories, by offering the 'sympathy' of the House to Mr Lawson. He had 'taken the only honourable course left open'. The former Chancellor had been driven to this desperate act by the 'arrogant, dictatorial' behaviour of the Prime Minister. 'She', cried Mr Ashdown, 'must go.'

But she wasn't there on the front bench to hear him.

Mrs Thatcher was said to be too stunned to speak about her loss.

Mr Lawson leaves behind a devastated Cabinet, a distraught City and a sinking pound. The late Chancellor is survived by the Government, but maybe not for much longer.

There will be private memorial services at the Treasury and in his constituency. No flowers.

REFUGEES IN THE SAME OLD BOAT

Melanie Phillips
27 October 1989

When is a refugee a real refugee? Only, it would appear, when Britain isn't involved. An ignoble history seems poised to repeat itself yet again. The Government's threat to force the boat people back from Hong Kong to Vietnam is entirely consistent with Britain's policy towards refugees over many decades. This country has time and again sought to keep refugees out of British territory by insisting that they are just not refugees at all.

The buzz phrase is 'economic migrants'. Refugees? says the Government. What nonsense. These people are just in search of a better way of life. They don't conform to the international definition of refugees. Er, well, actually, some of them do. Why some and not others? Well, those 13,000 who got to Hong Kong before the official policy of screening started in June last year are all bona fide refugees, it seems, simply because at that stage no one had devised a wheeze to prove that they might be something completely different. Since screening started, some 10 per cent of these wretched people have been classified as refugees. The remaining 40,000 or so have been categorised as economic migrants, and if they won't go back voluntarily it now looks as if HMG will force them back, despite fears that in their economic desperation to migrate they may even more economically kill themselves out of fear of violent reprisals if they return to Vietnam.

The list of these fortune-hunters is growing all the time. Take the Tamils of Sri Lanka. Just out to better themselves, shrilled ministers and backbench MPs. So they were thrown out back to Sri Lanka where, surprise surprise, some of them were duly tortured and ill-treated, just as they had said they would be, before being restored to Britain courtesy of the British judiciary, who declared the Home Office to have acted illegally.

Take the Kurds, people who seek admission to Britain on the grounds that they face well-documented torture and oppression in Turkey and who said their fear was so great they would kill themselves rather than return. Economic migrants! shouted ministers and their acolytes. So two Kurds economically set fire to themselves in Harmondsworth detention centre and one of them actually died. What horrors are in store when some 40,000 upwardly mobile boat people in fear of their lives are forced on to the planes to take them back to Vietnam?

The distinction between economic migrants and genuine refugees appears to be a bit of semantic legerdemain. When do economics stop and politics start? If people want to be free, they're called refugees; if they also want to be better off at the same time, they're called economic migrants. By that definition, the East Germans flooding out of Hungary are definitely not refugees either, yet somehow British officials seem able to get their tongues round that awkward word when people are fleeing to freedom from behind the Iron Curtain, but not when they're fleeing communism in Vietnam.

Could it be simply because the East Germans are not directly a British problem? Or could it also be that refugee becomes a forbidden word when Britain's interests are at stake? Turkey, after all, is important to Nato, we supply Sri Lanka with arms and military training and China is demanding that the boat people must be removed from Hong Kong before sovereignty is transferred in 1997. If persecution is actually only economics, lexicography is certainly politics.

The unfolding tragedy in Hong Kong displays some striking similarities with another glorious chapter in British Colonial history. On September 2 1939, the day after war broke out in Europe, six years after the Nazis came to power in Germany and started the systematic persecution of the Jews, a British coastal patrol opened fire on the first of many illegal immigrant ships carrying refugees to Palestine from Europe. During the following two years, when Germany was not actually obstructing Jewish emigration and when thousands of Jews could have been saved, Britain did everything in its power to obstruct the refugee ships because it considered it was not in its strategic interest to let them in.

As Bernard Wasserstein documents in his majestic book *Britain and the Jews of Europe*, it did its best to seal the escape routes. It exerted huge diplomatic pressure on a range of countries to stop the ships from leaving Europe for Palestine; it ignored legal advice that it was flouting international law in intercepting these ships on the high seas; when ships successfully ran the blockade, it interned their diseased and starving passengers; the Colonial Office tried to cut off aid to an immigrant ship blocked by ice on the Danube in dire need of money and food; it considered returning the immigrants to their country of origin; passive resistance by one group of refugees resulted in their being beaten back on to the boat; ships were wrecked and blown up.

And all the time the British Government insisted that they were not refugees at all. The term economic migrants was used even then; the refugee influx was classified as 'an organised invasion for political motives'. A memorandum by the Foreign and Colonial Offices distributed in January 1940 opined, in terms which the present Government would surely applaud: 'Illegal immigration is not primarily a refugee movement', although it conceded there were some genuine refugees among the immigrants. When the ship the *Salvador* was wrecked in the Sea of Marmara and more than 200 refugees drowned, including 70 children, the then head of the Foreign Office refugee section, T. M. Snow, commented: 'There could have been no more opportune disaster from the point of view of stopping this traffic.' Sir John Shuckburgh, the deputy under-secretary at the Colonial Office and no friend to the Jews, was driven to ponder aloud: 'What is to happen to these wretched creatures when they are driven back into the open seas, it is difficult to imagine . . . However, these are days in which we are brought up against realities and we cannot be deterred by the kind of pre-war humanitarianism that prevailed in 1939.' The new Foreign Secretary might consider whether he wishes to continue the tradition.

OUT OF OUR MINDS

Leader
31 October 1989

Good evening. You may have read in the newspapers of the resignation of the Chancellor of the Exchequer. This is tittle-tattle. We have done very well together for the last six years and very well for Britain and I think the results are clear to see. Nigel and I worked very well together with great success. He went with great dignity. Now let's get on with the future.

The economy has been run extremely successfully, we've created more wealth than ever before and spread it more widely than ever before, a standard of living people have never had before and a reputation of Britain overseas that is second to none. We are unassailable. I take the blame for most things that go wrong, and now and then a little credit for what goes right. And let's face it, Brian, Nigel was Chancellor! His reputation was second to none. He was unassailable. Advisers are there to advise: ministers are there to decide, and that was what we did. I have been asked about this five times, and I have replied five times. I am not going on like this. I am going on and on and on, but not like this.

Brian, the Europeans talk about being European and *communitaire*, but we practise it. That's life, what's the problem? I really can't have Britain worsted by other people having a different set of rules from the ones we have. We play fair, and the more liberal economics they have, using it with a small 'l', the better it will please me and I will be delighted when they have it. They will go with great dignity. They will be unassailable. At present, let's face it, they are higgledy-piggledy. They cannot go on like this. I like a strong pound. I don't like tittle-tattle, and I don't like higgledy-piggledy tittle-tattle.

Let's start the question again in a different way. I am staying my own sweet reasonable self. I like strong men, Brian, and I like strong women about me, and I like a strong pound. That way we have strong government. A strong pound is unassailable. It isn't higgledy-piggledy and it isn't tittle-tattle. Most Chancellors and most Prime

Ministers like a strong pound. Nigel and I and a strong pound worked very well together with great success. And, let's face it, he was Chancellor! He was not there to advise, he was there to minister. That's life, what's the problem? Strong ministers are unassailable. I really can't be worsted by other ministers having a different set of rules from the ones I have.

Now let's get on with the future. I am staying my own sweet reasonable self. Strong leadership will continue. Tittle-tattle will not continue. Unassailable higgledy-piggledy tittle-tattle will not continue. And, let's face it Brian, I am Chancellor! I am unassailable! Now let's stop this tittle-tattle. Strong leadership will continue, and now and then I will take a little credit for what goes right. That's life; what's the problem?

That was a party political broadcast on behalf of the Prime Minister.

AT THE BOTTOM OF THE PILE

John Ezard
6 November 1989

Mrs Pao Ha was walking in the yard of her old people's tower block in Kowloon this weekend when men suddenly began unfurling a red carpet in front of her.

The sight added a spring and a mischief to her step; for a moment she was tempted. However, she knows her place. She walked beside the carpet, not on it. The men were rehearsing for Princess Diana's 30-minute tour of the charity-run home next Thursday. Pao Ha, aged 78, will be a face in the crowd then.

Many of this colony's high and mighty will walk on red carpets in the reflected lustre of this week's royal visit, which starts on Tuesday. But nobody has ever considered laying one out for Mrs Pao Ha or for her fellow residents Mrs Ho Fook Hing, 70, and Mr Kam Fong, 82. Nor, more practically, do they, their children or grandchildren figure in the currently desperate diplomatic arithmetic about how many hundreds of thousands or millions should be given legal right of abode in Britain, or at least a tenuous promise of international refuge, if the saddest Armageddon scenario comes true here after 1997.

For no one expects her or her kind to leave. They are the *da gung jai*, a street phrase which means people at the bottom of the pile, subsistence wage-earners of the past or present, those who can't build up capital by doing business. Their families have been refugees once, from China, and victims three times – of the Japanese occupation, of the subsequent Chinese civil war and of the throes following Mao's revolution.

Their families may become victims again, if Hong Kong's transition back to China goes wrong. But they regard themselves, and are officially regarded, as too poor to become refugees again to anywhere.

'There is nowhere we or our children or grandchildren can go, nothing we will do,' Pao Ha said. 'We are not afraid who have no money. Only people who have lots of money and big cars, people who wonder where to go, are afraid. Our hearts are settled. We die with Hong Kong.'

And as she, Mr Kam Fong and Mrs Ho Fook Hing contemplated the fears and choices of the comparatively rich, of the red carpet people, a chuckle of gallows humour came into their voices. It was the tranquillity, inflected with irony, of men and women whose choices have run out.

The Helping Hand charity home, where they live, is

funded chiefly by the Royal Hong Kong Jockey Club and the women's Rotary-style Kowloon Zonta Club. The charity started 10 years ago, when tens of thousands of widows and widowers were discovered at the bottom of the pile, living in privately rented tenement bed cages six feet long, three feet wide, without cooking or sanitation.

Through what Helping Hand called an 'incredible' spirit of mutual care, they had survived these conditions for up to 16 years.

Each carries the blood of a village dynasty tough enough to have outlived times of historic chaos only to hear these times re-echoed in the June gunfire of Tiananmen Square. Pao Ha, Ho Fook Hing and Kam Fong grew up in China's Guangdong province as subjects of the emperor before the last emperor. Each talks of the hinge years of their lives as 'after the peace' – after the 1949 Communist civil war victory which temporarily lifted a blight that began with the 1938 Japanese occupation.

'We had meat again when the peace came,' Pao Ha said. Her family lived by buying and selling salted fish. The Japanese disrupted this trade and took chicken and pigs. 'We had to work hard to eat two rice meals a day,' she said. Yet, by the standards of that time and place under the Japanese, she wasn't doing badly.

Kam Fong, who fathered six children, said: 'We could not afford to keep my three daughters. I gave them to relatives who were richer than us. But they could not afford to keep my girls. All my girls died.'

Ho Fook Hing couldn't afford full rice meals. 'We lived on two meals a day of *congee* – rice cooked with lots of water. Also we ate roots from the centre of banana trees. All 60–70 people in the village lived like that.

'My ten-month-old baby girl died of diarrhoea. There was no doctor around. Then my two-year-old boy died after three or four days of high fever. We had no money for a doctor. Then my three-year-old boy had high fever for ten days. We sold my clothes to hire a doctor. The doctor came to my son in the morning. The same night my son died. I think of their deaths and feel very sad.'

Ho Fook Hing wept. Our interpreter, Ng La-Ging, a girl young enough to be her granddaughter, hugged her in empathy. In a taxi on the way to the interviews, Ging, a Birmingham University linguistics graduate whose family comes from the same province as the three elderly people, had said, 'The topic everyone I know in my generation talks about every day is leaving Hong Kong. It's so sad. Over the years you come to love the place. You are so proud of it and yet you have to leave it.'

After the 1949 Communist victory, buying and selling revived in Guangdong. Pao Ha said, 'The army moved into the village hall where people went to worship their ancestors. They lived there and they were nice, but people did not really like them. We had to work to pay them taxes.' Kam Fong said, 'I had to give land belonging to my ancestors to the communes. I would have been shot otherwise. It was very, very sad.' All three took advantage of the short period before Maoist China closed its borders to go to Hong Kong.

Pao Ha said, 'Life was better here. It was easier to find jobs. We got two proper meals a day to make us feel warm. We were not so disillusioned.'

Ho Fook Hing said she also had land confiscated. 'We worked for the Communist Party, chopping wood. Then they rationed rice.'

In Hong Kong, she bore four more children. The brightest of her eight grandchildren has twice been moved up a year at Hong Kong University. But she said, 'I do not think he will have enough money to go anywhere else if there is trouble after 1997.'

Kam Fong said, 'My children say, we have not got any

money, where can we go? If they had got money, they would go to Britain or Canada. As it is, I think they will have to go back to our ancestral village.'

SEIZING THE NATIONAL MOMENT

Martin Woollacott
11 November 1989

This has been Germany's year. From the crisis over Nato modernisation in March to the casting down of the Wall in November stretch an astonishing nine months in which Germans on both sides have reached out with increasing boldness to take their destiny into their own hands.

The rest of Europe has watched in fascination and sometimes in fear.

The international landscape with which we began 1989 – the old, familiar structures of the two alliances, the Anglo–American special relationship, the European Community's halting progress towards greater unity, and the newer but also beginning to be familiar element of reform in the Soviet Union – is being transformed, and it is Germany which is leading that transformation. In so far as the old remains, it is like an empty chrysalis, preserving the shape but not the substance of what existed before.

How distant now seem the quarrels of the spring over the introduction of new short-range missiles. West Europeans and Americans were arguing angrily about whether the Soviet Union was conspiratorially seeking to gain military advantage by negotiating away the West's remaining tactical nuclear weapons and then stalling on conventional reductions.

Strange to recall, we were still thinking in terms of Eastern Bloc tank armies and fighter squadrons, still counting divisions on the map of Central Europe, and still, some of us, acting as if the USSR remained a dangerous antagonist.

The revolt of the Bonn government against this antique thinking can be seen as the starting point for the great burst of German national assertion which culminated yesterday in the streets of Berlin.

Although Chancellor Kohl later agreed to an apparent compromise, it was clear even then – how much more so now – that West Germany had killed the programme, and it had done so because it sensed far better than any of its Nato partners how completely President Gorbachev had changed the situation in Europe.

The West Germans had cast an unprecedented veto against new nuclear weapons. They had done so after a period of co-operation and consultation with East Germany which looks in retrospect like a laying of the groundwork for what was to come in both Germanys.

The Federal Republic became the strongest advocate of arms control within Nato and the German Democratic Republic played the same role in the Warsaw Pact. Here was the partial and still nuanced defiance of their respective Alliance masters that indicated both a German refusal of the role of victims in the superpower struggle and a sense in both German states that the room for manoeuvre was growing.

If the March crisis over missile modernisation now seems something from another era, so too do the fears of the summer.

Germans on both sides realised that the Soviet Union had made not one but two fundamental international decisions. The first, of course, was to seek peace with the West. The second was that force could not and should not be used to maintain Communist authority in Eastern Europe.

For East Germans, watching Poland and Hungary, the message was there: things were moving towards the point where you could leave the country without real risk, and you could criticise the Party without real risk.

Out of that realisation came the explosive mixture of a massive emigration from East Germany and an overwhelming popular challenge to the Party inside it. The reaction of Americans and other Europeans to the summer exodus was, however, still embedded in the old thinking. The Soviet Union would permit a united Germany only if that state was to be neutral, the argument went, and that way lay the old nightmare of a Germany swinging between East and West. But the whole idea of neutralisation presupposes the continued existence of a world polarised between East and West, a world which is literally disappearing before our eyes.

It must now be clear that whatever form of unification or quasi-unification is eventually arrived at will not involve the neutralisation of West Germany in any meaningful sense. Instead what we have before us is a German triumph that could not have happened without Gorbachev and Walesa, a triumph that was not planned and which is in many ways an accident, but which nevertheless has come about because both West and East Germans have seized the moment of national opportunity. In doing so they have pointed the way to a European future in which Germany will be the single biggest power, economically, politically, and perhaps militarily, so far as that still matters.

For the rest of Europe this assertion of German nationhood has its unavoidably bitter dimension. Britain has spent the last 100 years fighting against the facts of German power: indeed, our modern national identity has to a great extent been forged in the fires of the great conflict with Germany, while our sense of our moral worth rests in part on our role in the defeat of Nazism.

Even in the post-war period Britain's understanding of itself has continued to be fashioned by our taking a leading part in the containment of Germany that was the unspoken second function of the Nato alliance.

For the French, too, the trauma must be a serious one. Their recent history is also centred on conflict with Germany, but their solution has been a different one from that of the British. Their post-war policy has been based on the effort to create an enduring Franco–German axis that would maintain French power in Europe. Who can say now that this solution can survive in a larger Europe in which a unified or confederated Germany is the strongest element?

There are darker problems than these for all Europeans, problems that have a special anguish for Slavs and for Jews.

Can we entrust the future of Europe to a Germany which has still not wholly rid itself of a nationalism that hankers, whatever is said officially, over the 'lost' territories in the East, that still sees Germans as superior to other nations and races, that still relishes power over others?

The historian Golo Mann wrote 20 years ago that Germany's post-war recovery took place against 'a historical background of which Germans had reason to be profoundly ashamed.

'Many were honestly ashamed; others said they were within limits; many were not.'

The temptation for Germans now, even though the generation of which Mann was writing has largely passed away, is to see in the great breakthrough of the last few months simply a kind of vindication of Germany's efforts to achieve hegemony in Europe, to see the first and second world wars and what is happening now as three chapters of the same story.

There is no denying a basic sense in which this may be true, and yet the last chapter will surely be different.

Europe is a different place, Germany is a different country. The international order the British presided over had no proper place for Germany, but that which the United States brought into being after 1945 has given the Federal Republic a privileged if somewhat constrained position.

And the closed cultural and political world of the old Germany has gone. Germans now are Europeans in a way they were not before, and indeed the demand of East Germans that they be allowed to be Europeans, with the same wide-ranging and unquestioned rights to travel, study, and residence as the rest of us, was both a catalyst and an indication of how much things have changed.

It is also true that the phenomenon of German power is not so recognisable inside Germany itself, where on both sides there is a sense of vulnerability and of continuing risk that militates against any revival of chest-beating nationalism.

We may have our worries about the different future we see opening up before us – it would be odd if we did not – but surely we must see what is happening at the Brandenburg Gate as a European as well as a German triumph.

THE FRONTIER GONE

Leader
11 November 1989

They crossed the border with incredible joy, amazement, tears and good humour. They sang and sparkled, above, below and beside the Berlin Wall. It was one of those very rare, absolutely electrifying, moments when the ordinary lay people take over and all the professionals – from prognosticators to border guards – get quietly out of the way. From the sidelines we should now be thinking big, electric thoughts about a future where so much, as yet barely definable, is possible. Germany is a country on the verge of reunification in spirit – never mind too much yet about the jurisdictional details. Something will take shape, probably closer to confederation than a total merging of frontiers and institutions. The process under way simply sweeps aside the natural hesitations of history (from Mr Gennadi Gerasimov yesterday in Moscow to the ex-army paper-seller up the road) about seeing one Germany once again. It also sweeps aside, with only a touch-wood percentage of remaining doubt, any real chance of tanks or troops or anyone else standing in the way. The victims of Beijing died so that everyone else would realise that this is now the unacceptable and dead-end alternative.

The crumbling of the Berlin Wall also signifies definitively, beyond the powers of any assemblage of international strategists to deny, the end of the superpowers' Cold War in Europe. Those flickering black and white images of the Berlin airlift can go back to the film archive room. Europe has emerged from the post-war transition which was no less transitional for lasting over four decades. The long-obvious truth is now openly revealed. Politics, internal and external, not weapons, kept Europe divided. Counting missiles and armoured personnel carriers was never a more mature exercise than collecting train numbers. Our own former Defence Secretary, Mr George Younger, seen briefly yesterday going on about the 'absolute preponderance' of Soviet troops in Europe, needs to take a deep breath and have a word with his American friends, who have themselves fallen into reflective silence. Anyone who now proposes to modernise short-range nuclear weapons should have his (or her) head examined. Does anybody currently believe in any conceivable scenario which would set the Warsaw Pact in motion, or the Soviet army on its own? If the Wall can come down, so can the alliances. Perhaps it will need a deal of tact, and tactical redeployment of generals without jobs. But we should start the advance planning for the decommissioning of the deterrence machine now. And it would be sensible to do it together, in bilateral pact discussions. Indeed, it may be prudent for the European chunks of the alliances to get together at the double, before they find themselves abandoned by the superpowers who – from Moscow to Washington – may see the point of commitment in Europe transformed overnight into a negative asset.

There is no denying that the centre of European gravity is going to shift as a result of the German earthquake. No one can be quite sure that some new fault line will not appear. It is very important not to encourage, in appearance or reality, a situation where East Germany simply joins 'the Western camp'. That would be to create a fresh imbalance – another reason why the dissolution of one monolith must be accompanied by that of the other. It would be the surest way of providing Mr Gorbachev's critics – apparently at the moment disarmed like everyone else by the speed of events – with destructive ammunition. The Soviet Union (unlike, we should note, the US) has always insisted that it is a European power, and will be rightly alarmed if a new Germany merely enlarges the other Europe. It is preferable to see (and we can hardly prevent) the re-emergence of a Germany linked to the rest of Europe, but essentially its own arbiter. Since that was the sovereign role we deliberately created for West Germany, we can hardly deny it now to the East as well.

There are shadows in many minds: of course there are shadows. But West Germany, over forty years, has developed the most prudent of democratic credentials, the most wise and cautious of voting patterns. Germany with its entirely new human face is the formidable economic power on the European – and world – scene. If reunification is a challenge, it can only be met by more wider European co-operation. As the horizons enlarge, even 1992 begins to appear a somewhat limited concept which will move sharply down the agenda in Strasbourg next month. Looking even further ahead (but if ever there was a stimulus to vision it is now) we begin to understand the potential behind the idea of Mr Gorbachev's common European home. A Europe where national rivalries are subsumed by economic co-operation, where military budgets are cut to ceremonial levels, where the wealth is at last available not only to tackle long-neglected evils at home but to pay for a genuine fight against poverty, injustices and ecological disaster in the rest of the world.

THE SOUNDS OF UNITY

Ed Vulliamy

13 November 1989

The anthem of the reunification of Berlin established itself in the west of the city over the weekend, and it was neither a political speech nor a verse from *'Deutschland Über Alles'*.

It was the amicable, scooter-like chugging of thousands upon thousands of little Trabant cars, brimful with families map-reading their way through the biggest weekend party of the 20th century. The cars formed convoys along the cobblestones and boulevards, or parked – illegally but unpunished – on the pavements.

Two million East Germans invaded West Berlin, making history with a good day out. The cork-popping on the Berlin Wall at the end of last week had been portrayed to the world as the symbolic theatre of reunification.

That drama was played by a few thousand. The millions that followed them came for a first, awestruck inspection of the lavish shop windows and the capacious bars of the *'Modell Deutschland'*.

All over the city, seven-hour queues crammed the pavement, waiting for each visitor's DM 100 gift from the government. In the banks, they collected a white slip of paper, walked over to the *Kasse* and exchanged it for either a blue note or two brown ones. A girl dressed in brushed denim, which is the uniform of the reunification, burst into tears when she was given hers. It was more than money – it was a certificate of freedom.

'We waited more than seven hours,' boasted Kerstin Haneis, a teacher from Karl-Marx-Stadt. 'We came at 8.30 this morning to see my cousin and now we will go round the shops – this is a lot of money for us.'

But she said she would not leave her family and her home.

Not so Karl Lochner, a telephone engineer. He planned to spend half his money on an unforgettable night out, then collect his bags from the station and begin a new life . . . he wasn't quite sure where or how.

The multitudes gathered even in the souvenir kiosk at subway stations: fluffy animals, chocolates, souvenirs and trinkets were second only to electronic gadgets in the order of preferences.

But the biggest congestions were around the marvels which even the DM 100 windfall could not secure.

A young couple at the front of a five-deep huddle stared at a Mercedes 500 on its rotating platform as though beholding some divine miracle; a windowful of watches, televisions and CD players similarly enraptured an elderly man in a beret – he wore a badge reading *Ich Bin Frei* – I am free.

They took photographs of domestic equipment or bicycle shops; a man and his son discussed the diferent sorts of ratchet on display in a hardware store. A child pealed with glee on using his father's new Walkman.

Many toured on the subway system, studying their maps carefully. They travelled for the first time on the Western subway underneath their own city, for the trains criss-crossed the Wall, yet the stations in the Eastern zone are sealed and closed.

But the usually guarded *Passcontrolle* between the underground western S-Bahn and the ground-level eastern streets was open and jammed full of people either returning home from or setting off for the wonderland over the Wall.

Thousands returned east through the autumn dusk and the *Invalidenstrasse* checkpoint on foot or in cars, tempers fraying a little, their babies starting to cry – but visibly glowing with quiet joy nevertheless.

Mr Gunter Moll's chugging Trabant had broken down and needed a push complete with Frau Moll, Frau Moll senior, two children, a new electric toaster and two pink fluffy toy monkeys. 'I think it is the battery, but no matter, it is the best day of our lives.'

Ralf Meyer wore black leather, and had bought a cassette player and records by Police. Dr Mathilda Absburg had bought suede gloves: 'When I came through with my mother I was thinking much about history and all that has happened before and now. But for a while today, I could just show my mother the city and do some shopping.'

By now, attention was shifting towards the teeming city centre, for the festivities were getting under way on the *Ku'Damm*, Berlin's main street. The calm but deeply moved East Germans thronged the streets, a group of lads wondered at a Yamaha 125 and couples holding hands meandered in to sample Sexyland and its peepshow booths.

The arcades of the *Ku'Damm Karree* shopping centre were bursting with window shoppers, some gravitating slowly towards the sound of a rock band called Eurocheck playing live tonight at the Museumschnepie bar in the depths of the Plaza. 'The sun is up, moon is down, I look up at the sky and I like it,' sang Sabina, the peroxided singer vocalist in her leather jacket and tight leopardskin trousers.

'*Alles Gut*,' said men to each other standing at the gents' urinals – 'Everything good'.

Franz Koener, a librarian from near Leipzig, was – like everyone else in the bar – spending a steadily increasing portion of his DM 100 on Kloster schwarz Pils. 'Today, yes, they came to see the shops, but that is just today. It will keep changing. Forty-eight hours ago we were shut in East Germany – now we are here. What happens now?

'The great thing about now is that nobody knows what happens now . . . but what I will do is to see my friends, even my friends from Czechoslovakia, we can all meet in West Berlin.'

By 4am on Sunday, the labyrinthine shopping arcades had turned into a dormitory resembling a Henry Moore sketch during the blitz. Rows of young people – most of them one over the eight – wrapped themselves in their brushed denim to settle down for the night.

Outside, thousands still patrolled the window displays and a few with some strength left had proceeded from Eurocheck's last encore to the *Joe an Ku'Damm* discotheque.

Just before light, as Torsten Timmler left the disco, he said: 'I will not come here to stay, although the policies in the DDR are of course not good – just think! I live in this city but I never saw it before! But maybe this changes now . . . we have seen West Berlin, it is like a dream. It is my dream of socialism.'

By mid-evening, the East Germans were flooding back into their sector of the city. They carried their booty with them in carrier bags – some of the boys wore Batman caps, and one group paraded its newly acquired ghetto blaster. Some lads were showing signs of wear and tear after a hard weekend. In a bar on the grim Alexanderplatz two boys slumped over their beers and had to be carried by friends.

All over the city, in the rooms of the awesome tower blocks, the spoils of a momentous weekend were being carefully unwrapped, coveted, perhaps, as emissaries of whatever happens next.

THE BEAR TURNS BULLISH

Richard Gott
20 November 1989

Start beneath the faded masonry of the Kremlin wall, at Lenin's polished marble tomb (it may not be there much longer), and stroll across the flattened cobbles of Red Square. Here, between St Basil's onion domes and the GUM department store (itself a cathedral to late-19th-century consumer capitalism), you come upon the entrance to Kubaishev Street, a broad if irregular thoroughfare with stuccoed buildings that still retain an air of crumbling splendour.

Number 6, down on the right, might cause you to pause a moment on an architectural tour of the city. Its brass plaque proclaims that it currently houses the USSR Chamber of Commerce, but its two noble Ionic columns and its handsome pediment, within which semi-naked figures disport themselves with pre-revolutionary abandon, suggest a more intriguing origin. For this was in fact, in earlier times, the Moscow Stock Exchange. It's a measure of the strange world that Mikhail Gorbachev now presides over that the resurrection of the concept of a stock exchange, if not the immediate refurbishment of the actual building, should now be on the winter's agenda.

For what strikes one most forcibly about the current mood in the Soviet Union is the lack of any sign of a renewal of socialism. This may once have been on Mr Gorbachev's programme, but it has long since been abandoned by his supporters in the Gadarene rush towards capitalism on which almost everyone is now embarked. This historic movement is not as visually dramatic as the breach in the Berlin Wall, but there is no mistaking the fact that no one now stands guard in Moscow even at the postern-gate of socialism. All have made their escape. Socialism is for the history books. 'It is now hard to defend Marxism in public,' writes a contributor to *Moscow News*, 'and the revolutionary spirit does not produce much admiration either.' Gorbachev may still speak of socialism, but capitalism is all the rage.

I have come late to Gorbachev's Russia, though hitherto cautiously enthusiastic from afar. Tariq Ali has already written a book about it, so has Anthony Barnett, so too have Martin Walker and Patrick Cockburn. The British Left, in their several and separate ways, have celebrated the downfall of Brezhnevism and the emergence of an official Soviet line on the Stalin era that echoes the traditional Trotskyist position at almost every point. So delighted is everyone by the Soviet Union's dramatic abandonment of its pretensions to be a global superpower that most writers also throw in a measure of wishful thinking about the resurrection of socialism in some hopeful, utopian form. With Stalinist deformations out of the way, is not the old road to socialism now open?

Would that this were so.

I have read their books, followed developments in the press, and watched each unfolding drama on television. But Russia cannot be adequately experienced at second hand. And it has to be said, from all the experience of the briefest of visits, that there is now no great undercurrent of support in Russia for the social and political ideas that inspired the October Revolution of 1917. Far from it. 'What would Lenin do were he alive today?' asked Yegor Yakovlev, the combative editor of *Moscow News*, in playful vein. 'One thing's for sure: he wouldn't quote what he wrote 70 years ago.' Would he, too, endorse the capitalist enthusiasms of the Revolution's eighth decade?

Capitalism is what everyone now longs for in the Soviet Union, without perhaps enquiring too deeply what it really is. But people want to know more about it, how it works and how it succeeds. No one is interested in its failures. Shamelessly under way already is a campaign to join the World Bank and the International Monetary Fund. Once perceived as overt agents of American imperialism, these two Washington agencies are now seen as the external saviours that will help the floundering perestroika project survive.

Discussions about the nature of imperialism have long since been abandoned. 'There is nothing wrong with seeking outside assistance,' says Guzel Akulova, an economist who specialises in international finance, 'at a time when outmoded economic structures are disintegrating.' Look, she says, 'industrialised countries like Britain and Italy took IMF credits in the 1970s, and complied with the programmes suggested by the Fund.' Why, she tacitly implies, shouldn't the Soviet Union? Why indeed not?

'We are novices to a market economy,' she says, 'and it would be quite appropriate for us to follow suit now.'

There is, of course, an additional bonus: 'If we heed the advice of the World Bank and the IMF in setting our house in order, then foreign companies will feel more secure in our market.'

But if creeping capitalism is on the agenda, how realistic is it to think that it could actually be achieved? Russia, after all, is short of experience of the entrepreneurial spirit and historically unacquainted with the Protestant ethic. I met several budding capitalists in state enterprises, embarking on self-management with considerable zeal (and an eye open to hard-currency opportunities), but most of them enjoyed the feather-bedding provided by the state. Few seemed prepared to contemplate the construction of an enterprise that would stand or fall in the market, and when will that kind of market exist in the Soviet Union?

Official opinion in Russia downplays the return-of-capitalism theme. 'Restoration of capitalism is impossible,' writes Nikolai Andreyev, the parliamentary correspondent of the political weekly *New Times*, 'for the simple reason that it calls for private initiative, enterprise, a readiness to take commercial risks, and to risk all one's own in the event of financial failure. These are qualities seldom to be found among the members of our society. Worse still, even if there are people who risk and try to become entrepreneurs, the system dampens their enthusiasm and quashes it.'

Back in Red Square, Lenin, you might think, should be turning in his grave. And not before time. Indeed, it's a toss-up whether the Stock Exchange in Kubaishev Street will be rehabilitated before Lenin's embalmed body is finally given a decent burial. For the historical revisionists in Gorbachev's Russia, having given Stalin's memory short shrift, have now moved a few years further back. They are giving active scrutiny to the years of Lenin's revolution. 'Interest in the Stalin era is waning,' wrote *Moscow News* in its issue celebrating the 72nd anniversary of the October Revolution. 'Ever more frequently today we return to the events of October 1917.'

It's not so much a question now of rehabilitating Trotsky as of reassessing Kerensky.

Moscow News reprinted some of the fresh analysis now being prepared by a special commission of historians, set up by the Central Committee of the Party, dealing with certain aspects of the Party's history. One article, by Vitaly Starkev, restored Trotsky to his proper role at Lenin's elbow in the weeks before the Revolution. Another, by Vladlen Loginov, explained, with an unusual note of regret, how the struggle in 1917 had moved 'from the sphere of political dialogue between different forces to a scene of violence, bitterness and civil war'.

A third article, by Yuri Polyakov, took up a similar theme, recalling the human cost of revolution – 'to bring home the idea of the monstrous dangers of embittered enmity and violence'. 'For a long time,' Polyakov went on, 'Soviet history books idealised and romanticised revolutionary violence. Today we know that this idealisation does no good.'

To contemporary Soviet historians, revolutionary violence has not got much to recommend it. 'Revolutions which strike down the old and propel history forward', Polyakov went on, 'resolve contradictions that have come to the boil. But they can't make all people happy. Marxist historians have tended to ignore the tragedy of the vanquished, and the mutual bitterness that tends to escalate endlessly and become stained with blood.'

The debate about revolutionary violence is of course important in the context of the 1980s. It is vital for the present Soviet establishment to emphasise that there will be no return to the years of Stalin's terror. But the way the debate is going, it can also be read as the first zephyr bearing an implicit criticism of Lenin, a man well-schooled in the Jacobin (and Jeffersonian) tradition of support for necessary terror.

After all this, it is hardly surprising that *Moscow News* should have devoted its back page to a reassessment of Alexander Kerensky, the socialist revolutionary overthrown by the Bolsheviks. At least there is no nostalgia yet for the tsar. The paper regretted that an alliance between Kerensky and Lenin had been so fleeting.

Gorbachev himself has not quite gone this far. 'Some people say that we should go back to *February* 1917,' he told a group of economists the other day. 'But what kind of progress is this if we have to go back and start from square one?' But Gorbachev has certainly given the green light to this re-examination of the nature of revolutionary violence. His most influential ideological adviser, Alexander Yakovlev, wrote in July, at the time of the 200th anniversary of the French Revolution, that violence could no longer be perceived as the midwife of history.

More pressing than the state of history is the development of the present. Gorbachev's experiment with perestroika has grown increasingly friendless. The present regime is particularly unhappy with the criticism that has come from the Left. 'There is now a left-radical school,' says Leonid Abalkin, Gorbachev's economic guru, 'which demands that perestroika be carried out rapidly and resolutely, often without regard for the actual situation.' Abalkin suggests that this is often 'where the main danger to the cause of perestroika is to be found'.

Equally worrying for Gorbachev and his friends is the formation of 'a right-conservative alliance of social forces', created largely through nostalgia for the past and discontent with the present. 'The adherents of this school', argues Abalkin, 'are in favour of returning to old methods. They appeal to the feelings of the masses, flirt with the working class, pass themselves off as its only adherents and advocates, and often exploit the ethnic feelings of the Russian people.' They 'pose a very serious threat to perestroika.'

This conservative element is deeply embedded within the trade union movement, and perestroika enthusiasts can often sound like Mr Norman Tebbit in the early 1980s. One member of an old Bolshevik family told me how he had paid his union dues all his life, and what did he get from them? 'Many trade unionist functionaries', says Abalkin, 'have been drawn into this array of forces, wittingly or unwittingly.' Their demands, he says, 'are camouflaged by the slogans of socialism. But what kind of socialism? The one we are travelling towards, or the one we are trying to escape from?'

Len Karpinsky, a columnist on *Moscow News*, puts it more starkly: 'The ideological foam of Stalinism is again visible on the crest of this conservative wave, this time in a populist version, with lots of clamouring about socialism and communism. But all this "socialism", which the conservatives are busy protecting, is full of Stalin's dogmas.'

It would be nice to report that Gorbachev's friends and allies are engaged in a fruitful and vigorous delineation of their own plans and programmes. But the truth is that an ideological vacuum stands at the heart of the Gorbachev agenda. 'We're up against a scarcity of ideas,' says Vyacheslav Ivanov, a people's deputy, 'the threat of an ideological crisis is real. We must set up think-tanks.'

'There is cynicism too,' says Vitaly Tretyakov, the deputy editor of *Moscow News*, 'cynicism that results from tiredness, from our unsettled state, from our "foundations torn up", from politics and political intrigue, and from sheer material dissatisfaction – they haven't fed, clothed, and housed us fully and at once – and from the fact that there are too many victims, too much hurt pride (we never did catch up with the West), and too great a lack of faith. And finally, of course, it results from the fear that the past might return.'

Gorbachev never meant to be a revolutionary. His speeches often harp on the failures of the Brezhnev years, on the opportunities for reform that were missed. Many leading figures now claim that they were always reformists, but never had the opportunity to carry out their reforms. Yet in the late 1980s their 1970s dreams of reform seem rather small beer. Gorbachev himself tells of a time in the early 1970s when the Central Committee discussed adapting the socialist system to the scientific and technical revolution. 'Everything that was done at that time was consigned to the archives – on the eve of the world oil crisis when the most profound restructuring and adaptation of capitalism was beginning. Capitalism threw millions out of work on to the street and restructured itself. But we . . . retarded the process of rational change which had come to a head in all the socialist

30·10·2257
Y'KNOW—I'VE BEEN CALLED MANY THINGS...
LAWSON IN LEAGUE WITH SUIC
CULT
....BUT I NEVER EVER THOUGHT ANYBODY WOULD STOOP SO LOW....
ATTENTION! ATTENTION!! BIG MOTORWAY MADNESS PILE UP!!
IS IT MORE THAN TWELVE FATALS?? ARE THEY WHITE?? IS IT IN A MARGINAL??
SUICIDE SUMO CULT LINK SHOCK
....AS TO CALL ME AN "AMBULANCE CHASER"
--© Steve. Bell 1989~
WILCO... —WE'RE GOING IN!!
NIGEL LAWSON IS INNOCEN
AMBULANCE
WAR ON ALL FRONTS.... ENEMY WITHIN WITHOUT BEARING 90 DEGREES EAST!
NIGEL LAWSON IS FAT BUT INNOCEN
31·10·2258
NOW HEAR THIS! NOW HEAR THIS!! ARE YOU ONE OF US??... I'LL REPHRASE THAT: ARE YOU ONE OF ME??
SAVE THE BLIP
©Steve Bell 1989~
WHOEVER IS NOT WITH ME IS AGAINST ME! PUT YOUR HANDS IN THE AIR AND MOVE AWAY FROM THAT UNFORTUNATE DISASTER VICTIM.....CHIEF INSPECTOR: TAKE HIS PULSE!!
?

I THINK HE'S BREATHING, PRIME MINISTER. AN INITIAL DIAGNOSIS WOULD SUGGEST HE'S... ER.... NOT VERY WELL....
STOP THE SLAUGHTER OF INNOCENT FATMEN
1·11·2259
...SHALL I BRING HIM IN ...OR SHALL I LET HIM ORFF WITH A CAUTION, BEARING IN MIND HE'S DONE NOTH-ING EXCEPT GET RUN OVER?
© Steve Bell 1989
ASK HIM IS HE FOR ME OR AGAINST ME??
SAVE THE BLIP
HANG ON — - HE'S WHISPERING SOMETHING...
CHRIST!! HE SAYS HE'S ONE OF THE U.K. FIFTY SIX MILLION!
THE EFFRONTERY!! I STAND ALONE!!
MA'AM - WE'VE JUST HEARD OVER THE RADIO — THERE'S BEEN A MEGA-SMASH IN THE MIDLANDS! 
POP
KLANG
2·11·2260
...IT INVOLVES PLANES, TRAINS BUSES, CARS, A CANAL BOAT AND A HORSE AND CART; THE VICTIMS ARE MOSTLY WHITE AND IT'S SPREAD ACROSS THREE MARGINAL CONSTIT-UENCIES!!
WHAT ARE WE WAITING FOR?? ONWARD!!!
BUT MA'AM — IT'S A REAL BIGGIE! ARE WE REALLY EQUIPPED FOR A MAJOR DISASTER? I MEAN - WE GOT PLASTIC BULLETS, A BIT OF GAS, SOME HIGH EXPLOSIVE SHELLS....
...BUT NOT A LOT IN THE WAY OF MEDICAL NECESSARIES!!
©Steve Bell '89
PIFFLE!! ALL I NEED TO BRING IS MY CHARISMATIC, NAY, QUASI-RELIGIOUS PRESENCE AND THE OXYGEN OF SELF-PUBLICITY!

Men – a user's guide

Mark Haddon and Clara Vulliamy

♪ ...the one and only walking, talking Living Doll... ♫

What women want is complex: passion, commitment, independence, security, excitement, tenderness, stimulation, mutual support.

What men want is simple. Utterly fantastical, but simple.

The Mature Woman
Razor sharp suit, cool competence and a job almost as prestigious as his. Underneath these trappings, however, she is a NYMPHETTE (cf)

The Nun
The lure of the unattainable. Not a real nun, of course, but a BLUSHING VIRGIN (cf) who made a mistaken career move. All she needs is a Real Man to reveal the BIMBO (cf) beneath the hessian vest.

The Nymphette
What every Capri driver wants on his passenger seat. Thighs like a leopard, breasts like zeppelins and the brain of a kiwi-fruit. Has the desire to copulate incessantly.

The New Bimbo
The male id's answer to feminism. In essence, a NYMPHETTE (cf), with cropped blonde hair, DMs and a copy of "The Second Sex."

The Blushing Virgin
The larval state of the BIMBO (cf), NYMPHETTE (cf) or NEW BIMBO (cf).

The BIMBO
A basic combination of titanic breasts, skyscraper legs, no GCSEs and a willingness to please that would make a sheepdog sick.

The Mythic Mother
Cooks, irons, sews; washes, mops up baby sick and will listen to him until the cows come home. Also turns into a BIMBO (cf) or a NYMPHETTE (cf) as required.

The Vamp
A racy blend of NYMPHETTE (cf) and the geography mistress. Will treat him like a naughty 6-year-old. Very perceptive...

Men — a user's guide

Mark Haddon and Clara Vulliamy

THE MALE BODY — SOME COMMON MISCONCEPTIONS

It's not only women who think their legs are too hairy or hips are too wide. Men, too, are unable to look at their bodies objectively.

THE HAIRY CHEST

Not all women turn to jelly at the sight of thick, bestial hair.

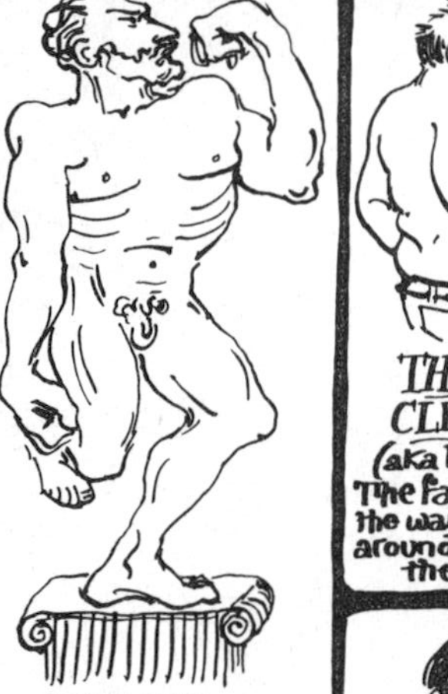

GENITAL DIMENSIONS

The favourite male Paranoia; Strange, since the penis is used only for urination and sex, rather than tenderising steaks, flagging down aircraft, etc...

Where's the stopcock, love?

THE REAR CLEAVAGE

(aka Plumber's Bum)
The false notion that the waist is a line around the middle of the buttocks.

PEEPING ANKLE

Men often believe their legs to be 4 inches shorter than they are.

MONSTER MIDRIFF

Let's get this straight once and for all: if you drink 24 pints of Theakstons a night, buy a long T-shirt.

POSTURE

Sexual body language does not have to be bellowed through a megaphone.

Men ~ a user's guide

Mark Haddon and Clara Vulliamy

Men – a user's guide

Mark Haddon and Clara Vulliamy

countries. As a result, we lost 15 years at the very least.'

Those were years that the locust devoured. Now the agenda has changed. 'The economic situation', says Gorbachev, 'is so serious today that it is having an adverse effect on the social mood. This is hampering the political process and the normal method of decision-making. It is all very serious.' Gorbachev's one-time hope of giving 'a new lease of life to socialism through perestroika' looks very slender indeed.

From the point of view of the West, none of this matters much. Mr Gorbachev is a competent administrator, a man who has put an end to the Cold War, an embryonic democrat in a part of the world where democracy and freedom have no historical roots. For what more can anyone ask?

In addition, on the plus side for the West, the Russians – both the elite and the people – are now wholly and absolutely obsessed with themselves. Developments in Eastern and Central Europe, even in Germany, might as well be happening on the moon as far as the Russians are concerned. Top of the West's agenda, they have a much lower rating in the Soviet Union. In Moscow, all looks rather different. Mr Gorbachev is a centrist politician sitting on a mass of unresolvable contradictions. The central problem for Moscow is the civil war that has now broken out between Armenia and Azerbaijan, an unheralded and still under-reported explosion that threatens to destroy the old Russian empire not just in the Caucasus but in Central Asia as well. The second problem is the economy, and the third is the seismic fault line to the west, running from the Baltic states down through Byelorussia and the Ukraine to Moldavia. For if Russia loses its outlying empire, a nasty bunch of chauvinists and anti-Semites is waiting in the wings.

The 'Union for the Spiritual Revival of the Fatherland'

was formed earlier this year, and it has many supporters in the Party and the newspapers. It has the familiar fascist capacity to address the concerns of the Left with the language of the Right. It deplores the spiritual and moral depravity of the nation, expressed in the people's 'unquenchable thirst for goods', and in 'the selling-off of renewable natural riches to foreigners' which has created 'the threat of an ecological and social catastrophe'. One of its leaders, Michael Antonov, wrote years ago of how 'in all spheres of the Russian people's life there is but one mission: to repulse the attack of rootless and cosmopolitan elements, to throw off the foreign Western forms that have been foisted on the people, and to return to the immemorial origins of Russia.' And in case you're perplexed by the age-old reference to 'rootless cosmopolitans' spoiling the motherland, here is the testimony of Vera Bryusova, another Soviet academic with access to the columns of the newspapers: it is the Jewish power structure, she argues, that is responsible for the destruction of village life and for 'the anti-popular projects to change the courses of the northern rivers and the destruction of the Volga'.

Anti-Semitism and populist ecology. It's a rich mix. If Gorbachev fails, there will be little threat to the West. The cost to the Soviet Union will be immeasurable.

THE HOUSE GOES PUBLIC

Nancy Banks-Smith
22 November 1989

Perched up in the press gallery among, as Dame Edna Everage puts it, a poorer class of person, I had the spookiest impression of having been there before. Perhaps in a previous incarnation as the Duke of Wellington or a woodworm. Then it all came flooding back like a blocked sink. It was a public house.

When I was a child I used to stand at the top of the stairs in my parents' pub, peering through the bannisters while the same hot, rough, ascending roar rose like the head on a pint of Guinness. The same inchoate shout like one voice. The same irritable cry of 'Order, order'.

I would still be sitting there, wondering, if Mrs Thatcher had not begun to speak. Then I remembered. My mother or, if you've never had your ear chewed by my mother, Annie Walker of 'Coronation Street'. 'Of course it was . . . of course you cannot . . . that is nonsense.' Giving them what for.

It was my mother's ambition to turn a pub into a hotel by attracting what she called a nicer kind of customer altogether. The nicer kind of customer sat behind Mrs Thatcher, often wearing eyecatching scarlet. She, of course, wore royal blue. The rougher element sat opposite, snapping their braces and patting their whippets. There was, in fact, one dog, whose name, I am told, is Alf. I have little faith in this information. Occasionally a particularly synchronised roar would make it raise its head hopefully as if it thought it caught the word 'Time!'.

Sometimes a customer would try to catch the landlady's eye. She was gracious. 'We have two customers over here and a third over there. Now which one wanted to come first?' When she sat down the better class of customer rose as one – as if remembering her earlier barbed remarks about idle hands and picking up litter – and left Mr Paddy Ashdown to address a limitless length of leather like a herd of green cows.

At no point did Mrs Thatcher acknowledge the existence of TV, standing there in its corner, knowing its place.

Every other speaker mentioned it in a jolly rollicking way, as if getting the jokes in first. Mr Kinnock generously offered his *papier poudre* for removing excess cranial shine to Mr Gow, beaming brightly on the other benches. I admired Bill Walker, who turned up in a kilt knowing full well that anything below the belt is wasted on TV. Good knees are good knees for a' that.

As the market leaders in British soaps are centred on pubs with landladies who, with a spare sheet and toasting fork, could go on as Britannia without rehearsal, I foresee a limitless run for the Parliament Arms.

People who always spend their lives perched in this place say it was remarkably restrained yesterday. Nobody put their feet on the desk, a habit which goes down badly with house-proud voters. No one swore when their dinner was late, no one threw their plate in the grate.

It was all very 'Did I jog your pint? Tut-tut. Permit me to purchase you another.' Definitely a hotel; positively not a pub.

There was, however, the oddest little opposition on the front benches where Dennis Skinner, commonly known as the Beast of Bolsover, and Edward Heath, obliquely described by Mr Gow as the Grocer of Old Bexley, sat facing each other. Neither seemed to show any interest in their own leader's speeches. Nor the camera. Neither said a word. I don't know why they seemed to me to be ticking.

LIFE, DEATH AND MR RUSHDIE

Hugo Young
24 November 1989

For a man who heads the British campaign to have Salman Rushdie murdered, Dr Kalim Siddiqui exudes disarming joviality. Although he is a Muslim fundamentalist, he claims to be a liberal, and a British one to boot. It emerged, moreover, that he has something in his past which might seem to fortify that claim. This added piquancy to our conversation about life and death and Mr Rushdie.

We spoke some time after Dr Siddiqui's latest inflammatory speech, for which he had been denounced as deserving prosecution for incitement to murder. It was one of several, throughout this year, in which he has reiterated Ayatollah Khomeini's statement that Rushdie must die, on account of certain passages in his book, *The Satanic Verses*. Not content merely to say this, Siddiqui has taken to putting the proposition to the vote at his meetings, and finding most hands raised in favour of death. There could hardly be a clearer case of stirring up the murderous feelings of the Muslim community.

Dr Siddiqui affects incredulity at such a suggestion. He turns out to be entirely against the idea. After 25 years' residence in the same little semi in Slough, he has, he says, too much respect for British law. I asked him whether he personally would have felt obliged to plunge the knife, had I chanced upon Mr Rushdie and brought him with me to Slough. 'No, no, of course not,' he insisted. Murder, it appeared, was 'on the agenda of 998 million Muslims outside Britain' but not of the two million living closest to where the intended victim is in hiding.

On inspection, however, this seemed a less than watertight assurance that Khomeini's *fatwa* was in abeyance. Dr Siddiqui's words had a certain ambiguity. 'Muslims in Britain do not have to execute that *fatwa*,' he said. And: 'We don't have to execute it in this country.' Not, be it noted, 'must not', still less 'must never'. And since Mr Rushdie can have little intention of voluntarily travelling from Britain to any Muslim country, he would surely 'have to be' executed here or not at all. Moreover, when Dr Siddiqui, the day after we spoke, sent me a written message to make quite sure I understood his formulations correctly, he again used an ambivalent phrase. 'It is not for Muslims in Britain to execute Rushdie,' he wrote, adding: 'But if *The Satanic Verses* remains in circulation, in whatever form, the Muslim campaign against the author and the book will continue and intensify.'

When I put it to him that behind this casuistry stood the plain fact that endless repetition of the *fatwa* amounted to encouragement of the Muslim masses to carry it out, he denied the point: 'So if Rushdie remains in this country, he remains alive?'

'Yes, he does,' replied Dr Siddiqui. But then he added, with a world-weary smile, that of course Britain was a place where a lot of murders took place every year. 'I cannot take responsibility for the behaviour of every one of the two million Muslims in this country.'

Nor was the danger likely to be banished soon. The author and his publishers could still withdraw the book, apologise in suitable terms and offer their money back to every purchaser who asked for it. In that case, 'Muslims here would consider the matter closed'. But only in that eventuality, I noted, was Dr Siddiqui prepared to say categorically that he would be going round the country preaching peace. 'I would then do everything in my power to persuade Muslims in this country to accept that as the end of the story.'

Meanwhile, he appeared undeterred by the manifest failure of his campaign. 'The book is our target, not Mr Rushdie,' he insisted at one point. In that case, I replied, since several hundred thousand copies of the book were now in circulation, what was there left to fight for? Ah, he replied, history showed that these campaigns took many years. 'This is going to run and run. It is a matter, if you like, of honour.'

And what about the campaign's counter-productive effect? Its conferring on Rushdie of immortality? 'Hitler is immortal. Stalin is immortal. Vicious people. Attila the Hun is immortal. So what?' It seemed to me that Salman Rushdie would be unwise entirely to rely on Dr Siddiqui's assurance that his quarry was the book and not the man. The issue was not only honour but 'values': the values which Rushdie, with his scabrous abuse of the Prophet, had grievously violated. And here we come to what Dr Siddiqui sees as his Britishness: his allegiance, in fact, to a tradition still closer to home. This emerged in a disconcerting gambit at the start of our conversation. 'I see myself as a *Guardian* man,' Dr Siddiqui declared. 'I have read the *Guardian* almost every day of my life since coming to this country from Pakistan in 1954. I would like British society to develop broadly along the lines the *Guardian* has always advocated.'

Not only had Dr Siddiqui read the *Guardian*, and absorbed, however esoterically, its values. He had worked for the paper from 1964 until 1972 as a writer and sub-editor. Before he took up his present post as director of the Muslim Institute, the paper was his major source of employment. He reeled off the names of such familiar colleagues as Alistair Hetherington and Geoffrey Taylor, and greeted our photographer, Frank Martin, as a long-lost friend. 'I love the brotherhood of journalists,' he declared. He remains a paid-up member of the NUJ.

What, I wondered, had gone wrong? How could this *soi-disant Guardian* man, reared in the bosom of liberal toleration, now calmly be defending his role at the head of the most violently illiberal challenge to freedom of publication Britain has seen in modern times?

It apparently did not occur to him that this was a

contradiction worthy of remark. For although he had wanted Britain to develop 'broadly' as the *Guardian* wanted, he now felt that we, and not he, had taken a wrong turn. He remained, he insisted, a liberal. But we, not he, had gone wrong. 'The throwing overboard of sound values which the so-called liberal revolution has undertaken is not for the good of this country,' he said. 'It does not lead to the wholesome development of a healthy society.'

His denunciation was both specific and general. It challenged, rather awkwardly, the liberal consensus about publication. And it raised a broader question about the state of British society. One began to see the Rushdie affair as crystallising several issues, not the least of them a new one to me: the claim made by Islamic fundamentalists like Dr Siddiqui to be missionaries inside British society, bringing purity and morality to purge what he calls 'the filth of Western culture'.

On the issue of free publication, we reached an early impasse. Again the doctor's favourite newspaper was in the dock. He waved a letter he had recently received from the editor, in which Mr Preston explained his reasons for declining to publish as an advertisement the text of Siddiqui's recent speech. The speech contained, wrote the editor, 'material likely to encourage violence, or lead to the possibility of racial strife'. So it was as unacceptable as any similar ads. Dr Siddiqui found this a strange sort of liberalism. Nothing had done more to encourage strife and violence than Rushdie's book. 'Yet that book has been defended by the editor and his staff, but not my little speech. Because I am not, according to him, the kind of liberal he would like me to be.'

What kind of liberal was he, then? 'I take a very broad view of life. I believe you are entitled to your values, and

I'm entitled to mine. I must not abuse yours, and you must not abuse mine.'

Not only was abuse to be avoided, so, even, was giving offence. When I asked Dr Siddiqui why he liked living here at all, he immediately reeled off the freedoms he had enjoyed: to write, to publish, to be left alone. 'I can publish anything I like,' he said, 'so long as I don't offend other people.'

'Even if you *do* offend other people, surely?'

'I don't quite think so. No.'

'The *Guardian* offends people all the time, and it's free to publish.'

'Only within certain guidelines,' Dr Siddiqui doubtfully replied. The point he pressed was this: 'I'm not going to have Peter Preston or you or anyone else define what kind of liberal I ought to be.'

Nor, he was convinced, were we, rather than he, the true representatives of the British people when it came to Salman Rushdie. The freedom allotted to *The Satanic Verses* was 'invented overnight by the media, the Government and the literati in order to defend Rushdie'. His nomination for the Booker Prize shortlist last year was a piece of manipulation, almost certainly part of a plot. Why, only the other day, hadn't the shenanigans over this year's Whitbread fiction prize shown that prizes were manipulated to suit the organisers?

When I poured scorn on the notion of such a plot, and suggested that Rushdie's freedom was of concern far beyond the 'literati', reaching into society at large, Dr Siddiqui's retort, alas, was not entirely far-fetched. 'I don't believe British society thinks that. The average Englishman would say, "This fellow Rushdie is a so-and-so." I have spoken to people. They say the book is unreadable. They say he has introduced a level of social conflict into this society which no other freedom we have ought to allow to happen.'

It is, however, on the other flank of the liberal inheritance that this fundamentalist admirer of the Iranian revolution bears down with greatest fervour, and might possibly, if he could hoist himself out of the single-issue ghetto, receive in certain quarters the warmest response. Rushdie has to be stopped because 'if we accept defeat, we would be opening the floodgates to this type of literature'. This loathsome torrent, moreover, stretches well beyond insults to the Prophet to encompass the entire collapse of values in their broadest sense. Here we discover Islam in its missionary mode, wishing to do far more than survive as an oppressed minority in a foreign country. Not only does Siddiqui insist on his Britishness, proclaimed alike by his 25-year residence and his mastery of English argot, not to mention his journalistic pedigree. He offers Islam as the saviour of a society that has lost its way.

'Christians have surrendered to the onrush of secular civilisation,' he says. 'Rampant secularism is going to destroy mankind. It is trying to make us believe that the values Catholics believe in or Muslims believe in were acquired in the Dark Ages, when all was ignorance and superstition. It thinks all problems can be solved as long as there is tolerance and enough research institutes.'

Secularism declined to recognise any authority outside man himself. 'I think this is so ignorant, so arrogant and destructive of human personality in the long run, that we are heading for the abyss.'

Islam, he said – by which he meant his fundamentalist version of it, and not the corrupt facsimiles to be found in Saudi Arabia and, in fact, every country in the world except Iran – was alone preserving a God-centred value-system, which enabled societies to emerge that were 'wholesome' and 'healthy'.

Islam therefore offered itself for service. It could do for Britain what Britain had once done for the world. 'What did the British Empire try to do? You tried to change world society into your own image.' This provided Islam with its model, and we shouldn't sound so shocked. 'You're making us sound like criminals,' Siddiqui said in a high-pitched chuckle, 'coming to this society, trying to change the good old British way of life.'

The thirst for change, indeed, was what should bind liberals and Muslims together. Weren't we all in that business? Above all, surely, the *Guardian*? The doctor was ready to admit that he was actually, in certain respects, a conservative. But that didn't make him any less of a liberal. Or less of a *Guardian* man. He just disagreed with what Salman Rushdie said, and would attack to the death his right to say it.

DANCING IN THE STREETS

Michael Simmons
25 November 1989

Vera Handlikova is 66 and cried all night when she saw the tanks come into Wenceslas Square in 1968. Last night she was there again and crying again. 'It's perfect,' she said. 'It's marvellous.'

It was too late to buy a drink, but the square was full of people drunk with joy. Soldiers in uniform, mad slogans pinned to their backs, walked up and down, arm in arm, waving flags.

Waiters abandoned hotel tables and joined in. Taxi drivers flew flags from their aerials and waved at everyone. Passengers leaned out of car windows ringing hand bells.

Car horns blasted in cacophonous celebration. A student under the Wenceslas statue shouted into a megaphone, but he was inaudible. A non-musician blew a trumpet, hopelessly out of tune. It didn't matter.

Sub-rock music came from a record shop doorway with the inevitable chaotic result outside. 'I have never seen Czechs dancing in the streets,' said 22-year-old Karolyna Matouckova, her eyes gleaming.

A BBC man stood in the middle of the square and tried many times to make himself heard: 'In his farewell statement,' he read to the film crew time and again, 'Mr Jakes was very honest . . . '

But the square belonged to the students. Draped in flags, wearing flags on their heads, waving them, holding them high, they strolled, singing and shouting, up and down the square. 'Thank you, students,' the chant went up. David Valik, a 25-year-old teacher, said: 'This is the first-ever non-violent revolution. Gandhi would have been proud of us.'

The debate was interrupted by an old woman. 'Thank you,' she said to me. 'Thank you very much.' And she pressed the national flag she had been waving into my hands.

There was caution as well. Alexander Dubček and the leading dissident and playwright Váčlav Havel were at a news conference when it came through that the Jakes team had gone. 'I think', said the playwright, 'it is time for champagne.'

'I think', said the old reformer, 'that it is time for reflection. Perhaps tomorrow we will be wiser.'

Reflection was not out of order. Anyone who could get near a TV set last night was treated to pictures of riot police inflicting their brutal worst one week ago.

The appointment of the new party leader, Karel Urbanek, raised more than a few eyebrows. 'Long live free Czechoslovakia!' Mr Havel toasted to the jubilant crowd which jumped to its feet in an explosion of joy.

However, a few seconds before sheer happiness and an overwhelming sense of unity flooded the entire hall with the announcement of the Communist Party resignations, differences between the two leading protagonists of Czechoslovak independence remained.

'I do not share the opinion that socialism is unreformable,' Mr Dubček said when asked about the political future of his country on the eve of imminent change in the leadership. 'The Party must be more open,' he insisted.

Mr Dubček led the Prague Spring reforms crushed by Soviet-led armies of five Warsaw Pact countries in August 1968, after the hardline Soviet leadership of Leonid Brezhnev claimed that socialism in Czechoslovakia was under the threat of counter-revoution.

'I used to pass myself for a socialist, but I stopped using the word 15 years ago,' Mr Havel countered. 'This word completely lost its meaning in the Czech language,' he said. 'It became a magic spell with which the bureaucratic power would protect itself. This can be different in other countries. But I do not use the word [socialism] any more. What I want is social justice; there are many examples to learn from.'

SURVIVING – THE HARDEST ART

W.L. Webb
30 November 1989

Ueberleben ist alles – to survive is everything, said Rilke. He wasn't exactly a Czech writer, but he was born in

German-speaking Prague a few years before Franz Kafka, and brought up there before he set out on his poet's odysseys, and certainly no one has said more concisely what the primal need of the Czech spirit has been, not only in this century but for most of the time since the Counter-Reformation.

As this year's miraculous harvest of hope continues to ripen in Central Europe, it's worth remembering that in Czechoslovakia once more it has been a handful of banned writers, tired old poets and sacked philosophers who have stubbornly kept alive the memory of another kind of culture and society, another way of being citizens in the heart of Europe.

By now, responsibility for that survival must be part of the job description of all good Czech scribes. The task descends from Comenius, via those writers of the late 18th century who revived a language and culture moribund after a century and a half of ruthless Germanising with a great transfusion of Shakespeare, Milton, Voltaire and Goethe in new Czech translations. In the 19th century, with Prague still ruled from Vienna, it was the makers of Czech culture, Josef Tyl, Dvořák and Smetana, Bozena Nemcova and Jan Neruda, who made the Czechs a nation.

When the living idea became a constitutional reality, Czechoslovakia chose for its first president a philosopher who flew from Prague Castle a flag inscribed with the words: 'Truth prevails'. Kafka and Hašek survived to see the state and nation fully established and endowed it with great works. Karel Čapek in his plays and novels and journalism was a great educator of the young republic, making men think not only about the growing threat of fascism and some of the demons that science and technology were letting out of the test tubes, but also, with his brilliant teasing of cliché, about the spiritual and political dangers inherent in conformity's evasions and suppressions.

In some ways, the unstuffy incarnation of this tradition was Jaroslav Seifert, Prague's Nobel laureate of 1984, who died only three years ago – one of a generation of fine lyric poets born at the beginning of 'the electric century'. (They were all of the Left, though Seifert was the only true proletarian among them, a fact which made his early rejection of communism and criticism of the Party's leader Clement Gottwald the more resented.)

He has been variously immortalised, by his own lyric memorials of Prague's beauties, architectural and human, but also in that lively scene in Milan Kundera's novel *The Book of Laughter and Forgetting* (reported from the life, Skvorecky assures us), where an aged and legless 'Goethe' is carried bodily down the staircase of the Writers' Club on Narodni Trida by a swaying crew of equally bottled bards:

Finally they got him on to the pavement and up against a lamp post. Petrarch and Boccaccio kept him from keeling over while Voltaire went out into the street and hailed a cab.

'Do you have any idea what you're witnessing?' said Lermontov to the student.

'You're just a student, you don't know what life is, but what a fantastic scene! The poet descending. Do you have any idea what a poem it would make? . . .'

That suggests something of the affection Seifert's peers had for the old lover of women and words and wine, but it doesn't tell you that for quite ordinary Czechs he was *their* laureate, whose poems – which they could quote, too – had been life bread in hungry times. During the Nazi years, writes Skvorecky of Seifert in *Talkin' Moscow Blues* (Faber), 'In book after book of great linguistic beauty – and full of encoded messages clear to the Czechs, impenetrable to the Nazi censor – the poet boosted the morale of his nation and filled hearts with the perhaps sentimental but so needed love for the country and its ancient capital.'

I was able to see for myself how naturally he was called on in bad times in the offices of *Literarny Listy*, the Writers' Union magazine, one day in July 1968, when they came in with the proofs of a special edition being rushed out to put heart into the people while Brezhnev was reading the riot act to Dubček in a railway siding on the Czech–Soviet border. As well as Pavek Kohout's appeal to the leaders not to let them down, the front page had a photograph of Czech partisans mourning a Russian soldier killed during the liberation of Prague in 1945, and . . . a little poem by Seifert: he had to be there too at such a time – the people trusted his voice.

And after the Russians did invade a month later, he called a taxi and himself hauled his failing legs up that staircase on sticks into the Writers' Club to be elected president after Eduard Goldstücker had been driven into exile, refusing Husák and his crew the union's endorsement until in the end they disbanded it and, according to the hallowed Brechtian formula, elected another.

Probably the crucial continuity for Czech writers, though, is the abiding influence of Kafka and Hašek, those strangely complementary, non-identical twins, whose short lives began and ended within a few months of each other. What a legacy to grapple with! No writer has struck such terrible and instructive resonances in this century as Kafka, not least in the warning power of that 'peculiar atmosphere', as Eduard Goldstücker put it, 'in which the greatest bestiality is combined with the highest technology'. That moving hand writes on the wall for all of us. But Kafka's works dominate the Czech literary imagination as immediately as the looming bulk of Hradcany dominates the Prague skyline:

Someone must have been telling lies about Joseph K, for without having done anything wrong he was arrested one fine morning.

From its first sentence, *The Trial* finds direct echoes in the experience of tens of thousands of Czechs and Slovaks under the Stalinism of Gottwald and Novotny and the neo-Stalinism of the people installed under Brezhnev. And beyond the first circle of the afflicted, nearly everyone in daily life has experienced the implacable mad logic of the Law that will not show its reasons or its face, and known the desperation of trying to reason with that malign topsy-turvy, or seek a human response from it.

'My guiding principle is this', says the judge of *In The Penal Settlement*, so ardent with enthusiasm for the shining engine that executes by inscribing the Law in the condemned man's flesh: 'Guilt is never to be doubted.' Tom Stoppard, in his introduction to the American edition of Váčlav Havel's *The Memorandum*, quotes what the playwright said to his judges before he was sentenced in 1979 for helping the Committee for the Defence of the Unjustly Persecuted (whose Czech acronym is VONS):

The system is based on a prior assumption that the state can do no wrong. The decision of a court is regarded as infallible in principle . . . Anyone who questions it is automatically defined as an enemy and everything he does is qualified as hostile. If the institutions of the state can never be in error, then anybody criticising their actions is logically engaged in slander, vilification and so on. And why should somebody vilify? Naturally, out of hostility. And if out of hostility, then, naturally, in collusion with a foreign, hostile and anti-socialist power.

The indictment does not mention what should be the crucial issue – the contents of the VONS statements. The prosecution cannot allow any consideration of what VONS actually said, because to allow that would be tantamount to conceding the possibility of the state's fallibility . . . If you write that student X copied a piece by Váčlav Havel and gave it to his fellow students to read, it does not sound nearly so serious as it does when you write that 'Student X duplicated and distributed in an illegal manner an anti-socialist pamphlet by a right-wing exponent.'

A good student of Dr Kafka.

Given the fact that Kafka's physical world is all around you in Prague, and the malign way in which nature imitates art there, it's not hard to see why the remembering and the rescue of this writer in German should have been a prime duty for Czech writers as soon as the Twentieth Congress made such an attempt feasible. The Nazis had destroyed what was left of the edition of Paul Eismer's Czech translation of *The Castle* in 1939, and in 1948, after the Communist takeover, the complete edition in preparation was suppressed, and until 1957 nothing was published on or of Kafka.

The rehabilitation was mainly effected at a famous conference in Libice in 1962, in the teeth of bitter opposition from hardline East German critics. (The long Czech and Slovak contempt for Prussian and Saxon political primitivism which allowed them always to say, 'Well, but it's even worse up there', was the main reason one knew that Prague would blow not long after the crumbling of the Berlin Wall: to be behind even Red Prussia would have been the last straw for battered Czech pride.) Since then Kafka's influence has been omnipresent, in the plays of Havel and the novels of Ladislav Fuks and Ivan Vyskocil: even in so Czech a writer as Ludvik Vaculik in that fine wry novel, *The Guinea Pig*.

The situation is similar, though less dramatic and more

ambiguous in its effects, in the case of Jaroslav Hašek, the beer-stained anarchist who created that archetypal little-man-as-anti-hero who, since we don't call Dr Kafka Frantisek, we must learn to call The Good Soldier 'Svejk', as the Czechs know him. There's no need to claim some sort of equivalence with Kafka, though it's worth remembering that Max Brod, the contemporary, friend and discoverer, one might say, of Kafka and Janáček, talent-spotted Hašek too: 'A later age will put him on a level with Cervantes and Rabelais.'

Whatever about that, this unholy fool, this sly subverter of all authority and rude demystifier of power and pomp, has been a present help to his fellow-countrymen in their troubles with Habsburgs, Nazis, Stalinists and neo-Stalinists alike. The merry techniques of resistance and survival he supplies in a world in which the chap at the next pub table may *still* be the police spy Brettschneider are the strong form of his popular influence.

There are weak, even weakening forms, too; a kind of nihilism and lumpen anti-intellectualism which the Party itself hasn't failed to exploit in the past. Ludvik Vaculik, in one of the samizdat 'chronicles' in *A Cup Of Coffee With My Interrogator*, imagines *this* Svejk across the desk from him, ominously evolved into a lieutenant of police, but still with 'the very countenance that Josef Lada, Svejk's illustrator and co-founder, established as the symbol of a certain somatic type . . . applying logic as round as a shaven head.'

But Hašek's positive literary influence has been strong, too, most evident in the mix of meaty surrealism and poetry, and pub and street, that you find in the novels and stories of Bohumil Hrabal, author of the novella that was turned into Jiri Menzel's film *Closely Observed Trains*, and the magic lantern show of modern history as seen from provincial Bohemia published recently here as *I Served The King Of England*.

In another of the pieces in his *Talkin' Moscow Blues*, that good novelist Josef Skvorecky gives a picture of the rum milieu in which this utterly Czech figure, lawyer, steel worker, scrap merchant, writer, emerged; over the years Skvorecky has been publishing from his Czech press in Toronto the complete, unexpurgated Hrabal that Prague couldn't stomach:

'I met Hrabal under circumstances that sound like one of his own stories. In the early fifties when I was an editor at a publishing house, one of my duties was delivering obsolete galley proofs to the scrap-paper salvage centre. The fellow in the patched overalls there would examine my proofs with interest. Then he would launch into a fluent discussion of literature; Breton's *Najda*, I think, was his subject that day. Later we met at the flat of the poet and artist Jiri Kolár (best known in the West for his collages), a typical centre of the Czech avant-garde, where we discussed abstract expressionism or whatever was in the air. We also read aloud our verses and stories.'

The last time they met Hrabal was low and full of grumbles. 'I'm as good as done for,' he said. 'Those guys [in The King of Bohemia or some other Mala Strana pub] have heard about the money I'm supposed to be raking in by putting their stories down on paper, and so now whenever I walk into a tavern all I hear is "Here he comes, the great writer! Wants to make another hundred thousand just by sitting and listening!" And they clam up and scowl into their beer.'

Of course, in the great cycle of mean-minded if largely bloodless purges, involving a million and more, that followed the invasion of 1968, many poets have 'descended', many writers and philosophers, banned or evicted from their chairs, have been returned to the people involuntarily, working as stokers, waiters, night-watchmen and hospital porters when they weren't bumping into each other in the ante-chamber to Lieutenant-Colonel Noga's interrogation room in Bartolomejska.

Some of the people involved – like Vaculik, whose plain Moravian way of talking to top apparatchiks at the 1967 Writers' Congress, even the Minister himself, as if they were human beings was one of the things that made his confrères brave and broke the Party's confidence – give so ruefully tonic an account of all this that you may be tempted romantically to see it as a 'positive' phenomenon. Philip Roth, in his novella *The Prague Orgy*, tried to think what it would mean: 'I imagine Styron washing glasses in a Penn Station bar-room, Susan Sontag wrapping buns in a Broadway bakery, Gore Vidal bicycling salamis to school luncheons in Queens – I look at the filthy floor and see myself sweeping it.'

But as you read again what was written and said in 1968 and look at the writings that have since managed to escape the police and customs, it's impossible not to know the overwhelming sense of waste that the Czechs themselves know – the waste of lives and works and the chance of ordinary spiritual fulfilment. Solzhenitsyn had already warned us before the invasion that the Soviet leaders' clocks were slow in relation to our times. For Czechoslovakia, as Váčlav Havel hardly needed to remind the crowds in the snow the other day, it meant that the clocks stopped for 21 years before one of Brezhnev's heirs could catch up – too late? – with Dubček's notion of a socialism with a human face, and enable history to resume again in Central Europe.

Havel himself – five years in prison, twenty locked out of the theatre – has been the exemplary survivor and chief remembrancer of other possibilities in the latest round of

Czechoslovakia's struggle against power that Kundera says is the same as 'the struggle of memory against forgetting'. He connects, in a quite unvengeful way, present-day Czechoslovakia with the liberal-democratic pre-war order: his father was an engineer and wealthy entrepreneur, an uncle built the Barandov film studios, one grandfather was 'a bit of a writer' and even briefly a Cabinet minister. Doubly alienated – as a rich fat city child taken by a governess to the school in the village to which they were evacuated in wartime, then banned from higher education as a child of the *haute bourgeoisie* after the equivocal 'revolution' of 1948 – he has always known what it is to be an outsider, and the unfulfillable wish to 'join' was what developed in him the sense of the absurd which moves in his plays.

But Havel is younger (born 1936) than many of the 'reform' Communists and established activists of the Prague Spring. He has always shared with the generation younger than him the need to see reality without *a priori* ideological filters. In April 1968, in an interview with the film critic A.J. Liehm, Havel spoke warmly of this generation and of the art that the new consciousness, with its instinct for the human and the concrete, was going to produce in Czechoslovakia. Reflecting on this shortly afterwards, Liehm wrote: 'I thought of the people who deluded themselves into thinking that Havel was an exception, an untypical, borderline phenomenon, and not a true representative of this generation. That is a mistake, a terrible mistake. On the contrary, Havel expresses the feelings of his generation with absolute clarity, across the lines of politics and other loyalties. And he speaks for the generation that follows him too. Whoever fails to understand this will have lost everything in this country, once and for all.'

Well, that's a bird that has fairly come home to roost in Prague, where the clocks are chiming again and the dough-faced men in the Central Committee can't hold back history and reality any longer.

The economy apart, how dire the situation is now can be seen in *The Restoration Of Order* (Verso), the book on the 'normalisation' the Communists imposed after August 1968, written by Vaculik's Slovak friend, Milan Šimečka, university lecturer and author, latterly truck driver and builder's labourer. In it he describes the total destruction in 1969 and 1970 of all the wealth of literary, cultural and political magazines the Czechs always bought so avidly before the war and after the Thaw, 'many of them with long traditions and of a standard comparable with the better sections of the independent European press'. Thereby, he said, 'large sections of the recalcitrant intelligentsia had their tongues painlessly torn out.'

Then he describes the consequences of this and similar bulldozings of the social fabric. 'The fundamental aim has been achieved. The Czechoslovak intelligentsia has been tamed and now displays the characteristics it is intended to have in "actually existing socialism". In formal terms, its submission is even greater than in other countries with actually existing socialism . . . This orderliness has one principal defect, however. Should the regime require urgent assistance in the shape of bold thinking or objective analysis of a difficult social problem, it would have no one to turn to.'

Havel spoke the other day of his longing to become a private, play-writing person again, but if Czechoslovakia's survival is to be assured, I'm afraid it will be some time yet before he and Vaculik and Šimečka and the rest of the saving remnant can feel their historic task is done, and retire to cultivate their strictly literary gardens.

ON BORROWED TIME

Ian Black
1 December 1989

It was just before 11 in the morning when the young Palestinian began his slow, menacing march through the narrow alleys of Nablus's old kasbah, with clusters of excited teenagers following him at a respectful distance and others shrinking back in fear.

He could have been no more than 17, but he gripped his rifle with the confidence of a hardened fighter. The muzzle peeping out from under the black plastic wrapping and the slightly curved magazines in his jeans pocket made it look distinctly like an M-16.

The gunman was a thin, sallow youth with a mean face, an undersized Arab Rambo with a swaggering gait to match.

'His name is Hani,' someone whispered as the strange procession went past. Hani would allow no photographs. 'How do I know you're not from Israeli intelligence?' he shouted. It seemed pointless to argue.

Young Hani is a Black Panther, and he is living on borrowed time. Two nights ago, three of his friends were arrested after a chase across the rooftops of the Yasmina quarter of the kasbah. His turn will come, too. And he is unlikely to live to tell the tale. Palestinians with guns rarely do. Black Panthers are loyal to Yasser Arafat's Fatah group and – along with the rival Red Eagles, affiliated to the Popular Front for the Liberation of Palestine – they are the hard core of the intifada as it approaches its second birthday. Their flaunting of weapons – never normally seen in public – attests to a dangerous new stage.

Young Nablusis like these are the self-appointed guardians of the Palestinian uprising, meting out punishment to those fellow Arabs unlucky enough to be branded as collaborators with Israel's feared Shin Bet secret service.

Their justice is rough, crude, and designed to deter: last Friday, in broad daylight and in full view of dozens of onlookers, the Red Eagles executed a local woman suspected of procuring young women for prostitution and of betraying their members to the Israelis. Her corpse was spat at and kicked for hours.

About 150 Palestinians have been killed as collaborators since the intifada began in December 1987, and Nablus, the West Bank's largest and most militant city, has had more than its fair share. As the uprising staggers on towards its third bloody year, the killings go on.

The Israelis may not care for their informers, but they are worried by the danger of armed insurrection and the creation of no-go areas under their very noses. When a Red Eagles leader was gunned down here earlier this month, the head of the Shin Bet personally came to congratulate his men on a job well done. It is not an easy job: if the Panthers and the Eagles are fish, the kasbah is their sea. In the labyrinth of twisting alleys, and along the rooftops, they can move freely within the ancient walls even though Israeli troops are only a few hundred yards away in the modern centre of town.

Israel's military might can do little. Short of razing the whole area, the soldiers are helpless as whistles and prearranged signals warn of their entry.

The sea is friendly, but Hani and his friends may be going too far: after Tuesday's arrests the Black Panthers imposed a curfew and confiscated telephones from houses in Yasmina, desperate to discover how their cell structure had been penetrated.

Resistance is hierarchical, and after the Panthers and the Eagles come the ordinary masked men – Al-Mulathamin in

Arabic – who wear black Ninja suits, carry long knives and hatchets, and were busy yesterday painting new slogans and pasting up pictures on the kasbah walls.

They are not exactly friendly, either, but since they have no guns, and are thus less exposed to the informers, they posed happily.

PIGGING IT

James Erlichman
1 December 1989

They have been dubbed horizontal humans. Pigs are nice, intelligent creatures whose physiology closely resembles our own. Too nice, perhaps, to mince up into sausages. But they taste better than Golden Retrievers and don't look as cuddly or cute.

Pigs are also, by nature, very clean. Given half a chance they will collectively agree a toilet area within their living space and stick to it, or decidedly not, so to speak.

But the pig's fatal flaw is that it will withstand almost any abuse to which man subjects it. It is the near perfect inmate of intensive agriculture.

A further misfortune for the pig is that its carcase receives no subsidy from the EEC. So pork prices are relatively low and most pig farmers, especially the smaller ones, don't drive G reg Range Rovers.

Consequently, many closely packed pig units in the UK are a breeding ground for disease. In its 24-week life a pig for market is fed a steady diet of 'growth-boosting' antibiotics, over-the-counter drugs which speed weight gain. They themselves have questionable effects upon the food chain, but worse dangers follow from the conditions in which pigs are kept. The growth antibiotics are not strong enough to prevent illness. And even pigs, cramped and often tethered in their own filth, finally get sick and infect each other.

Veterinarians are legally forbidden to prescribe therapeutic doses of antibiotics to animals unless they are directly 'in their care'. Farmers are also required to observe the 'minimum withdrawal period' before slaughter – the time it takes for all residues of the drug to leave the animal.

And yet abuse is so rampant that residues of sulphadimidine, an antibacterial drug used to treat rhinitis, keep turning up in the pork we eat.

More than a quarter of pig kidneys sampled by the Ministry of Agriculture in 1985 contained sulphadimidine residues at concentrations 11 times higher than government limits. The Government's chief veterinary officer, Mr Keith Meldrum, describes the problem as 'a long-running saga' but says that educating farmers and vets has improved things. Now residues contaminate just one sample in 20.

Despite their image of being devoted to animals, veterinarians are self-employed businessmen, and livestock vets are in the business of helping farmers put 'the most meat on the hook' at the lowest cost in the least time. Many vets also dispense drugs and make an immediate profit from the markup on their own prescriptions. The more they prescribe, the more they make.

Even if residues have been cut, sulphadimidine remains the most overused and misused drug in intensive livestock rearing. Bad conditions mean a lot of pigs are genuinely ill and are on the drug. But farmers and vets also get round prescribing rules by declaring that herds

SUSPECT CHEMICALS PERMITTED IN UK

NAME	USE	SUSPECTED RISK	BAN
DRUG RESIDUES			
sulphadimidine	pig antibiotic	thyroid cancer	proposed US
chloramphenicol	livestock	leukaemia antibiotic	USA
Carbadox	pig growth	carcinogen promoter	proposed UK ban overturned
FOOD ADDITIVES			
tartrazine (E102)	widely to colour foods	asthma, hyperactivity	Norway, Finland,
red 2G (128)	colour meat products	asthma, hyperactivity	USA, France,
brown FK (154)	colour kippers, crisps, caramels	asthma, hyperactivity	USA & EC except Eire & UK
caramels (E160)	widely used food colouring	possible carcinogen	none
sulphites (E220–27)	food and drink preservative	asthma	restrictions in USA
PESTICIDES			
Alar	apple growth hormones	carcinogen	proposed US
captan	fruit fungicide	carcinogen	Finland
tecnazene	storage of potatoes	unclear	none

are 'in danger of getting ill' and need prophylactic doses added to their feed.

The rules also require sulphadimidine to be withdrawn at least ten days before a pig is slaughtered to ensure no residues remain.

Mr Bernard Peat, a pig specialist at the National Agricultural Centre at Stoneleigh, believes that many farmers are just a bit absent-minded. 'The drug is pre-mixed in the feed and farmers can forget to take animals off it in time.'

Others with a less charitable view believe farmers cynically flout the rules because their chance of being caught is remote and the prospect for prosecution, virtually nil. Ministers have hinted that drug residues may be tackled by the new Food Safety Bill announced last week, but enforcement by overworked inspectors seems unlikely.

Concern about sulphadimidine residues remained a back-burner issue until three weeks ago when the US Food and Drug Administration announced its intention to ban the drug (known as sulfamethazine in the US) because it had been linked to thyroid cancer in rat and mouse laboratory studies.

Gerald Guest, director of the Centre for Veterinary Medicine, said: 'We have several steps to complete, but I expect that in six months we will propose to withdraw this drug.'

While hearings to ban drugs in the US are held in public, decisions in the UK are taken in secret and then not even published. Mr Meldrum said that his officials and scientists had already re-examined the US data and had come (privately) to the conclusion that sulphadimidine was perfectly safe and could remain on sale. There was no reason, he said, to alert consumers.

The Government took a similar stance in keeping the apple spray Alar on sale even though the US decided it was a cancer risk to children and took steps to ban it.

It is instructive to see precisely why the American authorities disagree. Both countries start with the same method to assess risk. Laboratory animals are exposed to smaller and smaller doses of a chemical until a 'no observable effect level' (NOEL) is found. It has been decided (arbitrarily) that humans may be 10 times more sensitive to it than rats or mice. And then, that some humans may be 10 times more sensitive than others. So, the 'safe' human dose is set at 100th the amount (correcting for our much heavier body weight) which just failed to affect a rat or mouse.

The flaws in this are clear. Since we weigh at least 500 times more than a mouse we end up with a 'safe' dose of a chemical five times bigger than the one it got.

Second, the whole concept of a safe 100th dose is mumbo jumbo. Even Professor David Conning, director of the industry-funded British Nutrition Foundation, admits it has no scientific basis. Short-term, high-dose tests on animals tell us virtually nothing reliable about the risk to humans of low-dose, lifetime exposure to a chemical.

Third, and this is the nub of the matter, the causes of cancer are not always dose related. This is why the Americans no longer accept 100th dose safety margins when a chemical becomes a suspected carcinogen.

The American authorities have decided from computer models that the cancer risk from Alar is unacceptable, especially when it is quite possible to grow nice apples without it. They are now moving, in full public gaze, to ban sulphadimidine by the same logic.

This when-in-doubt, take-it-out attitude is good for consumers. It might also force farmers to treat horizontal humans a bit more humanely.

WHEN SEX BECOMES SIN

Duncan Fallowell
1 December 1989

In New York City, estimates of the number carrying the Aids virus vary from half a million upwards. The human infrastructure of the arts has been devastated by the loss of actors, directors, dancers, painters, journalists and so on. Trying to mount a play or ballet in New York is close to impossible – so many of the necessary class have gone. This is not the case in Great Britain, where the impact of Aids on the arts is more general and insidious. We have yet to be shaken into candour – although the process is beginning. References to anal sex have reached the Jimmy Young show, so certain taboos have collapsed.

But other taboos spring up. The initial effect of Aids is a rapid proliferation of NO. These days James Bond is allowed only one woman per film – but is yet to be revealed as a condom-user. The condom is a problem, as well as the answer to a problem. In an infectious, people-jammed world, the Catholic Church forbids its use. The British Government refuses to permit condom distribution in prisons because this would be an admission of what they and everyone else knows: that homosexuality is conventional in prisons. Hypocrisy kills. The Government Aids programme is not so much anti-Aids as anti-sex, a cause the British are always ready to support.

Fay Weldon has said that reading about sex in yesterday's novels is like watching people smoke in old films. Love and romance are supposedly making a big comeback. So at last Fay can write romances on a clear conscience. But love and romance have never been away, any more than sex and smoking have. The coming of Aids vividly reveals how helplessly romantic, superstitious, ignorant and bigoted our sexual thinking still is.

Maybe Aids will force us to be more realistic – and more fanciful. Certainly the forms of love and sex are altering. When did they not? The arts eat up these alterations, as they do everything else, without a qualm. Only the artists left behind turn nostalgic, sometimes aggressively so.

The arts are more discreet than they were 10, 20 years

back. The Rio Carnival too is quieter now. This is due to Aids, and due also to the air of congestion we're all having to cope with. Constraints in art can stimulate creativity, just as taboos are one of the ways in which humans – no longer reflexive animals merely, but imaginative self-conscious beings – bring about sexual arousal (entirely uninhibited lovemaking is entropic; monogamy often founders on this).

Taboos create fantasy, constraint may be stimulating; but art and caution are not healthy bedfellows. Aids encourages censorious attitudes and therefore censorship, which is not stimulation but constipation. Sex shows, sex shops, pornography have been largely swept away from our cities, where they hardly existed anyway. Safe-sex pornography has reached Europe from the US. This is quite as instructive as any government campaign but the British are not allowed pornography, although their prurience makes them imagine they are flooded by it.

Nudity is on the increase in life. The fashion for torn jeans is the body in bondage crying for release – the body is revealed by an act of violence. The whole modern 'look' for young people is the gay/lesbian stereotype with sadomasochistic overtones. Loss of physical embarrassment is also associated with the growth of sport and leisure activities. But representations of nudity are once more disappearing from the ordinary as well as from the pornographic world. Rees-Mogg is appointed to cleanse a television service which, as far as sex is concerned, was already so clean you could hear it bleat. The body may be used in sport but not contemplated in pleasure; used to advertise but not to gratify. The body, the temple of love, becomes the nursery of pestilence, tempting and lethal. The very sensation of sexual arousal is life-threatening. Sex in art will recover its old post-*Fanny Hill*, pre-*Lady Chatterley* malevolence. Only more so.

Television, incidentally, has behaved very responsibly over Aids, whereas the public has been subjected to raucous and misleading intimidation by the press, quality as well as tabloid. One concludes that television is taken more seriously than print and is therefore more aware of its responsibilities, whereas the press feels that it doesn't matter so much if, in the course of indulging its principles, it gets things a bit wrong.

On the whole, Aids is sexually transmitted. In the magnesium flash, the life seed may be swapped for the death seed. It is seen therefore not as a disease to be confronted rationally and sympathetically but as a sin, as a crime against humanity. During this primary phase the fight against Aids has inevitably revived anti-homosexuality. In an aberration from the realm of common values which governments are supposed to foster, Clause 29 singles out homosexuals as the one group in Britain whose attachments are not to be permitted the description 'family' (a word which essentially means 'household'). Petty and ridiculous in itself, this legislation none the less gave official approval to homophobia in the country at large. Ostracisation in the Aids era gives an embattled intensity to homosexual experience and so to art.

Art and literature have only begun to deal openly with sexual matters in the 20th century. It would be unfortunate if the subject were to be driven back into darkness by the challenge of Aids when precisely the opposite needs to happen. The British are especially bashful about utterances on sex and love, the result of their fear of the body and fear of emotion.

No European country can match the complexity of our sex-control laws, although the Aids crisis has of course posed difficulties everywhere. In Italy the Catholic Church continues to oppose programmes of public enlightenment. In Germany the national purity neurosis has resurfaced. The French, whose cult of '*amour*' dislikes any interference, are trying to brazen the whole thing out, notwithstanding the Pasteur Institute in their midst. But the cultural environment in which continental artists work is less philistine, more supportive and adult than ours.

Cyril Connolly's remarks, written in 1938, still carry weight: '. . . It is no exaggeration to say that every English writer since Byron and Shelley has been hamstrung by respectability and been prevented by snobbery and moral cowardice from attaining his full dimensions . . . it is the difference between being a good fellow and growing up.'

Hypocrisy, lies, distortion, secrecy, deceit, threats, self-disgust, cooking the facts, and shame – all these may make life more interesting, but they are no good when trying to cope with Aids and all are exemplified in the case of the writer Bruce Chatwin, the most important Aids casualty in the arts to date. Chatwin was unable to admit to having the Aids virus, presumably because it would have been tantamount to a confession of the homosexuality to which he was socially maladjusted. At a different level, it would also make this otherwise very successful man appear to be a loser in life.

People often view the early death of an artist as the extinction of a production line – oh, the masterpieces we shall never have. But a work of art comes out of all the circumstances of an artist's life. Aids and the prowling death gave Chatwin the opportunity to write an extraordinary book – his character, which gave us the books we have, meant that he couldn't take that opportunity.

The cause of Aids would have been immensely advanced had Chatwin come forward, but if he didn't wish to do so, that's his right. Writers usually refuse to join circuses, however worthy. On the other hand his fear of what was inside him gave his books an enamelled, sterile surface. And if his shame did nothing for his art, it did even less for his death, which instead of being tragic becomes the one thing he didn't want it to be – ignoble. Shame over what one is, sustained to the point of death, produces a curious depression in others.

This is because shame is very contagious. The dark secret was maintained after his death not only by a grieving family but also by many liberal colleagues. It was a campaign not of silence, which is permissible, but of deception, which is not. Public obsequies conducted by those who knew otherwise, ascribing Chatwin's death simply to a bone marrow disease, hit a new low in our ability to tackle the subject. When liberal intellectuals are frightened to mention Aids, what hope for Joe Bloggs? Doctors often collude with families to misrepresent the cause of death, so the medical picture is falsified as well.

Yes, Aids has given us a new subject to write about – but art is not propaganda. It arises from a deeper pit. Aids is our old friend Death in his latest costume. It will give a quiver of tainted fascination to the end of our millennium, as syphilis and tuberculosis did to their times. Meanwhile the artists themselves are being far from impractical.

Gilbert & George's recent exhibition raised £565,500 for Crusaid, the largest single private donation yet. And as we move into a more open, less callous decade, perhaps some good may come from this macabre affliction. Perhaps we may all become a little more honest about what we do, why and with whom. And is that so very important? Well, it can make us generally less abject, less unkind creatures, more capable of withstanding fear and using a candid intelligence to face our bizarre destiny.

STRAIGHT-LACED

Nancy Banks-Smith
2 December 1989

'My God, what was that!' said the headmaster of Mill Hill Mixed Infants, clutching for support at a mixed infant. He had the look of a man who, while painting a white line down the centre of the Circus Maximus, hears Charlton Heston coming round the corner.

My grandmother was withdrawing in good order after giving him a piece of her mind. She was in full war paint. The fox fur biting its own paw. The hat with the crashlanding crow. Though somewhat bowlegged she was straight as a truncheon from the hips up thanks to a Spirella corset with its world-famous, rust-free, spiral steel stay. 'The same wire that is used in high-grade pianos.'

By striking my grandmother smartly on her steel stays with a little hammer you could have played 'Rock of Ages'. Though it would have taken a better man than my headmaster to try.

Even my mother, though very much a child of the twenties and apt to break into a Charleston on unsuitable occasions, wore a Spirella. When she was dying the doctor diagnosed Huntington's Chorea, but it was only my mother's last Charleston. It says something for the world-famous, rust-free, spiral steel Spirella stay ('See how it bends in all directions') that you could even attempt a Charleston in it.

I never wore them. It's my fault that the Spirella factory, makers of made-to-measure corsets for 80 years, closed on Thursday. And yours and yours. Without corsets we cut a completely different figure. Tony Hancock once complained about the rigidity of Hattie Jacques's gravy: 'At least my mother's moved around the plate.' We move around the plate. They were moulded like a rather solid blancmange that used to turn up under the name Shape. It is too late now wishing you had Style 305, 'The most famous firm controlling girdle ever made', with its firm front lacing and flexible spirals. Made, if required, in tropical cotton to terrify the natives. 'It is no secret we have made in excess of a million of this style.' Too late now to whine for one. Money cannot buy it. Be off with you.

In the beautiful Spirella factory, a grade two listed building in Letchworth, Hertfordshire, there was row upon row of old Singer sewing machines. The bright November sunlight caught the sifting dust. Joy Kornowsky, 27 years there, was dusting the silent Singers; Jean Fitton, 33 years there, was hoovering. They were cheerfully heartbroken. Thames Television ('We've locked them in the room at the end') broke out and began filming.

Spirella has been dying for months and the staff were less than pleased at this good turnout for the funeral. 'I told them I don't want to be a cleaning lady,' said Jean. 'We were the cream,' said Joy.

Once the whole huge factory was turning out corsets, with another making only bras. There were 2,000 workers and 6,000 fitters. Then its fortunes, much reduced like our figures, shrank to the one small floor. And now to this. There were bundles of the spiral stay, whose invention in 1904 founded Spirella's fortune. Swung with gusto, one bundle would fell a water buffalo. There was elastic of a resilience to send you spinning down the room. Laces seven and a half yards long. Corset material of an impregnable texture that, come the four corners of the world in arms, would bounce them back again. During the war Spirella made parachutes. You wrench your imagination away from the image of corsets big as barrage balloons, majestic brassieres like double parachutes and strong, snapping suspenders floating down on the demoralised Hun. 'Mein Gott, vot vos dot!'

After the war there was a rush of orders from women whose firm controlling girdles with hose supporters of heavily nickled brass had only just made it to D-Day. Rather like the sudden hurry of 7,000 orders that came in when old customers heard the factory was to close. Joan and Betty Carter, sisters with 94 years' service to Spirella between them, were checking orders with 'What shall we do next year?' on them. As the Duchess of York (no relation) said in my favourite line from all Shakespeare: 'What stays had I but they? And they are gone.'

It is as obvious that the present Duchess of York does not wear stays as that the Duchess of York before her, the Queen Mother, did. That luscious hourglass shape comes with resolute elastic. And the Duchess of York before *her*, Queen Mary, was so straight-laced she could only incline slightly from the hips. As a girl, if you'll believe me, she used to turn cartwheels.

Spirella came to you as if you were royalty. The company had this nationwide net of corsetieres, a name later changed to consultants in a fairly foredoomed attempt to keep up with the times. Their 'Guide For Corsetieres' is helpful on the correct approach. 'Usually a few pleasant remarks will put the prospect at her ease. "The room is beautiful, Mrs – . It tells me you are artistic. Did you plan it yourself?" If a child is present or if there is a pet in the room, some comment to or about them always creates a friendly atmosphere.' Well, I don't know. I think it is the upbeat American influence of the founder. It never looked like that to me. A woman of the most repressive respectability would arrive and, failing to make any pleasant comment to or about me, disappear into the bedroom with my grandmother leaving me to lurid speculation.

What she was doing was lurid enough. She was fitting

the Spirella Patent Modelling Garment, an intimidating method of measuring. ('With its many lacings and its hook and eye adjustment, the Modelling Garment can look rather complicated'.) Once in, you were lucky to get out. ('Do not hasten to remove the Modelling Garment until the prospect has selected the material'.) The Spirella Manual has helpful hints on what to say when finally removing the Modelling Garment: 'As you open the back laces say: "There, do you feel your hips spread?" Then as you open the front laces say: "Feel that drop of your flesh and organs, Mrs – ?" Make her realise the comfort and support she is losing. People never really know how good a thing is until they have to do without it.'

And that's true too.

She would return to fit the finished corset, a process comparable to rounding Cape Horn in a tea clipper and a force nine gale. 'Ask the client to take an uplifting breath. Begin one or two eyelet holes above the holding knot and take up the slack to the pull-loop. Pull . . . grasp . . . tie . . . tuck . . . take up the slack! Feel that grip around the pelvis! Pull well down to aid in the anchorage! Remember, the flesh must go somewhere!'

Whatever happened? Where did the flesh go? Was it tights or dieting? Was it Marks & Spencer or Women's Lib? When I shut my eyes and see my grandmother, everything she is wearing seems extraordinary. The bird on the hat, the fox round the neck, the firm-control corset with its hooks and laces and rust-free patented springs. Look, the mixed infants are saying, it's all nonsense.

BOXED

Terry Wishart
14 December 1989

I am much troubled by a dwindling supply of cardboard boxes. The problem seems most acute in London.

Desperate to find one the other afternoon I approached what appeared to be just the sort I was looking for. I made to pick it up and to my utter amazement somebody was in it!

I cannot understand why what appeared to be a perfectly healthy young man should be idling his time away in the middle of the afternoon whilst responsible citizens are working desperately in the City to collect their hard-earned water share profits.

To add insult to injury the occupant had a northern accent. Said he'd come to London to find work (a likely story). What's the Government going to do about it, I'd like to know.

Then my attention was drawn to a newspaper headline: 'Economic migrants to be forcibly repatriated'.

I think there could soon be a lot of empty cardboard boxes when the Government gets moving on this one.

WE ARE YOUR GRANDMOTHER NOW

Andrew Rawnsley
15 December 1989

'Where's the old Iron Lady gone?' yelled a Labour back-bencher in the middle of question time. It was the best question, not only of this question time, but for some time.

Attila the Hen has been turned – apparently overnight – into Grandmother Of The Nation.

The woman who stands at the despatch box looks the same, dresses the same as the old Mrs Thatcher. But she sounds distinctively different. Instead of the familiar badgering, bulldozing, bellowing Thatcher, there is now this softer, subtler, smiling Thatcher.

It is uncannily reminiscent of the popular thriller plot, where a group of desperate men secretly replace a country's leader with an exact double – a plot most famously used in *The Prisoner of Zenda*.

Watching Mrs Thatcher at the despatch box – or rather the woman purporting to be Mrs Thatcher – one began to wonder. After all, one does not have to look far to find the desperate men, anxious to replace her. The Cabinet is full of them.

Of course, some say that senior ministers have simply persuaded her to adopt this new tone. But from all we know of her and them, that idea seems wildly implausible.

Which leaves, as the far likelier explanation, that the woman who has been carrying on as Prime Minister since the Strasbourg Summit is not the real Mrs Thatcher at all.

She is lying in a basement somewhere, heavily sedated, bound and gagged. The handbag has been put safely out of reach. A Cabinet minister is on permanent guard at the door. It is The Prisoner of Dulwich.

Meanwhile, the imposter Thatcher appears at the despatch box.

Consider this question time, which began with the Prime Minister's ritual list of her engagements for the day. On most days this might include a meeting with the odd general or admiral, a seminar with a privatisation think-tank and a banquet with the President of somewhere-right-wing-of-ridiculous.

Instead we heard that: 'This evening a reception will be held at Number Ten Downing Street on behalf of the Royal National Institute For The Blind.'

At this news, a little 'aaah' went up from the Opposition benches.

Neil Kinnock rose to press her on the latest escalation in the ambulance dispute. Now, the real Mrs Thatcher – in that basement, with a television set tuned to the Commons in front of her – would be bellowing back, eyes bulging, at the Leader of the Opposition through her gag. The bellow would be something about shameful strikers . . . extreme leftwing unions . . . endangering the lives of the old and infirm, etc, etc. You know the script.

Instead, the imposter Thatcher talked more in sorrow than anger. A generous pay offer for ambulance staff, a pity they didn't pick it up, that sort of thing. Not Mrs Thatcher at all.

She also agreed – sit down and pour yourself a stiff drink – to think about sending a telegram to South Africa, urging the release of Nelson Mandela before Christmas. And managed to sound as if she sincerely meant it.

The voice is the clincher. The real Mrs Thatcher did manage, now and again, that soft honey voice. But she could never keep it up. The woman at the despatch box yesterday was so soft-spoken that some Labour backbenchers were calling: 'Speak up!'

Altogether, the Opposition is having terrible difficulties coping with the new, improved model Thatcher, with added compassion and conciliation. Roaring at her: 'When Did You Know? When? When? When?' about the Rover affair rebounded only to her benefit. On the television screen, people will have seen a beleaguered woman surrounded by a mob of howling yobs.

Can it last? Possibly. But my guess is that, not far into the New Year, the real Mrs Thatcher will have escaped and will be back at large.

STATE OF FEAR

Nick Dallman
20 December 1989

A rap on the door. Nerves tighten. Nowadays in Hungary, when the dismantling of red stars – from public buildings, from railway engines, and perhaps even from the gravestones of party members – has become a minor industry, nobody worries about ominous knocks on the door.

Ten years ago, however, when memories of nocturnal visitors – coming in twos, but more often in fours, hardly bothering to produce a warrant – were still fresh, the noise made hearts miss a beat.

'We are expecting nobody,' I hear someone say, but the silhouette at the door, like an exclamation mark at the end of a command, demands attention. The silhouette materialises into a colonel in uniform, standing at ease, his face breaking into a tentative smile.

'Hello, old man, you haven't changed a bit in 35 years,' says the colonel. That is a lie for a start, I think, as I submit to the customary kiss on both cheeks. After an absence of so many years, this kissing among men seems an odd thing, but one ought to be thankful for small mercies: at least it is only two kisses and not three, as is the Russian custom.

I am much less worried by the kisses than by the question of the identity of the officer in front of me.

Who is he? I wonder, as I struggle to superimpose a young face on his middle-aged features. As his hand reaches out for mine, I recollect that at one point in those early post-war years I had a positive dread of men in uniform, and my terror grew in direct proportion with each extra pip.

My aversion to officers, especially those dressed in the dull green of the Wehrmacht, was already well established when, the war over, I ran into an old schoolmate of mine who was well versed in the ways of the then flourishing black market. Sensing, or knowing, that my days in my native land were numbered, he asked me if I needed foreign currency. Undeterred by an evasive reply, he told me he could even provide a reliable guide who would conduct me across the border.

The temptation was too great to resist. I turned up at his apartment at the appointed hour. A maid – a rarity in those puritan and egalitarian days – opened the door.

'Can I take your coat?' she asked sweetly.

Suddenly my eyes opened wide: I saw that my faded garment was being hung in the closet next to four well-tailored officers' overcoats, gold stars shining on pale blue epaulettes, the insignia of the AVO, the state security police. A trap had been set, but they had forgotten to camouflage it.

Before she could announce me, I retrieved the coat, muttered a few feeble excuses, and ran.

Barely six months earlier, however, another trap had been laid and I had fallen into it with a resounding thud. I was doing my third week as a young crime reporter and had just about finished my second and last story of the day when the phone rang.

The police press officer's secretary was on the line: 'I'm glad you are still there. We have a story for you.'

'Fine,' said I cheerily. 'I shall be round in a jiffy.' 'Don't bother,' came the reply. 'The inspector in charge is going your way, just wait for him.' A few minutes later a car drew up, its brakes screeching in the best SS fashion. Four men burst into the room. After the clatter and the slamming of the door . . . silence.

I was looking at them uncomprehendingly; they were eyeing me like a cat watches a captured mouse that might yet try to make a dash for freedom. Then one barked at me: 'Hand over your revolver!' 'My what?' 'Stop wasting time,' he said. I would have smiled at the Kafkaesqueness of the situation, had I not broken out in a cold sweat and had I at that stage not been ignorant of Kafka's existence.

The journey to the State Security offices was short; the stay there much longer. By way of welcome, I was told to stand facing the wall. This order was not countermanded until the early hours of the morning. By that time the room had acquired an axis and was gently gyrating around it. I was hungry and dizzy.

'Sit down,' said the night worker. 'I need your signature.' He shone his desk lamp in my face. I delved into my rather limited reservoir of defiance. 'You wanted to confuse me. You have succeeded. Now I can't even remember my name.' At this point his heavy hand came into harsh contact with my face. Later I saw in the mirror that the shape of his palm and fingers was etched in dark red on my skin.

If I had been able to see a copy of the local Communist Party paper, I would have learned that I – with many others – had been unmasked as a conspirator and an enemy of the state. I was in good company. The then Prime Minister – another, now forgotten, Nagy – was also accused of conspiracy. It was never explained how it was possible to conspire against yourself.

Our official unmasking was yet to come. One afternoon I was bundled on to an open lorry where about 40 others were already shivering in the late autumn frost. Destination . . . Budapest, Andrassy ut 60, taken over without any qualms by the AVO from its fascist secret police predecessors.

By way of diversion we stopped off at the army's counter-intelligence headquarters. Forty bunks to a barrack room. Still shivering, we were made to lie down, men and women in adjoining beds. Four soldiers with submachine guns patrolled the room, and an officer made his rounds at frequent intervals.

Loo time twice a day. The loos had no doors. We were taken out one by one and always a soldier stood behind, the barrel of his gun shoved between the prisoner's shoulder blades. We could hear the women beg: 'Can't you please move away?' This plea was always followed by laughter.

Nobody questioned us, and the soldiers never replied if someone dared to speak to them. In a desperate attempt at humour someone in a neighbouring bed muttered half out loud: 'The suspense is killing me.' A gale of laughter. 'Shut up, you bloody lot,' shouted a soldier, and he and his companions started rushing up and down the room.

The commotion brought in the new duty officer, a tall and muscular young lieutenant with a sad, world-weary face. 'John!' I cried out in relief and happiness: I thought I recognised him as a former schoolmate, a boy with whom I used to exchange groans about the maths problems whose solutions so frequently eluded us.

He had left our school in our final year, when his parents moved to another town. But 'John' did not respond. He looked in my direction briefly, but without a flicker of recognition. I am hallucinating, I said to myself at first: the strain has affected my mind.

During the next two days, before the dungeons of Andrassy ut 60 finally swallowed us, 'John' continued to make his rounds. My eyes followed his every move. The question of whether he was or was not John became the most important thing in my constricted universe.

I had to convince myself that my grasp of reality was not slipping away. If it were, the day would come when the man behind the shining table lamp would toss a fountain pen in my direction and tell me to sign a piece of paper, and I would say, what the hell, why not? But 'John' was no help. He just looked through me. I was a non-person in the making.

Thirty-five years later, as these thoughts of my encounters with men in uniform flashed through my mind, the colonel, who by this time I had succeeded in recognising as another former classmate, said to me: 'Come and have a coffee!' He grabbed my arm and guided me towards the road.

The coffee came with Unicum, a bitter spirit so much beloved by Hungarians that it is only available in expensive restaurants and hard-currency shops. Another coffee and two more Unicums later the colonel asked: 'Do you remember John, who was in the army with me?' 'Funny you should mention him . . . ' I replied.

He cut me short. 'John died of leukaemia five years ago. I saw him in hospital a few days before the end. He told me there was one thing which had deeply troubled him throughout his life, and that was refusing to acknowledge you when you were in trouble. He asked me to find you and to offer you his apologies and regrets. So I have made a point of looking you up.'

This called for another Unicum, without coffee this time, and a bottle of sparkling wine as a chaser. The colonel and I parted the best of friends.

Don't worry, John, all is forgiven . . . and almost forgotten. Just tell me one last thing: as everyone is so busy wiping out the memory of the last 40-odd years, do you still want to keep your military headstone with its red star?

THE DICTATOR AND I

Hella Pick
23 December 1989

It must have given the Queen a great deal of satisfaction yesterday when the Palace was at last able to announce that Nicolae Ceausescu had been stripped of the honorary British knighthood she had conferred on him during his state visit to Britain in 1978. Very probably she would also like to recover the rifle, complete with telescopic sights, she gave him on that occasion, as well as the diamond brooch Elena Ceausescu received.

It is unusual, to say the least, for the Queen to pass any comment about the state visitors she entertains on behalf of her Government. But in 1978, after a three-day stay by President Ceausescu at Buckingham Palace, the Queen let it be known that these were among the worst days of her life, and that under no circumstances would she pay a return visit to Romania.

Mr and Mrs Ceausescu had arrived at the Palace complete with a retinue of security guards and – the final insult – a foodtaster, who had to ensure that 'the lay God, the heart of the Party and the Romanian nation, the heir of Caesar, Alexander the Great, Napoleon . . . ' and so on and on, did not fall prey to a poisoned chalice from the British Queen.

James Callaghan was Prime Minister at the time; he had allowed himself to be virtually blackmailed by the Romanian leader to secure the state visit. British Aerospace had been negotiating for months to sell Romania's Tarom airline a fleet of BAC 111 aircraft, some of which were to be assembled in Romania. The Romanians, always slippery negotiators, seemed to be on the verge of signing – but baulked time and again. The contract was worth a lot of money, and British Aerospace and Rolls-Royce badly wanted to tie it up. As a bait, Callaghan offered President Ceausescu an official visit. But the Romanian leader insisted that nothing less than an invitation from the Queen would be acceptable.

The aircraft contract was subsequently signed, but continued to bring nothing but trouble for Britain. The Romanians didn't want to part with hard currency to pay for the aircraft, and being litigious they caused endless legal hassles as well. British Aerospace, like the Queen, no doubt prefer to forget their involvement with the Ceausescus.

But in 1978, commercial deals were not the only reason why Ceausescu was welcomed to Britain. In those days he was very much Communist flavour of the month. The West enjoyed and appreciated his independent foreign policy. Mr Callaghan praised his 'statesmanship'. Mrs Thatcher, as Opposition leader, queued up with other Westminster notables to shake his hand. Elena, who always laid claim to being an experienced scientist, was given a honorary degree at the Polytechnic of Central London. The Queen, pronouncing words provided by Her Majesty's Government, praised the Ceausescus for their 'heroic struggle' and said how much Britain had been impressed 'by the resolute stand you have taken to sustain the independence of Romania'.

Ceausescu had been much concerned that his state visit to London should attract full coverage in Britain. Suitably vetted, the Romanian media could then regale Mr Ceausescu's subjects with sparkling evidence of his acceptance among the living great.

A couple of weeks before he was due in London, Romanian diplomats did the round of London newspapers with the offer of an interview with the Great Man in Bucharest; but only on condition that his dulcet tones would be reproduced verbatim. The *Guardian* made the mistake of accepting, and I was despatched to Bucharest.

At the airport I was met by three members of the Romanian Communist Party's Central Committee, who informed me that the interview would, in fact, take place only if and when we could agree on the questions to be put to him.

Three days of negotiations followed, during which not only the general thrust of the questions was discussed but each individual word had to be agreed. It was both bemusing and amusing.

Finally, after the umpteenth draft questionnaire, I was solemnly informed that the President would receive me at 9am the next day. Bucharest was sweltering under a heat wave. But I was instructed to wear a long-sleeved dress, tights and gloves. I was told that three minutes precisely would be allowed for informal chatting – in French – and then the interview would begin. A tape-recorder was prohibited, although I would graciously be allowed to take notes. I would be given a transcript, in English, later.

I was escorted into the Presence by the Romanian Chief of Protocol. We were in a room of vast proportions. After a wooden smile from the President the TV cameras were turned on – it was an invariable rule that the 'Conducator''s public engagements were the lead TV story on the evening news – and we both sat down in deep armchairs, placed far apart and parallel to each other so that I could not really look at him, and vice versa. On a table next to him Ceausescu had a sheaf of prompting cards. Clearly there was no intention to say anything impromptu or improvised. By this time I felt the theatre had gone on long enough, and I did not keep to the script. I jumbled up the order of the questions and also slipped in some new ones about Mr Willy Brandt, the former German Chancellor, who was in Bucharest for talks.

The Romanian leader looked distinctly disgruntled; he fumbled amongst his papers; the ready flow of words slowed down. The interpreter was even more startled; and I never found out what Ceausescu really said, because I was quite obviously not being given an accurate account.

The transcript, couched entirely in indigestible loyalist jargon, came next day. In reply to a question about the maltreatment of Romania's minorities, Mr Ceausescu had apparently declared that 'Romania is among the few countries which have solved the problems of their nationalities in a democratic humanistic way.'

Similar self-delusion punctuated all his other remarks. It was tough to extract a few newsworthy lines, and I was reduced to quoting that Mr Ceausescu had warned that 'Africa must not be allowed to become an area of confrontation between the Soviet Union and the United States, or any other state.'

I had one more encounter with Ceausescu – in the winter of 1985. Sir Geoffrey Howe was on an official visit to Bucharest. The weather was bitter. Because of energy shortages there was virtually no heating and very little light. There were icicles in the room where Sir Geoffrey had meetings with the Foreign Minister.

But all was different when we came to the Presidential Palace. Up three floors it was still cold. Suddenly in a corridor it became warmer. The doors opened – and there was light and heat, and Mr Ceausescu.

I need hardly say that no flicker of recognition passed his face when I dared to approach the Light of Romania.

BECKETT: THE GLOOM AND THE GLORY

John Montague
27 December 1989

Samuel Beckett died on December 22 and was buried yesterday in a secret ceremony at the Montparnasse Cemetery. The son of a surveyor, he was brought up in Dublin as a Protestant, and studied modern languages at Trinity College, Dublin. He first came to Paris in 1928 to lecture in English at the Ecole Normale Supérieure.

After his father William Frances Beckett died in Dublin in 1933, his mother tried to persuade Beckett to curtail his literary ambitions. In 1937 he escaped his middle-class family, and settled in Paris.

He married Suzanne Deschevaux-Dumesnil, six years his elder, in secret in 1961. She died in Paris on July 17 at the age of 89. They had no children.

Beckett is dead, a consummation he long claimed to seek. 'I have no bone to pick with graveyards' is one of the best of his bitter-sweet comments on the whole business. The world mourns the loss of a great writer, for whom recognition was almost a burden, and those of us who knew him will also miss a courteous, punctilious, faintly lunatic friend; a soft touch for a sob story or a permanent loan.

I floated quite naturally into his company in the early sixties when we became Montparnasse neighbours. A.J. ('Con') Leventhal of Trinity was the catalyst, and if one was naturally wary of intruding on the great man, such caution soon dissolved in cataracts of drink and good conversation.

We usually met about 10pm in the Falstaff, an old

watering hole of the twenties still frequented by writers. Was that Sartre in the corner, or Ionesco? Probably, but after a friendly farmer's nod had been exchanged, we did not cross the lines, because that was the convention of our village.

Sartre lodged with Simone de Beauvoir in the rue Schoelcher around the corner, so everyone converged in the evening after the day's work to relax among friends. And relax Beckett usually did, the lined face suddenly crinkling with laughter, the seagull eyes sparkling. His bony reserve was daunting, but his beloved Con was a gentle subversive. Leventhal and I were discussing love in a leisurely fashion when Sam saw a chance to shove in his oar. 'No love!' he said with satisfaction. 'Only fuck.'

Startled silence, as Beckett moves in again. 'Eat-drink-fuck, that's all!' he declared, unconsciously echoing Eliot. How a shocked Con recovered to discomfit Beckett is a longer story; but he succeeded because he knew his friend.

Friendship clearly meant a great deal to Beckett, and he was fiercely loyal; the widows of his friends in particular can testify to his care and generosity. Although he was of the select company of those who, echoing Sophocles, would prefer not to have been born, he would do everything he could to ease a friend's suffering.

Contemplating the cheerful grimness of his work and days, I once asked him if he had ever thought of ending it. 'Out of the question,' he said brusquely, 'but I have thought about disappearance.' His best plan, he elaborated, was a boat with a hole in the bottom, to be dredged up by the divers. Then a sigh. 'That's legally impossible too. The widow wouldn't inherit for seven years.'

He lived without the protective outer skin of custom, and saw naked pain and suffering everywhere.

Chased out of a publishing party by a belligerent young

Irish novelist, he first disappeared under the table, emerging at the other end to plead on his hands and knees for a kiss from a pretty young woman. In a taxi afterwards, he mutely pointed to the signs for various charities adorning the inside of the car: 'Help the blind', 'Save the starving', 'Mercy for the mutilated'; they seemed to sing an answer to his call.

Over a cup of coffee, he confided: 'I see it everywhere. The human spirit is on its knees. Everything is on fire.' For him, only a few artists – the weeping canvases of Bram Van Velde, the ferocity of Céline's novels – were equal to the Goya-like darkness of our crematorium century.

Ireland was a sore subject, to be carefully handled: he had recognised Joyce's reservations and, though a firm Beckett family man and devoted to nephew or niece, he had no great desire to return. While he could speak with extraordinary fondness of the landscape, the land itself, and would praise books like Synge's *Wicklow Travels*, he suspected the inhabitants and their attitude towards art.

The famous misquotation about our being driven into writing because we were caught between the English and the Church was only partly right: we had also ruined ourselves. I had an early book savaged by an older Irish poet, and Beckett was relentless: 'Don't answer, they're not *worth* it.' He did not like bad manners, literary or otherwise, and regarded them as endemic to the great Hibernian bog.

Withall, he seemed to me deeply Irish, with his control masking volatile swings of mood from unshakable gloom about the human condition through ferocity at any surrender to lower standards; and underlying all, the quick redeeming flash of humour, the sudden surge of generosity.

We never mentioned Deirdre Bair's biography, not even my long, repentant review of it in the *Guardian*, but when I teased him about the confusions about his birthday, he still stuck to Good Friday, April 13, 1906, despite the birth certificate recording May 13.

'I have it from a good source,' he said. 'Not the Dublin City Records,' I replied. 'A far better source,' he grinned, 'someone at the heart of the problem.' Then with one flat Dublin phrase, he swept my friendly prodding away: 'The mother!' His look dared me to contradict that authority.

I watched once as a crafty journalist, seeking his confidence, lightly mentioned that he had played rugby with Ollie Campbell. Beckett's eyes lit up, and all the weary embarrassment vanished. 'Do you really know Campbell?' he said excitedly. 'What's he like?'

My cunning confrère confided that no more modest humble man ever pulled on rugby boot. 'He's a genius!' cried Beckett. 'But you're not supposed to have a television,' I reminded Sam. 'You're supposed to be against all that.' 'Only for the games,' was his furtive apology, 'and only when the Irish play.'

But the journalist had the hook in, and soon Sam was discussing with him a rugby team of Irish writers. Spoilers like O'Flaherty were easy to place, but the half-blind Joyce was a problem, and Beckett would not relegate his old master to the bench. 'Very crafty, very nippy, try him at fly-half. He might surprise you when the light is fading.'

When I moved back to Ireland, a decision about which he was mildly apprehensive, our meetings became rarer. In any case, his retreat for such occasions to the ultra-modern hotel opposite his flat was a sign not only of his advancing age but also of general change.

We rarely discussed writing, except when some technical problem was involved, but he was complimentary when I needed support. Once when I lamented the fact that Irish literature seemed to have gone backwards and that there was no longer any link between French and

English literature as in the great days of the Modern Movement, I was so eloquently gloomy that I finally let my head hang, declaring: 'There's no point in going on.' There was a sigh and a stir above me until I looked up into his concerned gaze: 'But John, you *must* go on.'

People sometimes wondered if Beckett's retiring modesty was genuine, considering his professional exactitude. In our second-to-last conversation, after we had moved away from that monstrous hotel to a little workers' café, he became his old relaxed self. 'What are you writing now, Sam?' 'Senilities,' he said with pleasant sharpness. 'But I'll manage something yet. Did you have that terrible choice at school between science and the Greeks? I wish I had read Sophocles . . . '

A phrase from our differing backgrounds intrigued him suddenly. 'John, what do you mean by a spoiled priest?' I explained, and there was a wry pause. 'Well, I suppose that I'm a spoiled hermit,' he said reflectively. 'My father was always worried about me and wanted me to do a Guinness Clerkship. I'd be retired by now.' 'And unknown,' I said. 'Ah, yes,' he said with a genuine sigh. '*Never heard of*.' He sounded as if he meant it.

TOWARDS A FREE ROMANIA

Ed Vulliamy & Nick Dallman
28 December 1989

The first night train from the Hungarian capital into the new free Romania left the glorious stone, steel and glass station, through the icy fog which hung from the sky, with something of a party on board.

The train was called the Orient Express – a title which might have run into trouble satisfying Western trade description regulations. But it was an impressive, burly, Romanian iron horse – East German-made and high off the tracks.

A clutch of foreign journalists, none of whom had visas, the Romanian guard in his Karakel lamb hat, a couple of Dutch students, and a Russian dressed in denim, were quick to crack open bottles of heavy red wine, politely declined by the Hungarian soldiers in the company only, they said, because they were in uniform.

The amiable Hungarians – a handsome officer and his barely adolescent sidekick – thought the passengers deranged; the last time this train ran before Christmas it had been shot at from a helicopter, and they jovially recommended passengers in couchettes to use the lower bunks.

The Russian with greasy hair and denims had left Moscow two years ago to work in Hungary and was returning to pick up his family and bring them back to Budapest. 'Why leave now when everything is changing in Romania?' asked a Hungarian girl with peroxide hair. 'Nothing is changing,' answered the Russian. 'Never believe the Romanians.'

One of the Dutch students was asking the journalists for a pen. A student journalist? No, he wanted to write a postcard to his mother to say he was going to Bucharest, but don't worry.

The Hungarian soldiers continued to banter in easy earshot of the Romanian guard, who was full of compliments for 'Magyari vino'.

'What's a Romanian sandwich?' quipped the soldiers. 'Answer: A meat coupon in between two bread coupons.'

At midnight: the frontier. An old station called Kurdij – a shell of wood and glass held up by dainty ornate pillars.

The Hungarians alighted and the Romanian soldiers mounted.

'I have never seen an army behave like this,' said an Italian radio journalist halfway through this border operation. The first soldier had greeted the rather excited compartment with an equally excited smile, not normally associated with faces beneath the square hats of Balkan armies. Here was the now revolutionary army going about its everyday duties but performing them with gusto.

He spoke in English: 'Yes, the President is dead and his wife shot. Bang . . . it may be interesting for you, and good for us, but there are so many Romanians dead.'

The Italian asked if he'd ever been in the Securitate; and instead of making an enemy surprisingly found a friend.

'Huh! Now they are supermen, you know? The supermen who kept that crazy guy as president for so long. No, we are with the people's army.'

The revolutionary army left it to young girls in smart blue suits to issue the visas for which payment in Deutschmarks would do very nicely thank you. 'Have a good time in Romania,' they smiled.

On the border platform, it was after 1am and a stream of giggling, skipping girls appeared – obviously attached to the troops in some way. While the chilling fog draped the great plains, they formed rings around the younger soldiers and skipped in circles, their laughter piercing the icy air. From the platform girders hung a new hole-in-the-middle, Stalin-free flag of free Romania.

Morning broke over the snow-draped, wooded mountains of Transylvania, a grey-yellow soft light, the colour of pale egg yolk. At Brasov, the train was transformed into a busy morning service into the capital, quiet crowds mounting the steps carrying their bags of tools or hessian sacks of agricultural produce.

Conversations between the new passengers and one or

two of the Western curious – held in a peculiar hybrid of French, Italian and classical Latin – ranged from the sudden drop in temperature (and the skiing opportunity this afforded) to Romania's group in the World Cup draw to the revolution and execution of the dictator.

'Now it is hard to believe that he stayed so long,' said a woman working for the state agricultural agency. 'But perhaps because we have guessed it would take so much killing and bloodshed to be rid of him.'

A man who worked in a fertiliser plant said that Brasov had seen three days of firing between the army and the Securitate, but that yesterday had been quieter. 'For us, remember, to lose people now again is a special pain because there was a massacre in our town just two years ago when they shot dead many of our people.'

A farmer, via three translations, said: 'Now they say that the terrorists have put poison in the water. The young people say this is nonsense, but many of the old people in Brasov are not drinking it.'

Outside the hill town of Poiana Tiaplut, down on the road below, a horsedrawn cart went by, driven by an elderly couple; it carried a coffin.

There was a holdup on the line – railwaymen working on the tracks in the icy cold, and above them on the embankment a posse of troops and armed civilians – the Romanian colours on their sleeves – kept watch, strolling to and fro and stamping their feet in the snow to keep the blood moving.

All along the track, clutches of civilian militiamen huddled round fires , blowing into their cupped hands, their rifles flung across their shoulders.

The train-snake wound its way through the white-speckled woods and valleys, past streams and waterfalls, villages of little wooden houses and grim new developments – and through the sheer, awesome rock of the mountains. But soon the mountains became hills, the streams became rivers, and the sun burned away the mist, making the snow dazzle as the train burst out on to the rich, dark-earthed Bucharest plains.

The chatter went on: Romania was in the World Cup, Hungary was not – this is still important. The farmer was looking forward to the summer's tournament, but his eyes were sad. His friend had been killed – he had heard only yesterday morning. 'The country must be built again,' he said. 'With the war we miss many things, petrol, very important. The soldiers need the petrol and lavatory paper, no lavatory paper. So you must get some on the train here and put it in your pocket.'

At Bucharest station, relatives and friends greeted each other apparently for the first time since the revolution: tears, hugs, kisses and fur hats falling off in all the embracing on to the slush underfoot. Passengers filed out into the slushier streets after a tough body and baggage search by lads in bomber jackets and ski hats – the young patrolmen of the new revolutionary militia.

Tanks were parked in the street outside; 15 hours and a world away from the mighty edifice of Budapest central station, the Orient Express, Romanian-style, had done its work for the night.

A LAD UNPARALLELED

Richard Eyre
9 January 1990

I didn't know Ian well until I worked with him on *Guys And Dolls* in 1982. I knew him then as an actor of charm, of wit, of skill, with a kind of engaging melancholy of the Mastroianni variety which he could dispel with a sardonic and self-mocking wit. He often looked truly beautiful, even angelic; then a mischievous smile would appear, and all thoughts of angels would fly away like frightened starlings.

I'd offered him a part in *Guys And Dolls* on the basis of his acting and hearing him sing at parties, where he revealed a pure and wholly unaffected singing voice. It was typical of him that he insisted on singing the score for me before he accepted the part and equally typical that when he'd finished singing he said to me: 'You enjoyed that, didn't you, Richard?' He knew he could make an audience (and a director) cry with a romantic ballad, and he loved to do just that. As much as he loved to torment me with his relentless mockery of my attempts to learn to tapdance alongside the cast.

He was a fine, light, unfailingly truthful, romantic actor, something that the French value more than we do. Like Cary Grant, he had the gift of making the difficult look effortlessly simple. But with Brick in *Cat On A Hot Tin Roof* and with his Hamlet he discovered a new gravity in his work, a real weight and depth. He became, in my view, a heavyweight.

We had talked about two years ago about the parts that Ian desperately wanted to play, Richard II, Angelo, Benedict and Hamlet. (Even, as he said to me one day recently, 'Lear, God willing.') He had a real passion for Shakespeare, rather rare in his generation. He really loved the density of thought, the great Shakespearian paradoxes, the lyricism, the energy of the verse. He didn't want to para-phrase it; the meaning was for him in the poetry, and the poetry in the meaning.

When I asked him to play Hamlet, I knew that he'd been ill, and even had pneumonia, and that he still had a chronic sinus complaint which gave him large, swollen bags under his eyes. On bad days it was barely possible to glimpse the face beneath the swelling , a malicious parody of his beauty. He was without vanity, but not without hope. He told me that he was HIV Positive and that he thought that the eyes would respond to treatment. When we embarked on rehearsals he was having regular, and immensely painful, acupuncture treatment and, later on, chemotherapy which exhausted and debilitated him. (Later in his illness he defiantly rejected all treatment; he wanted to be himself, however painful that was.)

About halfway through the rehearsal period we discussed the 'future', an unspecified projection. 'Do you think I can go on as Hamlet looking like this?' he said. 'You'll get better,' I said. 'We have to be positive,' he said. And we were. Our text was, of course, from *Hamlet*: 'There is nothing either good or bad but thinking makes it so.'

Hamlet is a poem of death. It charts one of the great human rites of passage – from immaturity to accommodation with death. Hamlet grows up, in effect, to grow dead. Until he leaves for England ('From this time forth/ My thoughts be bloody or be nothing worth') he is on a reckless helter-skelter swerving between reason and chaos. When he returns from England he is changed, 'aged', matured, reconciled somehow to his end. We see Hamlet in a graveyard obsessed with the physical consequences of death, and then, in a scene with Horatio prior to the duel, he talks about his premonitions of his end: ' . . . thou wouldst not think how ill all's here about my heart. But it is no matter . . . it is but foolery . . . We defy augury. There is special providence in the fall of a sparrow. If it be now, 'tis not to come; if it be not to come, it will be now; if it be not now, yet it will come. The readiness is all. Since no man of aught he leaves knows aught, what is't to leave betimes? Let be.'

We talked a great deal about Hamlet's accommodation with death, always as a philosophical proposition, his own state lurking just below the surface, hidden subtext. Ian was very fastidious about the 'Let be'. It wasn't, for him, a chiding of Horatio, or a shrug of stoic indifference; it was an assertion, a proposed epitaph perhaps: don't fuss, don't panic, don't be afraid.

I've no idea if it was Kennedy's coinage, more likely one of his speechwriters, but the definition of courage as 'grace under pressure' was perfectly suited to Ian. It was something more than stoicism. He defied his illness with a spirit that was dazzling, quite without self-pity, self-dramatisation, and, at least openly, despair. During rehearsals he was utterly without reserve. Where there had been a kind of detachment or caution, a 'Scottishness' perhaps, there was a deep well of generosity, of affection, a largeness of heart, and the only 'Scottish' characteristics that he showed were his doggedness and his persistence.

His last performance of *Hamlet* was less than eight weeks ago and he acted as if he knew it was the last time he'd be on stage. He'd had 'flu and hadn't played the previous two nights; he was feeling guilt about what he saw as his lack of professionalism. 'If they pay you, you should turn up,' he said. His performance on that Monday night was, as Ian McKellen said, like watching a man who had been rehearsing for Hamlet all his life. He wasn't playing the part, he became it. By the end of the performance he was visibly exhausted, each line of his final scene painfully wrung from him, his farewell and the character's agonisingly merged. He stood at the curtain call like an exhausted boxer, battered by applause.

When he became unable to perform it was a real deprivation to him. Without that there was nothing to hang on to. 'You know me, Richard, if there are two people out there who I can impress I'd be there if I could.' And he would, if he'd had the strength. We're often accused of sentimentality in the theatre but it can't be sentimentality to miss terribly someone whose company gave so much joy, whose talent really *did* add to the sum of human happiness and whose courage was beyond admiration.

I had a letter from him just before Christmas. He said: 'One day when I'm better I'd love to attempt Hamlet again and all the rest; and together we can revitalise Shakespeare. Anyway I hope this is not a dream and I can't tell you how much of a kick I got out of doing the part, if only for the short time I could . . . '

Let be.

COMMANDED TO BREED

Michael Simmons
10 January 1990

At the August 23rd Hospital in Bucharest yesterday, one of nearly a dozen in the city, 200 women had come in for abortions between 8am and noon; 12 newborn babies were handed over within hours of birth by parents who could not cope; and at least one mother had run, still bleeding, from her bed wanting nothing more to do with her child.

'It has been a routine morning,' said Dr Mihai Stanculescu, one of the hospital's senior gynaecologists, during a tour of the ward.

Ceausescu had, to put it charitably, a scientific attitude

to parenthood. He wanted a Romania of 30 million by the year 2000 (it is 23 million at the moment) and banned abortions for all healthy women under 45 with fewer than five children.

His attitude to newborn babies can only be called scandalous. He allowed many to be brought into the world unwanted, and those that were wanted he allowed to be kept malnourished and underfed. Others he contracted falsely to sell to would-be adoptive parents abroad. In some cases, the children were never delivered; and from others, it is said, he literally drained the life-blood to give himself a total fresh transfusion each year.

The result has been an unknown number, probably thousands, of babies handed over 'to the state' as unwanted, usually by single parents, and hundreds, if not thousands, of women dying in wretched circumstances after squirting deadly chemicals into themselves to secure illegal abortions.

Now, the National Salvation Front, in one of its first decrees, has legalised abortion. This means hospitals are flooded with women seeking abortions or desperately needed help to clear up the often poisonous injuries they inflicted on themselves in secret.

The corridors of the August 23rd Hospital, poorly lit and very inadequately heated, were filling with women in light dressing gowns queuing for attention, or recovering from the trauma of a now legal operation. (Previously, authorised abortions had to be carried out in the presence of a policeman.)

Each ward, the size of a small classroom, contains nine or 10 beds, not more than a couple of feet apart. Many of the beds contain two women; an alarmingly large number contain three. There are about half a dozen such wards, all austere and grimly functional. The plaster is crumbling,

(PREVIOUS PAGE) Home Thoughts from Abroad: The British community at play on the Costa del Sol. (24 June 1989. PHOTO: Frank Martin)

Dancing — but not for joy: The All Blacks in war formation against Pontypool. (18 October 1989. PHOTO: Frank Baron)

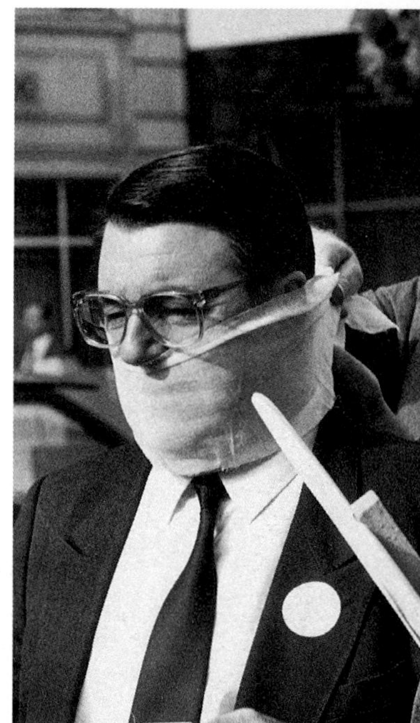

Speechless: Members of the National Union of Journalists protest against the ban on broadcasting speeches made by members of the IRA. (19 October 1989. PHOTO: Kenneth Saunders)

LIFT
THE
BAN

Human Writing on the Wall: Soldiers watch the
masses treating the Berlin Wall as fun.
(15 November 1989. PHOTO: Paul O'Driscoll)

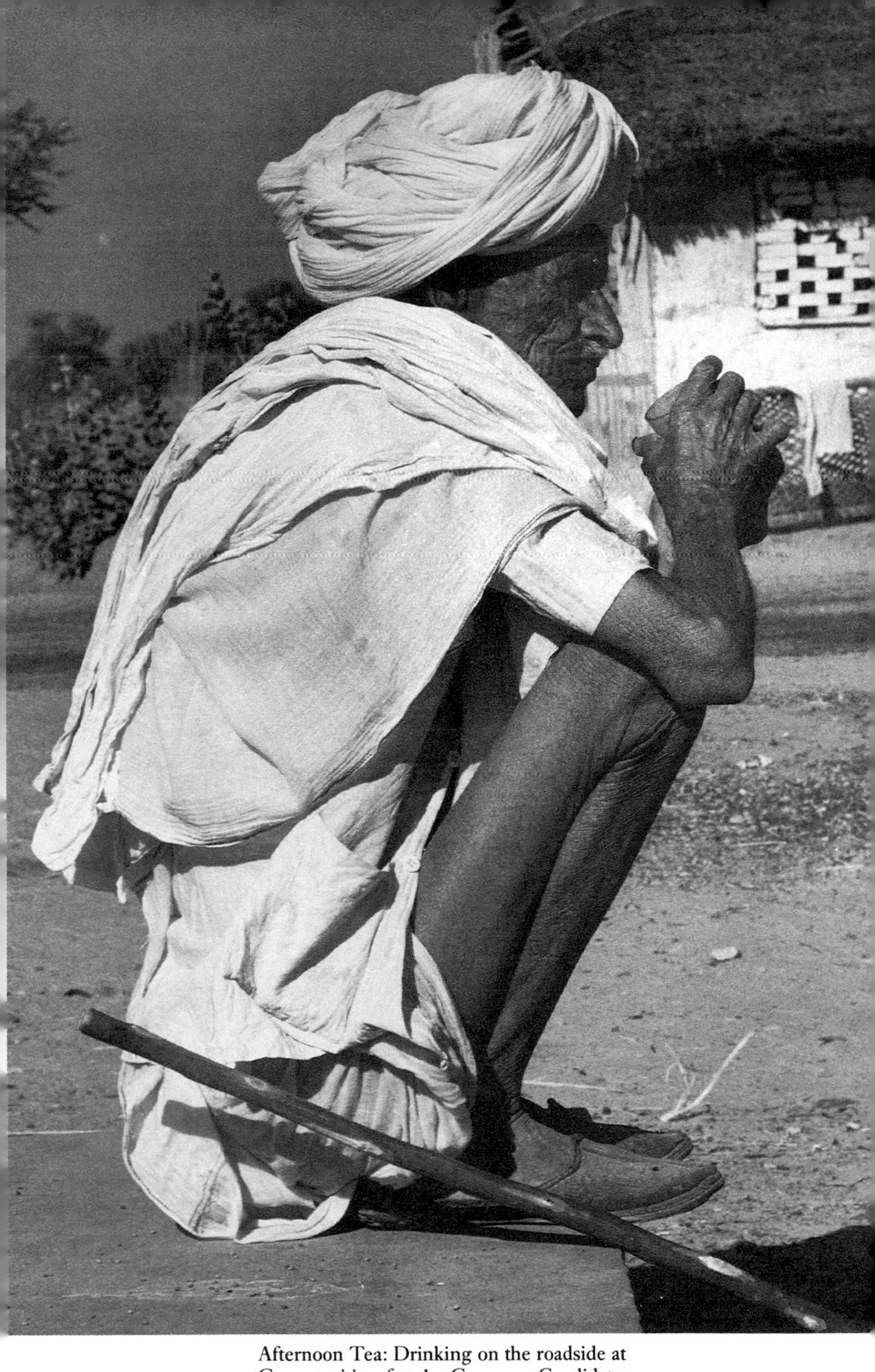

Afternoon Tea: Drinking on the roadside at Goner waiting for the Congress Candidate. (20 November 1989. Photo: Frank Martin)

Before the Fall: Ceausescu poised to give what turned out to be his last address to the 14th Party Congress. (29 November 1989. PHOTO: Martin Argles)

Room for a View: An East German soldier looks through a first chink in the Berlin Wall, made on the West Berlin side. (December 1989. PHOTO: Rupert Conant)

After the Revolution: In Bucharest flowers are laid down in memory of the victims of the uprising against the Ceausescu regime. (1 January 1990. PHOTO: Martin Argles)

Funeral Ceremonies: A victim of the uprising watched over in the town cemetery. (1 January 1990. PHOTO: Martin Argles)

Theatrical Gestures: The Trestle Theatre Company playing games in a plate. (11 January 1990. PHOTO: David Sillitoe)

Porthole in a Storm: The Prime Minister discovers a chink of light at the National Museum of Film, Television and Photography at Bradford. (1 March 1990. PHOTO: Don McPhee)

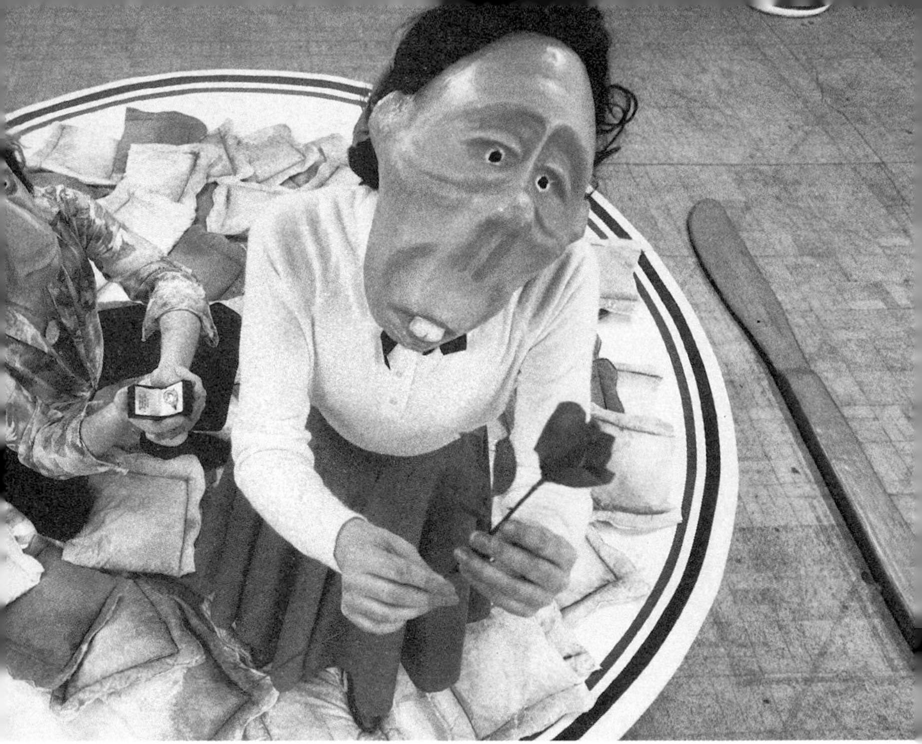

(ABOVE)Charity Beginning at Home: Young South Africans waiting for food hand-outs. (May 1990. PHOTO: Don McPhee)

(RIGHT) Spirits of Dunkirk: Little ships leave Dover for Dunkirk on the fiftieth anniversary. (24 May 1990. PHOTO: Kenneth Saunders)

(Above) Counting Sheep: The Crosscountry hurdles.
(25 May 1990. Photo: Roger Bamber)

(Right) Come You Spirits: Lady Macbeth (Kristine Ciesinski) rehearses Verdi's opera standing on top of a gas-holder, prior to EnglishNational Opera's Russian tour which was sponsored by British Gas.
(2 June 1990. Photo: Stewart Goldstein)

Legless: Boris Becker gets in his Wimbledon stride — before coming unstuck in the finals. (27 June 1990. PHOTO: Kenneth Saunders)

the bed linen is often torn, and there are almost no pillows.

The women are only too willing to talk. 'I have three children already,' said one, who is 39 but looks 10 years older. 'There is water running down my walls. I can't feed the children and I can't keep them warm. I would rather die myself than bring another child into such a world.'

'I squirted soap and alcohol into myself, but the hospital had to finish the job,' said another, who said two children was more than enough. Soap is a rarity in Romanian shops and alcohol is almost unobtainable.

The third woman had poisoned and killed her foetus last November, but only had it removed yesterday. The fourth had destroyed half her stomach, which also had to be removed. It was a miracle that these two women were alive, Dr Stanculescu said.

The hospital director, Dr Vireilius Ancar, said that until three weeks ago any of his staff caught helping in an illegal abortion or providing contraceptive advice or materials faced up to five years in prison and was struck off the register.

His staff is still paying the price for Ceausescu's ruthlessness. It works with obsolete equipment and sometimes no essential equipment at all. All sorts of surgical equipment, scanners and monitoring devices are urgently needed. Sterilisation apparatus is 40 years old. Drugs and painkillers are in acutely short supply and Caesarean operations are frequently performed without anaesthetic. 'We just yell at the patient to keep quiet,' one doctor said.

Ceausescu visited the hospital, named for the date in 1944 when the Nazi collaborationist regime was overthrown, where he inflicted such misery, only once – during the opening ceremony in 1972. One of the operating theatres has never been used.

In the last few days, people from France, Italy and

Britain have been flying into Bucharest anxious to adopt the babies promised by Ceausescu. Nobody calls it selling children, but the dictator had promised the babies on advance payment of £250 per child.

He broke his promises and the post-revolutionary regime has now been making arrangements, apparently with some reluctance, to rectify this.

Last weekend, a French aircraft returned to Paris with 64 children on board – some of whom had never been seen by the people wanting to adopt. An Italian plane left on the same day and some British adoptive parents are now in Bucharest – courtesy of a British newspaper – to see if more children are available to take home.

ON THE BOIL

Nancy Banks-Smith
16 January 1990

Andrea Newman's great success was *A Bouquet Of Barbed Wire* followed, when the characters were inextricably entwined, by *A Bucket Of Cold Water*. There is a sense of seethe and wallow about her seven-part series **A Sense Of Guilt** (BBC2) as though a rich stew were working up to a rolling boil. Images of sin and blood bubble up like baby onions. So do babies.

First we must get the players perfectly clear before we come to the permutations. Richard was married to Inge but left her for Helen. However, Inge, played by Malgoscha Gebel with the feel of real pain, refuses to let go, which makes Richard a sort of reluctant bigamist. She lives a life of Wagnerian gloom in a flat full of mulberry cushions and seems to have made a door by the heroically simple expedient of knocking a large hole in the wall. Intermittently she cuts her wrists or gets beaten up by the last man in bed, thus riddling Richard with guilt. (I was gripped to see from the book that she also does 'something complicated with sausages', but we'll come to that or perhaps, in prime time, we won't.)

Helen wants to kill Inge. Inge wants to kill Helen. Richard, an over-sensitive social worker, seems an improbable focus for such passion, given his tendency to wear purple shirts and plimsolls.

Into this cauldron of seething and sausages comes Felix, so called because no pussy is safe with him. Felix is married to Elizabeth but about to have an affair with Sally, Helen's schoolgirl daughter, and anyone else not actually wearing a wimple. This is because his mother ran away with a couple of lovers (one after the other, of course) and it has left him apt to stare out of windows with a slightly sinister squint.

Any fashion for fidelity seems to have passed Andrea Newman like the idle wind which she regards not, but everyone has a terrible time having a good time, so that's OK.

BODY COUNT

Chris Stephen
16 January 1990

About 200 people were in the cemetery when we arrived. The bodies, 10 of them, had been exhumed during the day and several more, all believed to be victims of Securitate, were expected to be found.

You could tell where the bodies had been found by the huddles of people surrounding the places where they were being dug up. The onlookers' faces showed neither surprise nor anger, shock nor shame. Young and old, women and men, gathered round, many of them commuters returning home in the late afternoon. A unit of conscripts vaulted a wall to see what was happening.

In the largest grave, a huge mound of earth had been dug to show five bodies lying side by side, four in plasterboard boxes, one in a smart coffin.

Securitate, it was explained later, had tried to hide the corpses by burying the dead among the graves. Coffins buried a few weeks before were exhumed, the corpses dropped in, and the coffins returned.

Yesterday, the cemetery was full of workmen turning over each recently dug grave. On the far side were more bodies, without coffins of any kind, simply lying together.

The corpses were waxen; not really people, they looked like dummies. Three of the four were white, and almost naked, the other, an elderly man, was fully dressed in casual clothes. It was impossible to tell how they died. One man had a scar from the top of his chest down, looking neat enough for an autopsy. The woman was naked save for white material draped about the lower half of her abdomen: caked hair, reddish-brown smears around face and mouth, her body was waxen.

Up to yesterday, only 22 bodies had been discovered here, although the authorities say that 90 more were taken to Bucharest and burned. Now they say there may be up to 4,500 from all over the Timisoara area.

After about 20 minutes in the graveyard, I had the sensation of corpses popping up out of the ground everywhere.

My guides were eager to show me the newest discovery.

'Wait here, they are digging now, maybe they will find one.'

I got out of the graveyard with bodies appearing everywhere. The smell was stronger. The graveyard, not far from the city centre, is surrounded by chemical works.

I looked at my guide's face and that of the other man and young woman who had been giving me a lively insight into the political debate until we came upon the scene. They were little changed by the experience.

They explained this was not the first time: 'You should have seen the ones we saw before,' my guide said.

PUBLIC MEN AND PRIVATE LIVES

Leader
19 January 1990

In an interview with *Newsweek* last autumn, the American Congressman Barney Frank movingly outlined the emotional pressures which face a gay person in public life. 'What kind of life is it when you meet someone?' he explained. If he had asked a man to be his steady companion, he said, they would have had to live a secretive life because of public disapproval. The result, Frank admitted, was that he had felt driven to seek the company of Washington male prostitutes rather than gay lovers. 'I was really in a depressed state,' he said. 'I had denied myself any kind of healthy emotional life.'

We do not know – because they have not been revealed – whether the facts are remotely similar in the case of Lord Dervaird, who resigned as a Scottish High Court judge at

Christmas. Because they are British, the judicial authorities and ministers involved are trying to hush everything up as much as possible. But the two cases have this much in common. They both expose the fact that a homosexual can still face public ruin merely for being, or even merely for being accused of being, a homosexual.

The Scottish dimension of this business is important. Scotland is, in general, a morally uptight society. Compared even with England, it is an aggressively macho world of heterosexual conformity in which there is no worse insult than to be gay (though that is not the word they use). Homosexuality had been legal for a decade in England and Wales before the Scots grudgingly brought their law into line. But a particularly potent brew of moral hypocrisy still flourishes in those wind-blown Edinburgh streets and behind those façades of stern stone.

All the same, the features of this case and the way it has been handled are glumly familiar in all countries. Homosexuality may be legal, but it is still generally treated as unacceptable and homosexuals are discriminated against as a result. In this case, as in so many others before it, there has been an effortless conflation of adverse inferences and a brisk effort to brush the whole matter under the chambers carpet which, inevitably, has gone wrong. Perhaps there are criminal matters involved here, but from the off-the-record briefings, it seems not. The questions of whether Lord Dervaird has committed an offence or no offence at all, whether he has been blackmailed or might have been blackmailed or whether he has never been blackmailed, have all been rolled into one. The only thing which really seems to count is that, perhaps, his homosexuality may have been about to be revealed. These are risks which heterosexuals, rampant or closet, do not run.

It is time that we all got used to the boring, everyday fact that there are homosexuals in all walks of life; inevitably and rightly so. They are as good, or as bad, at their jobs as anybody else. A homosexual Cabinet minister, a homosexual judge or a homosexual anyone is as much or as little of a risk as his or her heterosexual colleague. Those who think otherwise should read the report commissioned last year by no less an authority than the Pentagon, which showed just that. The more we accept the fact, then the more homosexuals can live honest lives. The more they are allowed to live honest lives, the less the temptation to clandestine sexual encounters and the less the threat from those who run greedily to the authorities or to the nearest prurient tabloid.

McDONALD'S IN MOSCOW

Jonathan Steele
1 February 1990

A quarter of an hour to closing time, the queue outside the first Soviet McDonald's was down to 300.

'We'll go on to midnight if necessary to serve all these good people,' Mr George Godden, the operations manager, promised as he stood at the front of the line in Moscow last night, letting batches of 30 or 40 people in every five minutes.

On the first day of its opening more than 20,000 people streamed into the fantasy-land restaurant which is not only bigger than any other in the world but also more lavish in its decor. Most of the customers had never had a hamburger in their lives.

Natalya Kaltshekh, a doctor in her early forties, gazed at

the huge plate-glass windows behind which happy Russians were tucking into food twice as fast as anything else Moscow has ever offered.

She had only been queuing for 15 minutes and was already at the front of the line. In her hand she held a copy of the multi-coloured menu given out to people in the queue. 'I have never eaten this kind of food,' she confessed. She had heard about McDonald's on Soviet television.

People did not stay inside as long as the management had feared. They had worried that customers would be much slower than the food.

'Not a bit of it,' said Mr Godden. 'They've stayed on average just the same time as anywhere else in the world.'

Many people had bought several portions to take home, he said. 'They're feeding their families on this.'

A couple of young computer science undergraduates, Volodya and Natasha Leshinsky, emerged smiling after about 40 minutes inside. Asked how it compared with typical Soviet cafés, Natasha said: 'The service is so good.'

They had eaten hamburgers before at one of the new co-operative cafés, Volodya said. 'But the meat is poor quality, and it was relatively more expensive, at least for what you were getting for your money. This place is world class.'

Half a dozen policemen stood around near stacks of crash barriers.

Earlier in the day the queue had been up to 2,000, snaking back through a zigzag of barriers on the edge of Pushkin Square, Moscow's Piccadilly Circus, a favourite spot for strollers, except that it has been remarkably devoid of neon until today. Now it is lit up by McDonald's trademark golden yellow arch.

The restaurant is a joint venture between the Moscow City Council and McDonald's Canadian subsidiary. It has taken 14 years to get McDonald's to Moscow. The first overtures were made at the Montreal Olympics in 1976. Unlike most other joint ventures in the service field, this one only takes roubles.

Westerners in Moscow are surrounded by joint venture hotels, restaurants, Xeroxing offices, film processing kiosks, and food shops. None of them caters for the vast majority of Russians who have no access to hard currency.

McDonald's has done it differently. Its vice-president, George Cohon, remembers the moment when one Russian looked at the plaque outside the door which says that service is for roubles only.

'This is perestroika,' he beamed.

A MAN WHOSE TIME HAS COME

David Beresford
12 February 1990

It was 4.16pm South African time on Sunday, February 11 1990, when he finally came out of prison – 27 years, six months and six days after he was captured in the little town of Howick, supposedly betrayed by a CIA agent.

As it happened, the timing was all wrong. President F.W. de Klerk had promised he would be out at 3pm, so he was one-and-a-quarter hours late. Which, when you think about it, is a little strange for a man who must have been longing to get the hell out of it for more than a quarter of a century. But then that was just one small element in a surrealistic day and, besides, he was having a cup of tea in prison with his family.

But by the time Nelson Mandela made that magnificent, if fleeting appearance at the gates of Victor Verster prison the air was electric with all the waiting and the excitement. The press had been there in growing numbers from about 8am.

Others were gathering as well: a crowd of well-wishers swelling to some 2,000 who danced and sang their way through the day.

There were about 100 uniformed police standing at the prison gates; a few dozen loitering under pine trees on an adjoining rugby field; two truckloads overlooking the scene from a mountainside; groups of plainclothes men in surrounding vineyards and troops in nearby bushes.

The end of the long wait was heralded, inevitably, by the networks when four of their helicopters, tipped off by radio, came hurtling over the hills and went zigzagging over the ground like an angler's floats signalling a shoal of hooked fish.

In this case it was a joint catch and as realisation dawned on the waiting crowd that it was Mandela's car they were tracking, on its way from his prison bungalow, the shouts and cheers reached hysterical proportions. The car drew up and he stepped out to give a clenched fist salute before taking the hand of his radiant-looking wife, Winnie, and advancing towards the gates 10 yards away, which symbolised freedom. The photographers stampeded and jumped upon each other with the air of desperation born of the fond belief that fame and fortune lay in a clear shot of Nelson Mandela. After shaking a few hands their target made a strategic retreat to his car and was whisked off in what was just one of the strange sights of yesterday: the 'desperate criminal' and 'bloodthirsty terrorist' of yesteryear protected by motorcycle police with all the pride of a presidential escort.

They took the back roads to Cape Town – where Mr Mandela was to address a rally – which was a pity, because the 50 kilometres of the national road from nearby Paarl to the mother city was lined by well-wishers waiting to glimpse the living legend.

When the cavalcade reached the city it found a huge, seething crowd of 60,000 gathered on the Grand Parade in front of the city hall. On a porch under a huge ANC flag the two anti-apartheid clerics, the Reverend Frank Chikane and the Reverend Allan Boesak, had urged patience as the hours passed. The heat in the middle of the crowd was almost unbearable, even in the evening. Fainting youths were passed over heads and hauled up to the podium for air.

A water main was broken open and people scrambled for handfuls of water. On the edge of the parade ground the crowd surged now and then to the thud of gunshots as police in adjoining streets fired at alleged looters.

In one corner a mobile medical clinic tended the injured lying on stretchers, some of them children.

The crowd waited on, heedless, for the man. And then suddenly he was there, to a bellow of welcome. Gaunt in his grey suit and donnish in spectacles, he read his prepared speech, concluding by recalling his speech at the Rivonia trial so long ago: 'I have fought against white domination and I have fought against black domination. I have cherished the ideal of a democratic and free society in which all persons live together in harmony and with equal opportunity. It is an ideal which I hope to live for and to achieve, but if needs be, it is an ideal for which I am prepared to die.'

Then the crowd broke into the hymn 'Nkosi Sikelele i'Afrika', and the waiting was forgotten in the moment: Nelson Mandela had returned to his people.

HONG KONG BETRAYED

Hugo Young
13 February 1990

From the Peak above the city it is impossible to believe that the lights are going out all over Hong Kong. On the contrary, they shine at night with ever more copious brilliance. The view from London seems usually to be that this capitalist enclave is about to crumble off the edge of Asia, depositing three million personifications of the yellow peril on the shores of Chingford, Essex. In Hong Kong they would have some difficulty in recognising Chingford, or indeed the City of London, as a place to offer them a particle of the way of life they still enjoy here.

The miracle advances with hardly a break. This place is the sixth largest trading entity in the world, and its trade has multiplied six times since 1979. The average household income, at nearly $10,000, has doubled in five years. But most of all, the miracle has a Chinese aspect. The bursting midget feeds the emaciated monster from which it is suspended: supplying 70 per cent of its investment, receiving 40 per cent of its exports, multiplying trade by 40 per cent a year for 10 years, employing two million citizens of China's southern region which abuts the colony.

Already, therefore, Hong Kong is a crucial key to China's well-being, if not quite so crucial as China is to Hong Kong's future. This week, when negotiation of the Basic Law which will shape the future is finally completed in Beijing, that bonding of interest is as strong as ever it was: a piece of objective reality the visitor perhaps finds it easier than the natives to cling to, in the frenzied agitation that passes for dialogue in this lately politicised business homeland.

The visitor, nevertheless, also faces some contrary truths. One is the massive infusion of mistrust now dogging the negotiations that appeared to begin so smoothly with the Sino–British Joint Declaration in 1984. Hong Kong cannot see the future other than through the prism of June 4, 1989, and the events in Tiananmen Square: events which China affects not to regard as even marginally relevant to Hong Kong.

For their part, Chinese leaders cannot believe that any British action is other than devious, with the covert purpose of maintaining a grip on Hong Kong after 1997. They have not penetrated the depths of Britain's post-colonial anomie. They don't comprehend the simplicity of our ministers' ambition, which is for a smooth exit from empire and no more bother.

There's a second strand of confusion. Nobody in Hong Kong agrees about anything. You spend a few days trying to find out what the business people think, or the rising professionals, or the churchmen, or even the British authorities, until being assailed by the blinding revelation that they have no collective idea what to think.

There is no business view about how to handle China; there are merely a lot of rival businessmen with massive stakes in preventing the other guy from getting ahead in Beijing. Much the same is true elsewhere. Passionate individual convictions add up to a profound collective agnosticism. This bewilders, but may also embolden, the outsider in search of some kind of truth.

Above all, there is no settled view about how to increase public confidence that China accepts the implications of the objective reality in which good Marxists like to deal. Confidence, without a doubt, is the elusive grail. For although capital is not in flight, people are. According to government projections, more than 50,000 young, educated Chinese professionals will leave this year: driven out, in the main, by an undeviating hatred of communism and a fear of what it might do to their children. How can the flow be stopped? The question is at the heart of every argument. It also exposes the historic British failure.

Economically, Hong Kong is a fitting site for the end of empire, the most brilliant jewel in the diadem. But politically it is the site of a great betrayal, and never has this been clearer than now. For the expedient now put forward to increase the confidence and end the outward flow is something called 'democracy'. This is supposed to be the bulwark against what China fearsomely proposes. Yet it would be hard to say which made this idea seem the more absurd: its history in Hong Kong, or the dilute version of it which could yet derail the Basic Law negotiations.

Consider the history. In the 1950s and 1960s, democracy was variously proposed for Hong Kong. A Foreign Office official, looking back the other day, dismissed this as having been the notion of 'crackpots'. Nobody wanted it, he said. By which he meant that China was against it, and the Hong Kong business community had always done very nicely without it. Consequently, Hong Kong has never had a single politician directly elected to power.

Democracy returned to the agenda before and after the Joint Declaration. It was canvassed especially in 1987, when demand appeared to be growing. But the government retorted with a cynicism remarkable even in recent annals. An opinion survey was held, which invited public views on different years in which direct elections might begin. The most popular year was 1988, but because this did not receive an absolute majority, government coolly asserted that there was no popular will for direct elections.

Many local notables have been caught up in a similar cynicism. Dame Lydia Dunn, who recently went to Downing Street to tell Mrs Thatcher that only direct elections to some legislative seats stood between Hong Kong and a total collapse of confidence, gave her more durable opinion of democracy to the House of Commons foreign affairs committee as recently as April 1989. 'I have an open mind,' she said then. Against the cooked book of the 1987 survey, Jimmy McGregor, spokesman for local business, blustered last November: 'It is completely clear that the Hong Kong people overwhelmingly support the concept of democratic government.'

These are not people who raised a finger for democracy at the time when the kind of advantages they now claim for it might have been infused into Hong Kong in preparation for the descent of the Visigoths in 1997.

Nor were the British: they went to some lengths to depoliticise Hong Kong and thus stamp on such shoots of democratic desire as might arise. An official ordinance still makes it unlawful to teach democratic practice in schools. And no public gathering of more than 30 people may take place without official permission.

Such is the basis from which Hong Kong's democratic spring is supposed to burst forth. Not surprisingly, it will fail. The price must now be paid for the Mother of Parliaments' rather shocking lack of faith in its own revered system as one which would have been worth imposing on this sophisticated economic outpost as the best guarantor of their protection.

The demand, in any case, seems trifling. Only in Hong Kong, lacking all democratic experience, could it be regarded otherwise. What China proposes is 18 elected seats out of 60 in 1997 (18 more than under the whole of British rule): what Hong Kong alleges its people want are 20 by 1991. There is also a complex wrangle over how the legislators shall vote, which again has a pettifogging importance which engages near-hysterical attention among these apprentice politicos. What neither side stipulates is legislative control over the executive, or the other normal appurtenances of parliamentary democracy.

No doubt it still makes a kind of sense for the 'democrats' to push their case to the limit until the Basic Law is set in granite. And it would certainly be sensible for the Chinese to concede a seat or two, since that would evidently be enough, at no serious cost, to persuade some Hong Kongers of Beijing's good intentions.

Whether Britain, having abdicated any semblance of a democratic mission for the last 20 years, should at the last minute seek to restore her tattered reputation by suddenly confronting Beijing, seems rather more doubtful. It would be a gesture classed among so many that are visible on every side here: the last writhings of people trying to render permanent the miraculous circumstances over which they know they will soon no longer have control.

Most of the people who recommend it – who are indeed demanding it with fanatical prophecies of doom – were, I noted, those who had no reason or need, *in extremis*, to stay here.

Those committed to the future, whether personally or as the representatives of impressive quantities of capital, take what is arguably the fatalistic but certainly the realistic line that nothing matters much except the future of China. To them the idea of Britain grandly throwing down a gauntlet at this late hour seems like sheer anachronism.

Tse Ka Kui, general manager of the Shui On investment company, was one of the few youngish professional Chinese with no plans to look for a bolt-hole. He calls himself a cautious optimist about the future. He would quite like more elected seats but he suggests we look at this from China's point of view. In 1984, China thought it would be painlessly inheriting the autocracy Britain had created and which Beijing found quite easy to understand. 'Now, on the brink of getting out, Britain suddenly says it wants democracy.' Tse's intention is to stay, among other things, to 'make a contribution to China'.

Something similar can be heard from a top man at the great business house of Hutchison Whampoa, Simon Murray. The well-tailored quintessence of a long-serving expat, he told me that at this late stage democracy, which he didn't sound too interested in anyway, was 'the wrong issue'. We should understand what 1997 was really about. 'I feel this is a commercial deal, perhaps the biggest commercial deal of the century.'

He has regular private talks in Beijing and is convinced that the leadership, well aware of the carat-value of the golden goose it will soon possess, is fearful only of being blamed for turning it into base metal. As an investor, of course, Murray knows that in China lies Asia's vast untapped resource: cheaper labour than Korea and Taiwan, less chaotic than the Philippines, a market of immeasurable potential.

The perspective of the British authorities in this last outpost is rather different. They are expert China-watchers, and share with most analysts the view that events in Eastern Europe offer no guide to what will happen to Chinese communism. Nobody sees a Gorbachev, still less a Solidarity, waiting in the wings. The leadership is unlikely to change dramatically.

But the British are more conscious of Chinese power than of the promise of Chinese realism. They can sketch with horrified relentlessness the scenarios that might follow the sudden appearance of a gauntlet after all these years of submissive diplomacy.They do not see much of an up-side.

But then they also are on the way out. That is the wider truth about Britain on the financial front as well. Some people call it the sunset syndrome, with Japan and the US, whose investment multiplied tenfold between 1985 and 1988, moving in as Britain surrenders its colonial privileges, and once-British houses – including Simon Murray's – are taken over by Hong Kong Chinese.

This was not all meant to happen. In part it derives from a defective sense of history. The most telling statement I've heard here came from not one but two British officials who both said, when reflecting on just why it was that we let democracy go by default, that somehow 'we didn't foresee the implications of 1997'. Somehow the Foreign Office mistook the importance of what happened in 1898: the humiliation that had to be avenged, and the face recovered.

Ineluctably arriving, 1997 caught Britain unprepared. And has left her with but one more duty – to be discussed here on Thursday.

TOWARDS FREEDOM

Leader
13 February 1990

On the prison door of Nelson Mandela's cell a tattered card used to read: 'Sentence: Life plus five years.' Yesterday he stepped to freedom and tore up a chapter of South Africa's racist history. There will be time enough to itemise all the snares which lie ahead before the South African people can achieve what most of them have been denied. Today we must simply celebrate an immense human and political victory.

The man who walked free yesterday had been labelled only ten years ago by former President P.W. Botha as 'an arch-Marxist supported by Marxists in Moscow' who should never be released. Five years later Mr Botha was compelled by the turning tide to offer to release Nelson Mandela – but on condition he 'renounced violence'. Let Mr Botha renounce violence first, the prisoner replied. Since then the moral balance has shifted so far that for the past year it is Mr Mandela who has been in effect laying down conditions fo his release. Now he emerges from prison with hands untied. It is the Pretoria government which desperately needs to negotiate with the ANC – and knows that it must end fully the state of emergency to do so.

It remains a historical tragedy that it should have taken more than three and a half decades for the South African white leadership to begin to contemplate the simple propositions put forward in the ANC's Freedom Charter. Black and white alike, it said, should 'live in brotherhood, enjoying equal rights and opportunities'. This moderate demand came from a movement which had been practising non-violence for half a century, and only turned reluctantly to selective sabotage after being banned – and after Sharpeville. South Africa was part of the great anti-colonial movement sweeping Africa and Asia, except that the colonialism was internal and intransigent. The determination to hang on to white supremacy in South Africa led to the death and suffering of millions of innocent people. That is why it is inappropriate to 'congratulate' President F.W. de Klerk on his 'realism'. The time to understand the real facts of life and death under apartheid was far overdue.

Even now the killing is not over. The brutalisation of the South African state and security apparatus cannot be eradicated by a presidential statement. On Saturday evening in Katlehong township, five demonstrators were killed by police, who then cynically claimed to have been using only 'teargas and birdshot'. More shots were fired directly and excessively into the crowd at Cape Town yesterday. It was a baleful descant to so much rejoicing. Not just the equipment but the mental outlook which produces torture, false evidence, and deaths in captivity is fully in place – a Frankenstein machine which could still undermine Mr de Klerk. As we rejoice with Mandela, we must mourn for those who have died and may yet die. It is another reason why 'congratulations' are out of order.

The sight on television of Mr Mandela emerging yesterday with a frail victory punch in the air was doubly moving: a myth made flesh, a crushing burden of responsibility. And then, voice strong above the Cape Town hubbub, he began to lay the lines for the future. There was to be no going back, no relenting, no facile cessation of the armed struggle, no break in the pressure for change that sanctions can exert. His release was not the end, but a punctuation mark in the obituary for apartheid.

The morning-after doubts about whether he can manage it are to be expected. There are divisions on the black side as well as on that of Mr de Klerk. He may have to mediate as well as negotiate. The opportunities for misunderstanding as well as for mischief-making are compounded by the vast gap between Pretoria and the black nationalist movement. Mr de Klerk talks of a constitution which is 'fair to all' – meaning that separate rights for the whites must be preserved. Mr Mandela talks of full political equality – meaning a unitary state where the majority will rule. But he also spoke yesterday – and everything in his past indicates that he means it – of a unity to be forged 'not just between the oppressed but between all South Africans'. He spoke explicitly of restraint. It is a disciplined hand which after decades of oppression could well have been withdrawn. Now is probably white South Africa's last chance to grasp it. Whoever can genuinely do so will indeed deserve the congratulations of history.

ON THE COKE TRAIL

John Carvel
16 February 1990

It was the day our drug-busting Home Secretary hit the pits in the heart of America and experienced a taste of the ultimate in urban failure.

Mr David Waddington, on the cocaine trail in Illinois, met the US Attorney who bans after-hours work by his staff because they would be shot if they went home after dark.

He saw the streets where raw sewage flows past the few houses and schools still standing in what looks like a construction site, but is really a muddy, squalid unplanned nightmare of deconstruction.

Mr Waddington heard how the city authorities are so close to bankruptcy they often fail to pay wages. For a period last year, the traffic lights were out of action because there was not enough money to replace the broken bulbs.

This was East St Louis on the banks of the Mississippi, once the prosperous junction of 32 railways which opened up the West and carried cotton from the South on its way to Mr Waddington's grandfather's mills in Lancashire. Now it is where gangs come to dump dead bodies.

He was introduced to Mr Richard Hess, the federal Attorney responsible for prosecutions in these drug-ridden badlands and the more comfortable neighbourhoods of surrounding South Illinois.

'In 1962 East St Louis was one of 20 cities selected by the President as All American Cities. Since then corruption in local government and rising crime have turned it into a place which is struggling to survive,' said Mr Hess.

The town's debt has increased to $50 million, while its population has halved to fewer than 40,000 – almost all black and two-thirds on welfare.

Property values are so low that its tallest structure, the 12-storey Spivey building, was recently sold for only $25,000. Industry has fled and the only thriving business left is drugs, mainly crack cocaine.

Mr Hess is the sort of big man who would look good on horseback with a sheriff's badge. He might do better that way.

'The town's debt comes from years of abusing various federal and state projects and mis-spending the money appropriated for the benefit of the citizens,' he said. 'A quarter of the council have been removed for fraud . . . We prosecuted a Baptist minister whose best defence was that he was the friend of the mayor. It didn't work, but at least it was a defence.'

The treasurer recently announced she did not have a cash flow problem 'because there's no cash to flow'.

This is the only town in South Illinois patrolled by state police. They encounter sniper fire. The ageing local force often cannot get its car radios repaired.

The town was chosen by the comedian Chevvy Chase as the location for a film on the ultimate in holidays gone wrong. When he stopped to ask directions, he had his hub caps removed.

Here in East St Louis, Mr Waddington at last found some absolutes. This is absolutely the wrong way to combat crack.

Over the river in St Louis – a different city in the different state of Missouri – the lessons were harder to evaluate. Here were schools where drug education starts at the age of three; where Mr Waddington was entertained for an hour by infants chanting variants on the theme Say No to Drugs; where police officers tell stories about addicted dragons and get children to practise refusing pills.

But this merely illuminates Mr Waddington's dilemma: does he put Britain on alert because of a warning that the drug cartels are about to open up the European market for cocaine? Or would this merely advertise crack to British kids?

KILLERS WITHOUT KNIVES

Ian Black
20 February 1990

In the heart of the old walled kasbah in Nablus, under driving rain and with an icy winter wind tearing through the narrow, slogan-scarred alleyways, an eerie calm reigns.

Most mornings, while the shops are open and the little wooden barrows are groaning with glossy fruit and vegetables, the Israeli soldiers stay well away, perched on their rooftop observation posts in Clock Square.

Strangers are treated with suspicion, most of all in the Yasmina quarter, deep in the kasbah. For here is the stronghold of the hard men at the centre of the intifada. Even the children carry carved black rubber daggers – a by-product of the burning tyres that often send fingers of smoke high into the leaden skies.

Yet it is quiet now. A few weeks ago two groups of youngsters – the Black Panthers and the Red Eagles – patrolled the alleys with knives, hatchets and even guns, harassing, questioning, and killing fellow Palestinians suspected of collaborating with the Israeli authorities.

By mid-December it was all over. Careful intelligence-gathering by the Israelis paid off, and most of these young desperadoes were gunned down or arrested. Around 30 Nablusis – including five women – had been liquidated, many stabbed or beaten to death with their hands tied and coarse sacks over their heads.

Today these cruel killings seem like a distant memory. In the high, vaulted room where at least seven of the executions took place, visitors are shown around as if the grim, rubbish-strewn shell was a historic site, a black museum of necessary but regrettable revolutionary excess.

'This is the most dangerous place in the entire kasbah,' says our guide, a thin, balding, moustachioed man. 'Now the killings of collaborators have stopped in Nablus, but we are still on our guard.

'Anyone who is decent and honest has nothing to fear, but anyone who has something to hide really does have good reason to be afraid.'

Yasmina is a breeding ground for desperation. With a population of 25,000 it is the largest and poorest of the kasbah's warren-like quarters. Twenty-five of its residents have been 'martyred' by Israeli bullets since the intifada began.

Its dark-eyed young men live without hope, without money, and with few prospects except continuing to fight, with meagre means and against heavy odds, for freedom. Most carry the green cards that state that they may not enter Israel.

Now, though, they are under control. Repeated appeals by the PLO leadership, inside and outside the occupied territories, have convinced them that killing collaborators is dangerous and counter-productive, playing into enemy hands by highlighting internal divisions, transforming the war of the stones into a bloody internecine struggle.

Leaflets signed by Mr Yasser Arafat's Fatah group – the largest of the PLO organisations – have called unequivocally for an end to all internal killings and kidnappings. The appeals have not only been heeded, but translated into a new organisation on the ground. Last month a new group of masked youngsters calling themselves General Security, the name used by Israel's Shin Bet, appeared to police the kasbah.

Nablus is certainly more restrained, although it is too early to say that the killings have stopped completely. On Sunday a man's body, shot four times in the head and neck, was found in the Balata refugee camp.

Last Thursday, in nearby Beit Furik, known as a Fatah stronghold, a 53-year-old man was publicly hacked to death in the village square. The day before he had confessed in the mosque that he had worked as an informer for the Shin Bet.

In Rafah, at the southern end of the Gaza Strip, such killings are a daily event. In Ramallah's Al-Amari camp another man was murdered on Sunday night.

The young men of Yasmina have sheathed their knives and put away their clubs – for the moment. But this fragile discipline may not hold. 'These boys are desperate and suspicious,' says a middle-class Fatah activist. 'They know nothing of the good Israeli who wants peace. They only see the soldier with his rifle and baton or the intelligence officer with his threats. If the political process does not succeed, there will be an explosion here.'

HONOURABLE MEMBERS?

Nancy Banks-Smith
21 February 1990

God invented sex so we wouldn't take ourselves too seriously. 'Harumph' he said or, possibly, 'Pshaw. Immortality? I'll give you immortality! Now listen very carefully. This is what you do.'

Impotence – One in Ten Men (Channel 4), produced and directed by Joan Shenton, was enthralling and original. Television, so apt to cover all the ills that flesh is heir to, has never touched on this before. It was also the funniest programme since 'Are You Being Served?' was handed its hat by a new head of comedy as being in deplorable taste.

For an hour no one risked even a wisp of a smile. You would think they were all at Cock Robin's funeral. Dr Alain Gregoire of King's College Hospital has a moustache whose natural exuberance can hide any hint of frivolity. He was demonstrating the properties of papaverine, which causes erections. 'Can't you show just how you give the papaverine injection?' asked our tireless scribe, Oliver Gillie. 'Certainly,' said Dr Gregoire, who clearly aspires to be on 'Blue Peter,' 'I've got a syringe and needle here, which I've actually prepared. Instead of using a real organ, I've got a demonstration piece here. It is slightly longer than life.' Opening his drawer, he extracted the world's largest cucumber. It looked like an anaconda of the Amazon sleeping off a goat.

Papaverine is a boon and a blessing but can have, Dr Gregoire conceded, one disconcerting side effect. 'On very rare occasions, perhaps one in 1,000, the erection *doesn't go away*. I give every patient a warning sheet dealing with this and they can quite simply go to a casualty department.' Quite simply? There speaks a man who never sat three hours in casualty with an erection and 15 football supporters.

America is, of course, in the van of such research. 'Good evening, Mr Dixon,' said a night nurse at the Texas Medical Centre. Mr Dixon grunted and buried his face in his paper. 'My name's Mary Adam,' she continued with unabated brightness, 'and I'll be putting your electrodes on tonight. Don't forget a technician will be monitoring you outside for your erections during the night.' Mr Dixon was by now only a pair of eyes, peering over the sheet. 'When you have an erection they will come in and take a picture of your erection with the camera and estimate the percentage of your erection from zero to 100. Any questions?'

Impotent men tend to believe or to be told that it is all in the mind. It may be, but it may equally be in the nervous system or the blood supply. Diabetes or multiple sclerosis, for instance, can cause impotence. There are surgical solutions. Some 50,000 men a year in America are fitted with implants; 300 in Britain. Top of the range is an endearing little affair with a bulb and two floppy ears like a rather dashed rabbit. Pump away and the ears rise like a rabbit who spots a field of Webb's Wonder and no sign of Webb. It can spring a leak, in which case you need a puncture repair. A simpler device, favoured in Britain for its cheapness, is like those plastic curlers with a wire spine.

Which brings us to St Peter's Hospital, Covent Garden, and the hero of the hour, Kemal Ali. Most of the impotent men who appeared were so achingly embarrassed that your toes plaited for their pain. Kemal Ali was a small, elderly man with diabetes and the first smile of the night. 'I came here for an operation because I married a young wife,' he said with sunny simplicity. 'After two, three years my erection failed. They explain to me to have an operation to make my wife happy.'

With its internal stiffening of two plastic rods, Mr Ali's penis waved encouragingly at his admiring audience. 'It can be bent downwards,' said the surgeon, exerting some force, 'to allow him to dress. It does become a little more malleable.'

Socialist Fenner Brockway once went to Eastern Europe, where he met one Comrade Penis. On his return he could not resist sending him a supportive postcard. 'Dear Penis,' he wrote, 'May you remain proud and upstanding.'

AN EDITOR'S DUEL

Jeremy Morgan
28 February 1990

A newspaper editor in Uruguay yesterday agreed to a duel with an irate police inspector – but quickly insisted he would refuse to use a weapon.

The editor, Frederico Fasano, was challenged to a duel by Inspector Saul Claveria after *La Repubblica* – a newspaper which prides itself on exposés – alleged that cars registered in the police officer's name had been seen carrying contraband from Brazil.

Inspector Claveria denied the charge, claimed his honour had been impugned and sent his seconds to Mr Fasano's office. Mr Fasano first said he would go to the duel without a weapon because 'I am not going to bear arms against another human being.' He said later that even if he were given a weapon he would not point it at his opponent.

No date has yet been set for the duel. The seconds will first negotiate and a tribunal will consider the justice of each side's case to decide whether there should even be a duel.

But Mr Fasano's decision has already stood convention on its head in a country where duelling is still allowed under a 1920 law.

He has the support of the press, many politicians and much of the public, aghast that such a thing might happen in 1990. The police officer spurned the libel courts and refused Mr Fasano's offer to use the pages of his newspaper to defend himself. In a fit of machismo, Inspector Claveria seems bent on humiliating or hurting his adversary.

Uruguayans see themselves as an island of sanity in a crazy continent, boasting solid citizens, liberal social traditions, slightly old-fashioned bourgeois values and stable banking. Now they are aware they look as capable of Latin American eccentricity as their more erratic neighbours.

This bizarre incident coincides not only with Carnival, but with the transfer of power tomorrow from President Julio Maria Sanguinetti and his Colorado Party government to Luis Lacalle of the opposition National Party.

The last duel between prominent public figures was in 1971, and involved nobody less than President Sanguinetti, when he was a government minister. He wrote an article which angered a senator and the two slugged it out with swords for 45 minutes before both retired hurt.

Permission for the latest duel was given by President Sanguinetti's government a few days ago. Inspector Claveria and Mr Fasano are free to fight each other with razor-sharp sabres or pistols.

SECRET TALK

Derek Brown
2 March 1990

The tomtom starts beating almost as soon as you check into the hotel. 'Hello, you are press reporter? I wish to speak about democracy movement . . . '

An appointment is made, of a vaguely clandestine sort. It may be a supporter of Congress or of the Communist Left, both banned, or simply a concerned citizen.

Whoever it is, these encounters make three deep impressions. One is fear, in which conversation on even innocuous matters is now conducted in the kingdom of Nepal. Another is the bravery and ingenuousness which marks the pro-democracy movement. The third is the deepening resentment of a Western democratic Establishment which seems blind to their plight.

The fear is most evident in the appointment with Marshal Julum Shakya, convenor of the central action committee of the outlawed Nepal Congress Party, and one of the last senior party men not under arrest.

Not that Mr Shakya is unacquainted with jail, having spent 15 of the 30 years since the 1960 royal coup behind bars. For the past month he has flitted from one safe house to the next, leaving his wife and five-year-old daughter in his own regularly raided home.

What is less logical is that the party contact comes to the most popular press hotel, the Yak and Yeti, and we make the subsequent shortish journey in a randomly hired public taxi. Even after 30 years of underground campaigning, it seems, the Nepal opposition has a lot to learn about security.

Even more audacious were the three smiling young

Central Committee members of the Nepal Communist Party (Marxist), who come to the hotel in broad daylight, and telephone its reportedly bug-infested switchboard under their own names.

One of the two who are willing to be quoted in print, Harish Chandra Acharya, spent three and a half years in prison 10 years ago. Unlike Mr Shakya, who said he was reasonably treated, he blandly recounts beatings so severe that he had to have a kidney removed.

Even after this, he and his comrades are on the cuddly side of communism. There will be a multi-party democracy in Nepal, he says. Private property will be respected. Even the King will be welcome in an interim role.

The three Communists are cheerful about recent events in Eastern Europe, seeing in them a portent for the success of their own movement. 'Socialism cannot leave the world. It is still there. What has happened is that authoritarian socialism has gone, not socialism itself,' Mr Acharya explained.

On this evidence, the Communists of Nepal seem far from the terrorising brutes portrayed by the local press and broadcasters. True, they have a record of occasional unspeakable ferocity, such as the public castration and lynching of a renegade leader in Bhaktapur some eighteen months ago. But the opposition says that at least 50 people have been killed in the recent pro-democracy protests. The government admits to 12; even that is an outrage in this traditionally tranquil land.

The blood has brought with it a heightened political consciousness among the middle class. Many have become more ardent in their support of the King and the non-party *panchayat* system which they say is the most suitable form of democracy for their country. Nepal's population is 93 per cent rural, linguistically divided, and desperately poor (in the far west there are mountain villages where per capita income is three pounds *a year*).

To which the opposition can reply that poverty is the responsibility not of the poor but of the rich. Nobody knows how wealthy the royal family are, but everybody says they are fabulously well off. Nobody can say how much ministers cream off the foreign aid, but everybody says it is unconscionable.

And yet the aid comes tumbling in without cease: half a billion pounds a year, according to one estimate.

Some countries, like the USA, try to link aid with human rights. Others, like Britain, think this undiplomatic. Britain is sending £16 million this year.

The aid, and the implication of support for one of the world's last untrammelled monarchies, baffles and enrages the new democrats.

'If the Berlin Wall can be broken, why not the system in Nepal?' asked one of the eager young Communists. 'And if Eastern Europe can get financial aid only with multi-party democracy, why are you giving all this money to help maintain the present system?'

ALBANIA'S FLAIR FOR SPYING

Helena Smith
3 March 1990

'I see no washing machines, explosives or refrigerators . . . but perhaps you have an English novel for me to read?' said the Albanian border guard as he shuffled through our belongings before we passed into Eastern Europe's last dictatorship of the proletariat.

Back on the bus being whisked through narrow, ill-lit lanes, normally the exclusive reserve of horse and oxen-drawn carts – private cars being banned in the People's Republic – we were treated to our first dose of ideological cant.

'You will notice that in Albania we have no litter. That's because our housewives don't waste their money on thousands of plastic bags . . . We have better things to spend it on,' said Michalis, a retired doctor, who played second fiddle to our principal guide, Komatos Damianos, an amiable professor of archaeology.

Entering Albania is to leap back in time 40 years. If, as in our case, it is everything but tourism that has drawn you to the only 'true' Socialist state in the world, a short stay there is also a relentless game of charades, with guides and the guided revelling in the mischievous delights of doublespeak.

We were, it must be said, some of the most unlikely tourists to have made their way up to the tiny Balkan country since organised trips from Greece first began in 1972. Armed with video equipment, recorders, and cameras, we passed ourselves off as ethnologists, archaeologists and teachers. But ultimately, the Albanians had the last laugh.

There can be no denying that when perceived through rose-tinted Western eyes, Stalinist Albania is a strange place.

Plastic bags aside, the Albanians have certainly invested a lot of time and money building one-eyed concrete foxholes. More than 500,000 of them are dotted around the intensely cultivated countryside, not only as a reminder of Albania's constant war footing, but also, as Mr Damianos explained, the siege mentality coming from being Europe's only state to 'have the courage to be guided by the principles of the people'.

Guided they might be, but it is a course of life that takes place under the watchful eyes not only of Big Brother, but also the all-pervasive Sigurimi secret police. Wherever we went, our polo-necked, flare-trousered, trench-coat friends came. They usually followed us on foot, although at times, like good yuppies, they were at the wheels of brand-new Golfs.

We noticed them for the first time in Sarande, a southern seaside resort town where we were inundated by cries of '*Ora, ora*' by watchless Albanians keen to learn the time. By the end of our first evening we had invited them down to the hotel bar, and they came with a nonchalant nod.

Despite the bleakness of everyday existence in Albania, the people, though lean in face and weathered by heavy workloads, appear better fed and dressed than when I last saw them in 1987 – in Tirana, the capital, I ran into pot-bellied students.

Now, with the promise by the Communist chief, Ramiz Alir, of more consumer goods, the three-million strong populace, though unsmiling, do not complain to visitors about their lives.

In fact, the nearest we got to an open display of malcontent came from a racketeer in Tirana who called himself Robert. 'Sex is our greatest problem. If you see a girl you like and approach her, she says "Go away, scoundrel". Without marriage they are so afraid. In England, I hear women use a pill.'

'Yes,' said a colleague, 'and men can use condoms.'

'Condoms, what are they?'

After a lengthy explication, they were produced by a male fellow hack, who had very quickly discovered he would be having no need of them in Albania.

Robert gingerly took them in his hands, gave them a rudimentary examination and said: 'Our women will be shocked. 'They are not used to these things . . . You know, by the year 2000, the state has plans for our population to increase to four million people.'

EXIT THE VILLAIN

Seumas Milne
6 March 1990

'Theatre is an arm of our struggle,' reads the inscription on the stage wall of the National Theatre in Bucharest. It is a slogan from another time and place, coined in the years after the Russian Revolution by the Communist poet and actor Vladimir Mayakovsky. But the recent experience of the Romanian theatre has given a new twist to Mayakovsky's words.

As the scope for political debate was progressively narrowed by the Ceausescu regime during the 1970s and 1980s, theatre became one of the last remaining weapons of passive resistance. 'The theatres were the last barricades,' remarks Alex Darie, a young Bucharest director. In the final Ceausescu years, when power cuts and rationing had reduced Romania's cities to a twilight existence, audiences came to the theatres to be fortified by the coded political messages – 'lizards', as the theatre professionals called them – acted out on stage. The choice of plays – *Hamlet*, *Titus Andronicus*, *Caligula*, *Vlad Dracula The Impaler* – reflected the overpowering concern with political corruption and autocracy.

Now, two months after the overthrow of the 'Conducator', Romanian theatre is having to face up to unexpected dilemmas. Many of the same productions are still running. But the dragon which was the focus of so many years of artistic subterfuge has been slain and the theatres have lost their role as purveyors of forbidden political fruit. The censor has gone – and so has part of the audience.

At the same time, political upheaval has put the country's intelligentsia back in the saddle after years of marginality or political subservience. Romanian artists who avoided the embrace of the Ceausescus – like the poet Mircea Dinescu and the actor-director Ion Caramitru – are the heroes of the hour and have thrown themselves into politics. Their art has to take second place.

Caramitru, whose production of *Hamlet* as an allegory of a corrosive regime is still playing in Bucharest, comments: 'Before the revolution, the theatres were packed. People came to hope and pray together. Now the theatres are empty. The best theatre is on the streets and the television. Now you can watch people in Parliament fighting and arguing with each other; we haven't seen that sort of thing for 45 years.'

By British standards, Romanian theatres still seem full enough and the productions have a vibrancy and seriousness which are often absent in the West. But there is no mistaking the still-tangible euphoria and drama of the new Romania. Every day there are demonstrations. Placard-wielding pickets march about. Groups gather and argue in the street at a moment's notice.

The day I met Ion Caramitru he had just been appointed a vice-president of the country. Outside his new office at the National Assembly building, soldiers and petitioners were milling about. Inside, the new vice-president, wearing jeans and trainers, seemed a little sheepish about his new role. He was one of the first to join the ruling National Salvation Front at its original TV station headquarters while the army battled with Ceausescu's Securitate in the streets outside.

On our way to the Bulandra Theatre to see his production of *Vlad Dracula The Impaler*, the front of his Dacia estate started to rattle alarmingly. It turned out that the bumper had broken loose. 'It's because of the revolution,' he explained as we tied it up. 'We were driving around like madmen.'

Vlad Dracula The Impaler – 'it has nothing to do with the stupid 19th-century American story', Caramitru explains – by the modern Romanian dramatist Marin Sorescu, is set in 15th-century Wallachia, Christianity's front line with Islam after the fall of Constantinople. The action opens with a debate between Vlad and two thieves he has impaled – one a Romanian who is being punished for defecting to the Turkish side, the other a Turk who is dying for exactly the opposite offence.

Vlad proceeds to burn and murder his way through Wallachia convinced that, given the country's geographical position, his methods are unavoidable. 'My stake thrusts its roots deep into the soul of this country,' he declares. 'I am cruel and it hurts. You only punish those you love.' But in the end he realises he has failed in his mission and impales himself as his own punishment.

The production is rich in echoes of the predicaments of modern Romanian history, though nothing could be as symbolically topical as Radu Beligan's eerie production of Camus's *Caligula*, which has been running at Bucharest's National Theatre on and off for a couple of years. Clearly the old regime found the dramatic final scene of the demented Roman emperor's murder by his exasperated cronies a little too close to the bone – the play was taken off last year, supposedly because the hard-currency cost of royalties to the Camus estate had become prohibitive.

Since Ceausescu's own execution in December, the cash for royalty payments has been found once again.

But the production which most clearly illustrates the problems Romanian theatre is going to have adjusting to its new situation is the satirical farce *Protocol*, currently playing at the Bucharest Theatre of Comedy. Directed by Alex Darie, *Protocol* is a savage portrayal in the Ayckbourn mould of crawling hypocrisy and corruption in Ceausescu's Romania.

A minor functionary holds an obsequious dinner party for his general manager in the hope of winning promotion. But everything goes wrong. The man whom he encourages his daughter to 'keep warm in the spirit of socialist morality' has in fact already lost his job. And the unprepossessing guest he invites to make up the numbers turns out to be a Securitate official who ends up sacking or promoting the other guests.

The production was ready on December 16 and was due to be seen by the censor on the 22nd – the day Ceausescu was overthrown. The author, Paul Everac, was frightened when he saw what Darie had made of it. 'I thought we had no chance of going ahead with it. The original text was more comic. He had made it very hard.' Now, even though Ceausescu and his party apparatus have been swept away, the Bucharest audiences still seem to delight in *Protocol* Darie remarks: 'The leaders hated the theatre and they never went. Sometimes things got through – it depended on their moods. If *Protocol* had passed the censor before the revolution, there would have been a riot in front of the theatre. When it did finally open in January we were afraid that the public would not react as before. But after 45 years of silence, these things are so important and they still seem satisfied.'

He is, however, well aware that artists cannot go on milking the past or using the established theatrical tricks for ever. 'We had an enemy and now he's gone. I think in a way we're going to miss him as a theatrical subject. The theatre has nothing to do with beautiful things, every play is about something bad or catastrophic.' Everac says that Romanian theatre will now have to turn its attention to 'more general, universal human themes'. But he worries when he looks at the arts in other countries which have lately managed social tensions more placidly. 'Look at France and Germany. They have no really great playwrights now. Their drama has withered.'

With the abolition of travel restrictions, Romania's actors and directors are about to be able to break out of the hothouse environment which has created such a powerful theatrical tradition.

In February, both the leading British producer of international theatre, Thelma Holt, and the director of the London National Theatre, Richard Eyre, were in Romania shopping for plays to bring to Britain. Caramitru's *Hamlet*, *Vlad The Impaler* and Darie's *Protocol* are almost certain to be staged here this year. But it remains to be seen whether the Romanians will continue to produce such a desirable export as the memory of the Conducator and his influence fades away.

IN DEEP WATER

Erlend Clouston
16 March 1990

Lovely, wobbly, wind-blasted Alston: ex-hippies stagger up the cobbled street in designer fell boots, dangling tots in fluorescent Peruviana. But this tumbledown Cumbrian paradise may have secret flaws: what is in the wind, the land, the water?

Up on Alston moor, still roughly scarfed in snow, the heather looks bitter and spindly, singed by acid rain. Up at soggy Nenthead, past the crooked sign pointing to The Highest Furniture Shop In England, rabbits wade through the black, peppery spoil heaps dumped by nineteenth-century lead miners. Great drifts of the stuff have flopped over the retaining walls and on to the banks of the river Nent, ready to be flushed downstream to the already suspect South Tyne.

'Once a week in summer they release raw sewage from the treatment works,' pants a large, moccasined lady outside Alston post office. On what day should tourists eschew paddling? She pauses. 'Tuesday. Or possibly Thursday.' And off she scurries.

Dr Lewis Routledge, who lectures on computing though his doctorate is in molecular biology, had heard about the sewage. 'Not healthy, and not legal,' he sighed. But it did not surprise him. Nothing surprises him.

'Our problem is that when things go wrong, we rely on the regulatory authorities to sort things out.' He laughed, sadly. Dr Routledge, a small, fidgety man with a bushy Charles Bronson moustache and excited fingers, has no more faith in the regulatory authorities than chickens have in stoats.

In Cambridge, engaged on post-doctoral research, he had witnessed frightful herbicide spills. In Newcastle the drinking water was so bad he imported his own from 25 miles away, three gallons at a time. Up here on Alston moor, he still was not safe: last year his son had been paralysed for two months after spreading sheep dip on his hands.

And the sheep dip was only one curse among many. The lounge of the Routledges' labyrinthine farmhouse rustles with reports recording, and anticipating, eco-doom. Here is one by Liverpool University, on the lead meadows of Nenthead: 'Culverting and/or bank reinforcement are needed to prevent further and possibly catastrophic contamination.' Here are some more, on leukaemia clusters, meningitis clusters and aluminium poisoning.

Here is a study Dr Routledge has written himself: *Health And Early Death In Eden* (the Cumbrian, rather than Old Testament, district). 'There are 678 wards in the Northern region of Britain,' reads out Dr Routledge, 'and Alston was 265th worst.' Well, that didn't seem too bad. 'For a rural area,' he corrected, sternly, 'that is VERY unhealthy.'

Next came, goodness, a pearly-breasted Italian lady, wrapped in translucent seaweed. But this turned out to be Signora Carlo Ripa di Meana, a saucy authoress married to the European Environment Commissioner, with whom Dr Routledge is in regular communication. Another flurry through the orange boxes and out came a letter from Carlo, informing his Alston correspondent that his complaint about UK sheep dip has been logged on at number 502/89.

Dr Routledge then began to talk about acid rain. He had worked for a period, back in 1967, for the Ministry of Agriculture in Scotland. They had known then about pollution coming from factory chimneys; some complicated monitoring technique had related plant growth to Glasgow's annual trades fortnight. All that time ago! And still nobody had done anything about it! See what he meant about the regulatory authorities?

Dr Routledge's constant ringing of alarm bells has brought him into conflict with the regulatory authorities. 'Northumbrian Water sent a delegation to the college to try to silence me.' Dr Routledge was unperturbed. 'I have plenty of lawyer friends.'

For years the mortal enemy has been Sir Michael Straker, businessman, landlord, chairman of Northumbrian Water. 'I think of him with caring thoughts,' smiles Dr Routledge, with all apparent sincerity.

It would have been interesting to learn if Sir Michael, too, prayed for his opponent. But at Northumbrian Water they went distinctly cool when they heard the dreaded name 'Routledge'.

'He seems hung up on a lot of things to do with water,' a spokeswoman remarked, crisply. Besides, Sir Michael was said to be utterly uncontactable.

So it was round to the National Rivers Authority (gen. manager, D. N. Rainbow) at Gosforth for an official response to Dr Routledge's claim that the Tyne Valley represented 'an ecological crisis in the making'. What did water quality manager Malcolm Colley make of that?

Not much. 'If there was going to be an ecological crisis,' soothed the bearded Mr Colley, 'it would have happened by now.' The chlorinated pesticides that were phased out in the mid-'80s had been 'much more dangerous' than the biodegradable organo-phosphorus compounds now deployed.

'Birds of prey are returning to the countryside in quite remarkable numbers,' he reported, triumphantly.

This brought the conversation round to dippers. Dr Routledge alleges that peat displacement through blanket afforestation had had a dreadful effect on river ecology in general, dipper breeding in particular.

'I must say I haven't come across that link before.'

Did the NRA take anything Dr Routledge had to say with seriousness? But yes. Mr Colley was very polite on that score. Take sheep dips. The NRA was going to institute a programme of farm visits, checking on all possible sources of contamination. Generally, however, Mr Colley did not have sleepless nights over Signor Ripa di Meana and complaint 502/89.

Would he let the Colley children play beneath a sheep dip outfall? 'Em . . . well . . . I probably have done.' (The hesitation, he explained later, was on bacteriological grounds.)

Mr Colley remained equally unflapped on the possible connection between chlorine and leukaemia and the lead levels at Nenthead: 'Dr Routledge is quite wrong to suggest that there is any threat to abstracted drinking water.'

Certainly he would not actually sip himself from the river Nent but, frankly, he asked, in this day and age, who would? 'No amount of treatment will make rivers safe to drink in,' he warned. The objective was to make sure that what came out of taps was drinkable. 'I am not dismissing Dr Routledge's points. It is just that there is bad science in them.'

Down at the North Shields fishing fleet, it was easier to be convinced of ecological apocalypse. 'Just had one wage packet since the New Year, mon.' Nigel King creaked about in his yellow oilskins, stitching nets that might be more use trapping rabbits in Nenthead. 'Out for five hours this morning. Caught half a basket of codling.'

He had not heard of Dr Routledge, but dumping was maybe the problem, right enough. He shook his head. 'Nothing gan.' Even the prawns had gan. Mr King shuffled a blue box out from under his ragged net. In one corner a dozen pink beetles stared back balefully. 'They're gigantic prawns, them, for these days,' he said, stirring them affectionately.

A sheet of paper was produced. This listed the going rate for prawns. Mr King studied it nostalgically. At the top it promised £51 for a stone of prawns, 'if two to a lb'.

'Get one that big now,' creaked Mr King, 'you put it in an exhibition.'

ALL THE FUN OF THE FUNERAL

Matthew Engel
17 March 1990

Pushing up the collar of his jacket, Leamas stepped outside into the icy October wind.

The Spy Who Came In From The Cold

I always wanted to be Alec Leamas. I wanted to sit in the café by Checkpoint Charlie, surreptitiously pouring whisky 50-50 into my black coffee, staring out at The Wall, wondering if the contact might make it past the guards, wearing that look that says One Knows What Other Men Do Not. As a technique for trying to seem important and feel better, it was always more convincing in Berlin than, say, Bognor.

Now it is obvious I am just another bloody tourist, collar turned up or not. The Wall is coming down. The ironclad mess of Checkpoint Charlie, rather reminiscent of Dover Western Docks, will soon be bulldozed. The café is already a museum, depicting scenes of state barbarism and the heroic ingenuity it engendered. The young folk of Europe flock to it and, as at the Tower of London, stare at the scenes of a distant, primitive age, in this case the 1960s, '70s and '80s.

It seems impossible that it ever happened in our time. Already, the Western side of the wall has been almost entirely chiselled away for souvenirs. There are huge gaps through which to view the rabbits – who could be among the big losers of unification – frolicking in No Man's Land. Graffiti-covered fragments fetch more than plain ones, so adventurous souls are now climbing through, spraying new graffiti on to the Eastern side before gouging out the stone and flogging it off.

Berlin has known some bizarre weeks in its history. Few can have matched this. West Berlin goes on much as ever. Through a combination of bombing, defeat, isolation, worldliness and wealth it has become Eurostadt, its main character the lack of it. The city is hardly German at all, merely Western: Canon, Seiko, Sony, video, sex, hey-hey-hey. In the subways, the buskers sing in that strange Euro-glish which is taking over the world: 'Naats in wide sadin, neh-va reachy Vienne . . . '

It is East Berlin now which is fascinating, caught at the end of its own, very different, isolation. As it prepares to join the real world, the place is thoroughly mixed up: confused-determined, bitter-sweet, repelled by the West yet fascinated, optimistic-depressed.

Earlier this week, four youths made what will presumably be the last-ever escape from East Germany. They walked on to a bridge crossing into West Berlin but still closed: when challenged by a guard they sprayed him with green paint and hit him with chains – brutally, according to the official account – before running off into the West.

Had they gone a few hundred yards down the road they could have strolled through one of the increasing number of legal crossing points with a quick flash of their identity cards. Why did they do it? Kicks, I suppose. But why on earth did the guard try to stop them? It was essential, said a government spokesman, to 'safety and order' that people leave by the right exits.

Safety and order! East Germany is close to vanishing point – the state that died of self-disgust. Tomorrow, the elections take place that will lead to its dissolution. Outside the Palace of the Republic the satellite dishes have been set up to send the swingometer-busting results round the world (Karl-Marx-Stadt, Christian Democrat gain).

Yet the Foreign Affairs Ministry continues to put out its regular bulletins announcing that the President of the People's Chamber has met the head of the political department of the PLO and expressed hope for the expansion of relations between the states – the terminally ill greeting the unborn. The population still turns up at 7am for the long day's work. Everyone still waits at the lights for the little green man before setting out across an empty road. On New Year's Eve someone managed to scrawl 'Vive L'Anarchie' on top of the Brandenburg Gate. Tourists, one presumes. Anarchy never had a chance here.

The dissonance of the time is everywhere. The International Bookshop still has a lot of *Dialektik* and *Socialist Housekeeping* (what they certainly don't teach you at Harvard Business School) and the small English-language section has P. I. Nikitin's *Fundamentals of Political Economy*, which explains the basic contradiction of capitalism: 'It develops the productive forces and thereby gives birth to its own gravedigger – the proletariat.' There is also a paperback volume, selling rather better, entitled 'DDR Kaputt'.

Over at the Leninplatz on Leninallee, the 60-foot statue of you'll-never-guess-who remains intact. He is making eye contact with a poster that reads 'Freedom instead of Socialism'. In the Centrum Warehaus, probably the premier supermarket of the Eastern bloc, Coca-Cola has arrived, along with strawberry yoghurt and a few kiwifruit, if you're quick. There is no shortage of frozen kohlrabi, tinned meatballs and cabbage juice, nor of toilet paper fit for sanding down a door. In the clothing section, you can almost smell the polyester but there are a few T-shirts with Donald Duck saying, 'I am the Surf Boss,' for 60 marks, two days' wages.

There are other strange innovations. At the Alexanderplatz underground station, the advertising space which used to be taken up with party slogans has now been given over to artists. There is a magnificent display of paintings and cartoons, and a collage of old East Germany: a plastic sandal, a tiny Soviet-made TV and rock-like loaves. Soon, this space will of course be required: Canon, Seiko. Sony, video, sex, hey-hey-hey. In the brief interregnum, there is a flowering. Nearby, one of East Berlin's first buskers plays a lonely alto-sax. My Berlin friend Matthew Rice says he must be West German because no one here could have a saxophone that shiny.

Above ground every day there are locals chanting the new mantra: monni-chenj, chenj-monni. But on a Saturday morning there are also real Hare Krishnas from across The Wall and Jehovah's Witnesses, who must be thrilled. In East Germany, people are accustomed to the idea that if something is handed out free, you accept it. Everyone takes a *Watchtower*.

That mentality has helped the election campaign. Everyone wants a leaflet, and a banana and a bar of chocolate if the Christian Democrats are in town and handing out freebies. The Social Democrats have been more dignified. When they held a meeting on Monday in the beautiful Immanuelkirche, a tramride out of the city, they had a packed house for two stars – Walter Momper, the Mayor of West Berlin, and the SDP leader Hans-Jochen Vogel.

Mr Vogel criticised the Kohl government for treating East Germany as though it were a tract of land with no people; Mr Momper urged them to think for themselves and appreciate the concept of freedom. They both made quite rousing speeches, but no one was very roused. There were a lot of elderly ladies in the audience and they seemed more conscious of being in church than in politics.

It is a complicated business, this freedom. The Immanuelkirche was the setting for some of the pre-revolutionary rallies when the despised Erich Honecker was driving down Leninallee with the Soviet leader, cheered on by the claque. That was five months and an aeon ago.

Have the East Germans yet worked out how they feel? One senses a nation scurrying from Moscow's skirts to Bonn's, without a pause for thought, a moment to consider whether just maybe it might not be possible to construct a wholesome society derived from their own harsh experiences – one that allows cartoons and collages to take up precious advertising space at Alexanderplatz.

Beneath the surface of this election, there are all kinds of emotions, many conflicting, some decidedly murky. I took the train out to Hellersdorf, a vast new expanse of apartment blocks half an hour out of town, built in the British-municipal style of 1965 and then left, Third World fashion, amidst the rubble. It is the classic Communist hyper-estate, like Basildon without the old-world charm.

The flats themselves are not that bad and may well be preferable to the old city centre blocks, unpainted since the war, where the walls resemble what is left of The Wall. But no one chose to come here and some foreigners say they can spot Hellersdorf people by their put-upon look.

Three stops down the line, I found the nearest bar. The natives were friendly. There was Andreas, who said everyone was already bored by the election and feeling apathetic. His mate Harry thought the West Germans were arrogant and that the Western media were preventing people making up their own minds. They turned out to be off-duty policemen.

Then I met Frank and Mario. Frank was a carpenter who had felt uneasy on his recent visits to West Berlin: 'It is hard to feel at home. I lose some self-confidence, I don't think I can compete. They were being kind to me but I felt like the poor, little one from the East.' Frank said his workmates were voting for the rightwing parties; living in East Germany had taught them that you had to go out and grab what you could.

Mario was a 21-year-old electrician who was not at all short of self-confidence. ('Eh, English? Liverpool, Depeche Mode, Frankie Goes to Hollywood? Friday, come to the disco.') But, without irony, he told a story that in every phrase said something chilling about life in the old DDR and something, perhaps, about the new Germany.

'Before the revolution, I was sent to work at the Greifswald, at the nuclear power station. Half the workers were Poles. They were filling their baskets with chocolate and butter and sending them home. We wrote to Erich Honecker to complain, and he sent back a letter saying we were racists. He also sent the state security service to watch us.' In the bar's toilet a few days ago, someone had stuck a few swastikas on the walls; but this was one of those rare occasions when the East Germans had been quick with the paintbrush.

On the way back to town, I stopped at an older bar, the 'Bright Corner'. It was full of older men too, coughing over their fags. The radio was tuned, softly, to one of the new East Berlin private stations. Just before the news, it played the West German national anthem. As '*Deutschland Über Alles*' began, the barman turned the volume up. When it ended, he turned it back down again.

The March wind was not icy. It was strangely mild, and confused April flowers were out all over the city: over the dying nation, the sun shines in. But as I left and headed for Checkpoint Charlie, I turned up my coat collar, Leamas-fashion, just the same.

OPERA IN THE FOREST

Jan Rocha
19 March 1990

Opera has returned to the Amazon rain forest. The legendary opera house in Manaus, built during the turn-of the-century rubber boom, will reopen this month to the sounds of Placido Domingo singing in *Carmen*.

The strains of *La Traviata*, *Aïda* and *Lohengrin* will follow in an exotic addition to the operagoer's round of Glyndebourne, La Scala, Covent Garden, and New York's Met.

Restoring the Teatro Amazonas to its original glory has cost £8.8 million. Since the last opera was sung there in 1907, the magnificent building perched above the city and the Amazon River degenerated into a scruffy venue for rock shows, carnival balls, and indoor football.

Previous attempts to restore the building, riddled with woodworm and mould, failed. But the latest restoration has been painstaking. Eight layers of paint were scraped away to show the original rose colour of the outside walls. Thousands of yards of red velvet were imported from France for the seats. The paving was dug up to reveal black cobblestones covered with latex to muffle the sound of horse-drawn carriages.

The opera house opened in 1897 with a performance of *La Gioconda*. It symbolised the extravagant opulence of Brazil's rubber boom, which turned Manaus, a thousand miles up river from the mouth of the Amazon, into an outpost of European civilisation.

Manaus had no rail or road links with the rest of Brazil, but it was awash with rubber profits. Everything was imported from Europe – Danish butter, German sausages,

French prostitutes and entire buildings made in Britain. Laundry was sent to Lisbon and French newspapers were sold on the streets.

The opera house had Venetian chandeliers, Sèvres porcelain and ironwork from Glasgow. The huge dome was covered in blue, green and gold tiles made in Germany. It would have had a staircase of Carrara marble, but that was lost in a shipwreck.

Caruso never sang there, but companies came from Milan, Madrid, Lisbon and Paris for 11 years. Inducements to sing in Manaus had to be introduced after yellow fever carried off nearly a dozen members of one company. Conductors were given gold-encrusted batons and sopranos received pearl and diamond earrings.

The rubber barons thought the boom would never end. Manaus briefly became the most advanced city in Brazil with the first electric tram system, clean water and telephones. But its extraordinary profits were based largely on the virtual enslavement of the Indian population who worked the rubber plantations.

An investigation in 1911 concluded that 30,000 Indians died from starvation, flogging and overwork to produce 4,000 tons of rubber which earned the Peruvian Amazon Rubber Company £1,500 million on the London market.

Manaus went bankrupt and the opera closed after the market was flooded by cheap Malayan rubber grown from saplings smuggled out of Brazil by an Englishman.

The rubber industry revived briefly during the second world war when Malaya fell to the Japanese. About 36,000 men were recruited in Brazil's north-eastern drylands and shipped to the Amazon to collect rubber for the American war industry. This 'rubber army' was largely abandoned to its fate in the jungle and nearly 20,000 died from malaria, yellow fever, snake bites and animal attacks.

Manaus is now a scruffy town of electronics assembly

industries and shops crammed with videos and colour televisions where high-rise buildings alternate with riverside stilt houses. But officials hope the revival of the opera house will bring tourists eager for cultural, as well as Amazonian ecological, adventures.

A SHIVER OF SHAME

Leader
23 March 1990

It is not Mrs Margaret Thatcher's style to apologise. You will search her speeches in vain to find her saying sorry. Until Wednesday evening, that is. For something notable happened when Mr Váčlav Havel came to dinner at Downing Street. Over the port and *petits fours*, the Prime Minister made a speech about Britain and Czechoslovakia. In it, she reflected that it was to this same building in the heart of London that her predecessor Mr Neville Chamberlain had returned in 1938 from Munich. Here, Chamberlain had uttered the fateful words that the agreement he had made with Herr Hitler, which in essence abandoned Czechoslovakia to the Third Reich, would mean peace in our time. 'I think each of us', Mrs Thatcher said on Wednesday, 'still feels some shame over that agreement.'

It was a short sentence, but pregnant with meaning. Shame is a powerful word, but it is not one which we readily associate either with the Prime Minister herself or with the ideology and culture to which she has lent her name. To be unapologetic is fundamental to Thatcherism. There, pride in enterprise, success, wealth and England are unshaded and indivisible. There is no room for guilt in this cosmos, much less shame about British history. The past is variously bunk or a triumphant national legend, but it is not our moral responsibility. Guilt is for liberals. Shame is for wets. Apologising is for guilt-ridden lefties. Worrying about the past is for wimps. So if Mrs Thatcher is expressing shame, then we should take note. Either (without a jot of supporting evidence) she is losing her nerve, or she is acknowledging the legitimacy of something which she derides elsewhere – notably in the debate about the teaching of history in schools – the idea that it is possible to be morally critical about British history.

The Prime Minister's embarrassment over the Munich agreement is certainly well founded. It would be echoed by many on the Left in this country – including leftwing Tories like Mr Edward Heath. But it is also a vernacular statement of the historical agenda of the radical Right which has believed, from the days of David Urquhart a century and a half ago to the Tolstoy–Aldington libel case of recent memory, that the Foreign Office is riddled with traitors who would make any immoral agreement with any dictator for the sake of a quiet life in the country. What is unusual, as with so much else in the Thatcher era, is to hear such sentiments being expressed by the leader of the Conservative Party. The Tories were, after all, the Party of Munich. No Conservative MP voted against the agreement, though some 30 abstained. Lord Home, today heavy with honours in his Party, went to Munich as Chamberlain's private secretary and continues to defend the deal. Lord Hailsham, the Lord Chancellor of Mrs Thatcher's first two terms, won the 1938 Oxford by-election on a pro-Munich ticket in a contest in which his opponents chanted 'A vote for Hogg is a vote for Hitler.'

For many reasons, therefore, Mrs Thatcher deserves congratulations for her frankness. Yet this can hardly be an end to the matter. So far, Mrs Thatcher's foreign policy has been based upon an instinctive dislike of the conspiracies of international diplomacy. That is why she made the Bruges speech and also why she condemns pre-war appeasement. But Mrs Thatcher has also readmitted moral judgement into the study of the national past. If a British Prime Minister can now apologise – rightly – to President Havel about Munich, then what next? There could be an apology to President Mubarak for Suez; or to President Rafsanjani for the overthrow of Mussadeq, to President Najibullah for Britain's three invasions of Afghanistan over the years, even to President Gorbachev for the war of intervention against the Bolsheviks. A word of apology to Mr Haughey might not go amiss either, nor would an expression of shame if and when she finally meets up with Mr Nelson Mandela. If Britain is now seriously settling its moral debts with world history, then it faces rather a long list of creditors.

BLACK JOCKSTRAPS WITH PINSTRIPES

Alix Sharkey
26 March 1990

At school it was so different. After playing football we would shower and dress in five minutes. Mirrors were for checking your necktie and hair; anyone spending more than a few seconds was fiercely ridiculed. Grooming was something to do with horses; the study of muscle groups confined to biology labs.

But if male members of the London Central YMCA are

representative of society at large, this spartan approach to physique and appearance has long since vanished. In the changing rooms of the Y, men of all ages, hues and physical types, from skeletal to simian, pore over themselves. Many discuss their bodies openly, swapping notes on everything from exercise routines to moisturisers.

The common bond is male vanity. Even those with a discreet kit and modest physical aspirations will emerge from the showers to spend an inordinate amount of time towelling themselves down in front of full-length mirrors. And there are moments of sublime surrealism for the eavesdropper.

'Yeah, this is 100 per cent Lycra, from a shop on Melrose Avenue. They do them with yellow and purple stripes down the side as well,' says one middle-aged man. He is wearing an electric blue body stocking, discussing his Californian workout fashions with a friend. He bears some resemblance to television's Bergerac, but is actually a taxi driver. He sometimes comes in wearing his badge around his neck.

Of course, male vanity is not confined to cab drivers. It's just that they are the loudest and most shameless of the London Central Y's 3,500 male members. Others seek the quiet anonymity of corner lockers, but go to equal extremes of self-veneration. As Mark Twain observed, there are no grades of vanity, only grades of ability in concealing it.

For instance, I can't help noticing that a number of young executives wear black jockstraps. Nothing unusual in that, except that they wear them under pinstripe trousers and change out of them to exercise. Surely this is a male equivalent of the suspender belt; are men now so vain that they grow coquettish?

Another area of concern is the club's general penchant for grooming products. Gels, creams, talcs, pomades, deodorants and baby oil combine in a heady vapour, redolent of exotic bordellos, more Miami Vice than Old Spice.

Don't get me wrong. I live in a glasshouse. My 'kit bag' contains many of these grooming products and I have my own timid ritual of conceit. But I thought I was a freak. It's the discovery that I'm normal that is so horrifying.

Dylan Jones, editor of men's magazine *Arena*, says I needn't worry. 'Men started to be more conscious of the way they look a few years ago, when it suddenly became OK for them to be interested in clothes. Now they've taken it a stage further and try to stay in trim. And there's been an enormous rise in the sale of men's grooming products in the past 18 months. We're certainly getting more advertising from that area.'

But is this vanity a decadent blight, a denial of manhood? 'If men can admit they're vain, that's fine,' says Jones. 'It's good for men to have a degree of vanity. The obvious alternative is the arrogant slob.'

The old stigma attached to male grooming may have gone, but what is one to make of men who shave their chests to accentuate muscle striations? Weight-trainers are conspicuously narcissistic, since the building of muscle tissue can be measured only by careful and loving self-scrutiny. And some will spend as much time dressing for the activity as checking its results. I've even seen men using their hair spray *before* they go into the gym.

It is also worth noting that the vainest are not necessarily the youngest. Looking after oneself gets more exacting beyond 30 – you have to look closer. And with the cheapest off-peak YMCA membership running at £132 a year, these are men prepared to pay substantial amounts to keep themselves in the pink.

Derek Hunt works out four afternoons a week. His distinctive kit – black vest, shorts, socks and trainers, red headband and wristbands – stands out amongst the more florid outfits. Hunt is an actor and pumps iron in order to keep trim. Now in his mid-50s, he started training five years ago because he was getting flabby.

'I wear the kit because it's practical, and because those colours make me feel sharp and active.' He argues that a touch of conceit can be therapeutic. 'Unless you've got a certain amount of vanity, you haven't got positivity. It's an aspect of self-confidence,' he says. 'Of course, there are the ones who come in, preen and pout, and won't talk to anyone else. We call them muscle snobs. But I don't believe it should be po-faced. I like a giggle; you can still get the work done.'

Sadly, this view is rare. The New He-Man is deadly serious about the figure he cuts. Toned, trim, slick and scented, with a bagful of designer gym togs – this would seem to be the Man Of The Future. But what about the backlash? Will women rise up and demand a less conceited, more rough-and-ready male? I'm going to the pub to ponder. And I won't be back until I'm stinking.

A CANDIDE IN BROMLEY

Angela Carter
29 March 1990

The Buddha Of Suburbia, by Hanif Kureishi(Faber).

The narrator of Hanif Kureishi's ebullient, dismayed farce introduces himself thus: 'My name is Karim Amir, and I am an Englishman born and bred, almost.' Karim, a.k.a. 'Creamy Jeans', is a child of Empire. When we first meet him, he lives with his Indian father and his English mother on the distant outskirts of London, enduring the last of school and the last of flower-power, in a state of near-terminal late adolescent angst.

But Karim's story will prove to be most English in its heritage – that of the glorious, scabrous, picaresque, savage, sentimental tradition of low comedy that stretches from Chaucer to the dirty postcards on Brighton Pier. *The Buddha Of Suburbia* is also as much of an up-yours for our times as *Lucky Jim* was for the fifties, although it comes in furiously from the left. Kureishi himself offers another signpost when Eva, Karim's father's lover, gives the boy a copy of *Candide*.

But, in some respects, Candide had it easy compared to Karim. 'I was sick of being affectionately called Shitface and Curryface.' Jamila, militant, feminist, black radical and his best friend, defines the problem: 'The thing was, we were supposed to be English, but to the English, we were always wogs and nigs and Pakis and the rest of it.'

Karim's world is soon turned upside down. His father, Haroon, leaves his sweet, downtrodden wife to live with sexy, trendy Eva and practise as a guru. (He is the Buddha of the title.) Jamila, to her fury, is bullied and cajoled into an arranged marriage with the amiable buffoon Changez, who demands, as part of a dowry, a complete set of the works of Conan Doyle. Karim moves to the big city. Life opens up. He starts a career as an actor, his first role, to Jamila's disgust, Mowgli, in what she dubs The Jungle Bunny Book. Punk happens. Charlie, Eva's son, turns into a successful pop singer, although Karim is keen to assure us he is a very bad one.

Karim falls worshipfully in love with Charlie in chapter one; by the novel's end, he has grown out of it. But *The Buddha Of Suburbia* isn't so much a coming-of-age novel as a coming-to-terms novel, coming to terms with a world in which nothing, neither pleasure, nor politics, nor power, can be taken on trust. Not even violence. When a girlfriend's father turns his dog on Karim, expectations are reversed with a vengeance: 'I knew by now what the dog was up to. The dog was in love with me – quick movements against my arse told me so.'

The sexual black comedy of this episode is shockingly cruel, hilarious and desperate; Karim is training himself, rigorously, to see the funny side. Irony is his defence and his weapon. The ribald subject matter is exquisitely set off by the louche prissiness of Karim's direction: 'I contemplated myself and my wardrobe with loathing and would willingly have urinated over every garment.' *The Buddha Of Suburbia* is wonderfully well written, tasty, interesting and full of glee. It is not 'well wrought' or 'finely crafted'. It is not like Penelope Lively.

In fact, it may be the first novel in what I trust will be a rapidly growing and influential genre – the novel designed on purpose to exclude itself from the Booker shortlist. There's not only the richly vulgar vein of body comedy – Hanif Kureishi finds every aspect of physicality from mastectomy to anal intercourse ruefully mirthful – but he remains wonderfully Right On, politically, and lets the middle classes play little if any role in this world of squats, anti-racism and dishevelled integrity.

He can't find a bad word to say about women, either, which is a lovely thing in this period of fashionable misogyny, but it does mean that Jamila and Eva and poor Mum are touched with a little bit of unexpected sugar. If some minor characters – such as Uncle Ted, the central heating engineer and part-time football hooligan – spring at once to pulsing life, others, like Jamila's mother, now a grocer, once a princess, haven't got much to do except stand around looking picturesque.

The novel ends with a wedding announcement – Haroon and Eva's – and a party. Karim ponders how things have been a mess but soon will get better. There's a sting in the tail; it is election night, in the fatal year of 1979.

A radical feminist I know paid *My Beautiful Launderette*, the movie scripted by Hanif Kureishi, her ultimate accolade: 'It almost made me like men.' His first novel almost made me nostalgic for that messy but on the whole optimistic decade, the seventies. It is a wonderful novel. I doubt I will read a funnier or one with more heart, this year, possibly this decade.

CULTURE CLASHES

Maev Kennedy
3 April 1990

Boris Botulism and the East End anarchists smiled at the idea of any links with Militant or the Socialist Workers, found Class War's middle-class ravings more than faintly comic, and laughed out loud at the idea of any connections with the Labour Party.

Between them they are veterans of every struggle from Greenham to Stonehenge, via hunt sabotage and animal liberation.

They came from Newham and Hackney for the demonstration, joined in the violence with enthusiasm, but insisted they didn't start it.

'It was the police,' Mr Botulism said. His friend, once a Greenham feminist pacifist, was not really called Sally Salmonella, but Mr Botulism changed his name by deed poll, and was once arrested by police who found that alone sufficiently provocative.

'We were in the square, not looking for a fight, and the police kept charging in causing little outbreaks of violence. And then people joined in, of course.'

Mr Botulism didn't join in any violence himself, because he has a bad back.

'We heard the sound of a riot breaking out, and we went to find it,' the former pacifist said. 'If you're asking if I approve of throwing scaffolding poles at the police, the answer is yes. Pacifism gets you nowhere.'

None of them had any sympathy for the injured police. 'They've signed on as defenders of the capitalist system,' Andrea, an American, said. 'Some people had calculated the kind of violence that would be useful. If the police beat up demonstrators sitting on the ground, that looks very bad for them.'

Fierce arguments about what happened on Saturday broke out all over Horseferry Magistrates' Court, but anarchists and pacifists found common ground in sympathy for the Spanish stonemason jailed for 28 days for stealing two dummy cologne bottles from the smashed window of a Regent Street chemist.

A young burglar reckoned he himself got off exceptionally lightly, because the judges were looking kindly on anyone not a poll tax rioter.

Most of the accused were young, male, pale, thin, and living in squats. Some gave as their only fixed address parents they hadn't seen for years.

One had been begging in Cambridge Circus, and was arrested on the top deck of a west-bound 53 bus, with a new clarinet which he said someone had given him.

One said he'd been handed five combat knives, looted from a sports shop, in the street. 'Look at them,' he'd urged the arresting officers anxiously, 'they're clean, they haven't been used.'

It was a culture clash, if not class war, in the court.

'Cultural studies!' Mr Roger Davies, the stipendiary magistrate, repeated, on hearing what one accused did in college.

One young man was told: 'You'd have been better off watching the boat race.'

'Wish I had,' he replied.

Alice Sheldon, one of the few women charged, pale, slight, in denims and an armful of bracelets, wanted to plead guilty so she could get home to the Reading travellers' camp and feed her puppy. She explained she'd seen four officers arresting one man who looked as if his arm was broken, and dived in to help. 'If it was four demonstrators and one policeman on the ground I'd have done the same,' she said.

Mr Davies worried about bailing her because of the travellers' camp. She reassured him that she wouldn't be moving because she had no motor to tow her caravan.

He urged her to see the court duty solicitor, and she came back in the afternoon pleading guilty after all.

'Can I speak?' she asked anxiously several times, and after she was fined £100 with £25 costs she managed to say: 'I was quite disgusted with the behaviour of both sides. Some of the police were very violent, and some of the demonstrators were no better than a football crowd. I don't really like to be associated with that sort of behaviour.'

Sarah Feldman was carrying Maurice Bloch's *From Blessing to Violence*, because she anticipated a long wait for her friend's case. Ms Feldman was the woman in the television film swallow-diving out from under the wheels of an accelerating police car.

She and another friend, Gareth Luis Burres, were troubled by the violence on both sides. They tried to leave early and asked a policeman the best way out. 'He just laughed at us.'

To their surprise their friend was bailed, despite living in a squat. He was charged with obstruction, but told the judge he had refused to move from sitting outside the National Gallery because they were hemmed in by police horses on one side, and a riot squad on the other.

'There was nowhere for us to go, that's why we sat down.'

They hugged him down the corridor, as he peeled back his shirt to show a huge bruise on his shoulder, and told how Hammersmith police heard he was a vegetarian and brought him chicken curry for Sunday dinner.

Stephen, also waiting for a friend's case, originally from Wales, took his black flag to the demonstration with all the other people from his squat in Brixton.

'We didn't come for a fight, we came for a party, we had a band and we had our flags and we all had our faces painted. We were about ten yards back from the gates of Downing Street, where the cops started all the trouble. We just wanted to get into Trafalgar Square. I didn't loot anything though, there was nothing worth nicking.

'This is only the beginning. The word is in Brixton this summer if it stays hot they're going to take it apart – but I don't want to do it in Brixton, I'd rather go and do it somewhere rich.'

THE BATTLE FOR STRANGEWAYS

Michael Morris
3 April 1990

It was a cold, bleak day at Strangeways. There was the usual Mancunian drizzle, with one or two heavy showers which brought out the golf umbrellas, even on the prison roof.

By 2.30pm riot police were girding themselves like medieval knights in protective armour for a second wave to follow the morning push, which regained control of four of the ten wings which radiate from a central rotunda.

The comings and goings were endless as fire engines and ambulances moved round the sinister-looking penal fortress.

Banners hung limply – one made of two white sheets – on the roof ridges. At one stage, prisoners used a long rope to haul up an object. There was a strangulated cry: 'We won't come down.'

Prisoners kept popping up through rafters shorn of slates in the previous night's dismantling of the prison. A long line of men used the cat-walk to get from one wing to another.

More slates were slung down in desultory fashion in contrast to the more insistent notes of something being smashed up out of sight.

At 10.30am police in shirtsleeves had queued at a big yellow van to be issued with riot gear, which they donned before carting large crates of equipment into the prison.

Ten minutes later a prisoner with a loudhailer on the roof kept shouting, among other things: 'They won't let us . . . ' but the rest of his words were lost on the wind.

He raised his arms in defiance. Some supporters in the crowd shouted: 'Stay where you are, lads!' By this time only 120 prisoners were still loose inside.

Ann Edwards told of her night-long vigil for her son, Geoffrey, aged 17, who is more than three months into his 12-month sentence.

'I don't know whether he is alive or dead,' said Mrs Edwards as rumours continued to circulate about 20 deaths. 'The police don't care. When you phone the police emergency number, it is either a continuous bleep or engaged.'

If her son was injured, she did not know which hospital he would be in. 'They treat them like pigs, so how do they expect them to behave?'

At 12.05pm Charles Kesaru, a Home Office spokesman, emerged from a police communications van, in a second appearance, to tell journalists that the morning operation to re-establish control of four wings had been successful. 'Control was established quickly and without direct confrontation,' he said.

The regained wings were G, H, I and K plus the hospital. No bodies had been found. Six inmates surrendered during the push. Mr Kesaru, plainly trying to be helpful with the little he could or was allowed to say, added: 'Attempts are being made to establish a dialogue with the 120 inmates still loose. Senior prison staff will conduct it.'

At 2.15pm a police helicopter circled over the prison without provoking reaction from the prisoners beyond a defiant wave.

Five minutes later, the prisoners were leaving the roof in what appeared like a changing of their own guard, probably to relieve those who were wet and cold.

An onlooker, Steven Crawford, aged 28, from Manchester, who came out of Strangeways in July after serving 2½ years of a three-year sentence, was asked what he would do with Strangeways. 'I would blow it up, and pull it down. You cannot build dirt on dirt and that is what they are trying to do with plans for extending it.'

Mr Ivor Serle, chairman of the POA at the jail, said last night that the number of prisoners actively protesting was reducing. 'The atmosphere is quiet and there is very little noise of damage going on.'

Later the police strategy for regaining control of the five

main wings was marking time as prisoners settled down for a second night on the tiles.

British prison sieges are usually a patient game, with no storming of cell blocks and risk to life.

The dialogue opened by the prison governor Brendan O'Friel was paying off as small groups gave themselves up.

TRUMP IN THE PINK

Simon Tisdall
7 April 1990

The garish pink and gold minarets, made of fibreglass and plastic, rise incongruously against the cold blue evening sky of the Jersey Shore. Nine Indian-style white elephants of sculptured stone guard the boardwalk steps, dolefully eyeing the deserted beach.

Up on the ramparts, outside an outlandish purple pagoda, a large man in orange turban and baggy trousers seems understandably self-conscious. It is 7.20pm, and at the main entrance spotlights are playing on the upturned faces of the crowd, which grows by the minute.

Colour-co-ordinated it isn't. Tasteful, it ain't. But who cares? In the court of Lord Donald, within the ever-expanding frontiers of the New York developer's empire, beauty is in the eye, not of the beholder, but of the shareholder.

Tonight everyone has a piece of the action. This is the official gala opening of the $1 billion Taj Mahal Casino-Resort, the most expensive, the biggest, and the most appallingly, amazingly, gloriously, vulgar gambling joint in the world.

On top of the main tower, one word, in giant neon letters, says it all: 'Trump'.

After Trump Tower, Trump Plaza, the Trump Shuttle and the Trump Divorce, welcome to the most spectacular trumpery of all. The great man will be here any minute.

In the casino, which has already opened, more than 3,000 slot machines stretch into a haze of glitter and glitz. All is bells and buzzers and the beep-beeping of rotating cherries and plums, like some supermarket checkout counter gone berserk.

The punters – mostly blue-rinsed, middle-aged women – sit entranced before their bandit tormentors, feeding quarters from plastic Trump-cups.

To cover his junk bond borrowings alone, analysts say Trump must take up to $1.3 million a day at the tables and 'slots'. In the first eight hours, the casino took $925,000, or $21 a second.

Lisa, the Harem Attendant (her official job description), who serves free drinks to the gamblers, says it's exciting. But she's not so sure about her skimpy uniform – red fez, blue feathers, and organza mini-skirt. 'It's very complicated to get on, considering it's so tiny.'

As a Trump Organisation woman estimates that there are 125,000 people in and around this temple of (pecuniary) doom, a great roar goes up. He's here!

Swaggering slightly, Donald Trump, the baby boomers' answer to Howard Hughes, enters. The band plays 'Eye of the Tiger'.

Down in The Inlet, a slum of boarded and abandoned houses plagued by crack, cocaine, violent crime, unemployment, and alienation, James Sharif offers a different angle on the Trump effect.

'When the casinos came to Atlantic City 12 years ago, there were lots of promises made, like new housing and that sort of thing,' he says. 'They never came to anything.

'This used to be a resort. They had Ferris wheels and fairgrounds, and movie theatres and restaurants. That's all gone now. Even the beach area has gone, the beach got eroded. It's all gambling now. This is Trump City.'

Seen from the dilapidated Bruce's Pool Room on Arctic Avenue, from the barricaded housing project on Delaware, the casino skyscrapers rise like islands of plenty in a sea of poverty.

Atlantic City is home to 12 casinos, three owned by Trump. But the town, as distinct from its superimposed guest-industry, is dying. Half the population is on welfare.

Patsy Scott, aged 23, has lived in The Inlet all her life. Does she think the Taj jamboree is fun? 'No I don't,' she says. 'He should do more. He should fix up the housing.'

Her eight-year-old brother, Paul, is more hostile to questions from a white man. 'Get out of here, man! Go get some money, man!' he hollers.

It's dark now in the court of Lord Donald and the vast throng wants action. Trump ascends the podium. To the chagrin of the gossip columnists, there is no estranged wife, Ivana, no Maria Maples, the jilted starlet. Just Trump, and a giant fibreglass Aladdin's lamp, which he ceremoniously rubs.

On a giant projection screen to his right, a genie appears. 'Master, I am at your service,' the genie booms.

'Open Sesame Taj Mahal,' intones Trump. With a crash of 'Star Trek' music, a vast red ribbon adorning the Taj tower is cut as though by magic, and fireworks explode overhead.

'You may not believe this,' says James Sharif, 'but there's a lot of people who like Donald. I like his style. He's a showman. And despite what they say, he's done a lot for this city.'

It is a view heartily endorsed at the White House Sub Shop, an eatery on Mississippi Avenue.

'The Taj is really pretty,' says Virginia, who works on the till and has lived in Atlantic City all her life. 'It's like Disneyland. It seems amazing that they could build something so beautiful – here. Amazing!'

Ralph Pileggi, another White House employee, says: 'You've got to admire Trump. He's brought a lot of jobs here. He's got a brain.'

And what does Donald himself have to say? All suggestions that this time he has gone too far, that when the novelty wears off the Taj could founder, are forcefully rebutted.

The Taj will make money for him, and for Atlantic City, he says.

'Well then, what about a British Taj Mahal?' asks the *Guardian*.

The great man pauses in the post-ceremony crush. 'Sounds like a good idea,' he smirks.

IRON LADY ON THE ROPES

Martin Kettle & John Rettie
7 April 1990

Britain created world headlines this week, with first the Trafalgar Square anti-poll tax riots and then the occupation of Strangeways prison fully reported.

But the events have also caused commentators in several countries to turn their attention to what Italy's *La Repubblica* called 'the political market's verdict on Maggie'.

The commentators and editorial writers of Western

Europe's press are in little doubt that they are now watching the death crisis of Thatcherism.

'The Iron Lady is seeing the beginning of the end,' was how the columnist Alberto Cavallari put it in *La Repubblica on Tuesday*.

'The poll tax revolt is only the most vivid manifestation of a deep-rooted social crisis.'

The riots have stimulated the cartoonists, too. 'Can't we turn to a different channel?' demands Mrs Thatcher as bricks explode from her television set in a drawing by Pepsch in Munich's *Süddeutsche Zeitung*.

Plantu, in *Le Monde*, took the Bayeux Tapestry as his model, depicting Mrs Thatcher on horseback leading a cavalry charge against medieval rioters and shouting: 'Shut up, you serfs!'

In its editorial column on Wednesday, *Le Monde* put the two outbreaks of rioting together and concluded that Britain faces a moral and social crisis.

'For several years,' the leading article said, 'we have witnessed a growth in violence in Great Britain. 'Such a thing is paradoxical for a country whose democratic traditions are among the most established in the whole world. The evidence has included brawling in football stadiums, clashes between police and strikers, and many other forms of hooliganism, including racial violence.'

It is clear, *Le Monde* continued, that 'the sense of injustice provoked by hardline Thatcherism' was behind many of these outbreaks. Minorities had sparked things off, the paper said, but they would not have had such success if larger numbers had not been prepared to let them. 'For many British people a moral crisis is sweeping their country,' *Le Monde* concluded.

'Free-market liberalism stimulates selfishness rather than common values. It is somehow symbolic that the uprising in Strangeways broke out in the prison chapel.'

If there is a note of satisfaction in the Western European press, most watchers on the other side of the Atlantic seem nonplussed. But there was a note of panic in the reaction of the Moonie-owned *Washington Times*.

'The political news for friends and admirers of Prime Minister Margaret Thatcher is grim,' wrote the columnist Arnold Beichman on Wednesday. But all was not lost, Beichman told his readers. 'The Tory worker will elect Mrs Thatcher if she sticks it out and runs again, as I hope she will.'

The Soviet press has barely commented on the local difficulties of Mrs Thatcher, who is a valued ally of President Gorbachev and remains a great heroine to many Soviet citizens. It is just as reluctant to criticise her over internal British politics as the Western press is about berating Mr Gorbachev over Lithuania, perhaps more so.

The nearest thing to criticism came in *Pravda's* report on Monday of the 'second Battle of Trafalgar'. Describing how 'the capital's usually decorous face was distorted by hate, violence and fear', *Pravda's* new London correspondent, Andrei Lyuty, said the blame could not be put exclusively on 'extremists from anarchist and ultra-left organisations', or on some of the police.

'It was rather a kind of riot against Thatcher's policies, a riot against the rich; the well-dressed crowd generally selected luxury limousines to attack,' he reported.

In its report the government newspaper, *Izvestiya*, said Conservative leaders, recognising that the poll tax 'they had approved and brought into force is now intensely unpopular', had tried to put the blame for the riot on the Labour Party leadership.

But, *Izvestiya* concluded, 'the deputy Labour leader, R. Hattersley, categorically and angrily rejected these accusations, which were clearly propaganda.'

TO STORM STRANGEWAYS

John McVicar
9 April 1990

As far as the battle for territory went, the Strangeways rioters had a walkover. Once they secured the commanding heights of the prison rooftops, the authorities backed off and adopted a policy of starving them into surrender. Unfortunately, as the prisoners had gained access to the kitchens in the initial assault, this was at best a long-game tactic.

A helicopter and strobe searchlights were used to keep the prisoners awake; and fires started by the rioters to keep warm were hosed down. The Home Office emphasised that the hoses were not being used on the rioters themselves. In the meantime, sections of the prison were retaken on a piecemeal basis by the warders.

There was no real departure from the softly-softly strategy that the Home Secretary, David Waddington, announced to the House the day after the riot started when he spoke of how many prisoners there were still '*to surrender*' [my italics]. It is difficult to establish who decided on this approach. Presumably the Strangeways governor, Brendan O'Friel, had a hand in it as he was part of the emergency committee that exists to deal with such crises. A high-ranking local police officer is involved, as are members of the Home Office's prison department. To some extent, though, their approach was inherited from the policy towards prison rooftop protesters established around the mid-'70s.

Yet very soon after the assault in the chapel the authorities knew that this riot was significantly different from any previous one – the rioters had gained control of the 'rule

43' wing that houses prisoners who are vulnerable to attack from other inmates. These offenders are the 'untouchables' of prison society; they are usually informers or sex offenders, particularly those who have abused children. They are segregated because they are targeted by the general prison population for attack.

Once they were at the mercy of rioters it was obvious that they were going to be severely beaten and even killed. Indeed, the details of what Roy Hattersley called the 'bestial acts' said to have been inflicted on these men – kangaroo courts, lynch mobs, torture, and, by some accounts, even forcible injection of drugs from the prison pharmacy – would not surprise anyone who is familiar with prison culture.

The authorities not only knew that this would occur but also had reports in the early stages of the riot of the grisly fate of the rule 43s. By virtue of the strategy adopted, they knowingly abandoned them to the persecution of the mob. Yet the principle for dealing with such situations is both clear and established: when kidnappers or hostage-takers begin to inflict violence on their captives the authorities use force to restore order or, at least, mount a rescue attempt. Of course, this is subject to whatever risk there is to those who would have to carry it out.

The question is: What risk was there? In fact, the risk would have been minimal. The most effective weapons available to the rioters were the prison rooftop slates which, once one masters their aerodynamic properties, function rather like flying guillotines.

High-powered hoses, though, can neutralise the slate-thrower. This would have allowed a storming force to gain access to the rule 43 wing, where it would have been a simple task to restore order. Tear gas, rubber bullets and batons would have been sufficient for the task, but if firearms were needed they should have been used.

The dereliction of duty by those who decided on the softly-softly approach – the final responsibility was the Home Secretary's – can be put in stark relief by considering what would have occurred if the rioters had taken hostage warders, the chaplain, or any other non-prisoners and begun to inflict violence on them. Even if it had meant calling on the SAS, Iranian Embassy style, the authorities would have stormed. They would have had to.

The question now becomes: What was it that obscured the duty of the authorities to protect the 43s? Incidentally, for what it matters, some of those housed in the 43s wing were not even convicted, and a number were neither sex cases nor informers. Obviously the prison authorities were in the thrall of the policy that had been applied in previous riots. None of the officials or the ministers concerned had the vision to see the real issue of the Strangeways riot. Perhaps, if Sir Douglas Hurd had still been the Home Secretary, things would have been different. What undoubtedly compounded the Home Office's myopia was the eagerness with which most of the commentators in the media and in Parliament blamed our dreadful prison system.

The liberals and prison reformers indicted overcrowding and, while they were shocked by the attack on the 43s, they are far too tender to grasp the nettle of using violence to stop violence. Predictably, the warders berated the Government for its unsympathetic attitude to their insistent demands for higher pay. This left the law and order brigade, who could only foam at the mouth.

The Woolf inquiry may be constituted only to look at 'events leading up to the disturbance and action taken to end it' but the Home Secretary has already conceded that Lord Justice Woolf can look at whatever he thinks is relevant. One area that is overdue for review is what is called the dispersal system.

In the late 1960s, the major problem was escape, and the Mountbatten Report recommended that difficult and dangerous prisoners be concentrated in one high-security prison. Another report argued for dispersing such prisoners to a number of high-security jails, and this policy was adopted. The escape problem, however, has been solved and the major security consideration for the prison service concerns disorders linked to protest. Indeed, protest culture is now part of convict lore.

The Strangeways riot exemplifies the disadvantages for control that are inherent in the dispersal system. It was led by convicts who are not escape risks but prison mavericks who have made a career out of fighting the system. There are far more of these inmates than there are escape risks, and it is becoming increasingly obvious that within the constraints of any likely prison budget the dispersal system makes it impossible to imprison them in a civilised fashion. Adopting the system of concentration would allow the proofing of one prison for high-risk escapers and trouble makers and would give the system the flexibility to make provision for sex offenders and other vulnerable prisoners in another specialist prison.

BRITAIN'S CLAP-TRAP

Walter Gratzer
12 April 1990

Sex, Death and Punishment: Attitudes to Sex and Sexuality in Britain since the Renaissance, by Richard Davenport-Hines (Collins)

Woody Allen's celebrated catechism of sex contains an article – 'Q: Is sex dirty? A: Only when it's done right' –

which perfectly encapsulates the Puritan spirit that enveloped the subject in a choking miasma of superstition, fear, lubricity and cant. It stems from what another great American, H.L. Mencken, defined as the haunting fear that someone somewhere may be happy. *Sex, Death And Punishment* relates how this attitude developed and took hold in Britain, how the good fight was fought and why it is not over.

The rise of syphilis – the finger of God (what, asked someone, must the rest of Him look like?) – gave the moralists their first big opportunity. As a hazard it immeasurably exceeded that of Aids today and its consequences were just as nasty. The lore that grew up around it and the treatments to which the unhappy sufferers were exposed were equally ridiculous. A quarter of a century after a cure (Salvarsan) became available, 'Zittman's Decoction', a valueless infusion of roots, first brewed in the sixteenth century, was, as Richard Davenport-Hines has discovered, still in use in the London Lock (that is, VD) Hospital. The danger of catching the disease was held to be related to the pleasure that the occasion afforded; this was because it was transmitted through the orgasm, as an effluvium of female passion. Thus 'the pox [was] fatal to most handsome men.' The first effective measure was 'a certain instrument called the Quondam (made of gut), which occasioned the debauching of a great number of Ladies of quality, and other young gentlewomen.'

With the Reformation came the first secular moves against forms of sexual deviance, including hanging for 'the abominable Vice of Buggery committed with mankind or beast'. But the law was, as ever, applied differently to the rich and the poor. Writing of Queen Elizabeth's courtiers, Donne wondered 'who loves whores, who boys and who goats'. (It needed the researches of Havelock

Ellis, some centuries on, to add ripe melons to the litany, and in our time, so one hears, there are also specialised tastes for acts involving vacuum cleaners.)

Near the end of the eighteenth century the Reverend Sydney Smith hit the nail on the head, as so often, when he described the dismal Society for the Reformation of Vice as 'a society for suppressing the vices of persons whose income does not exceed £500 per annum'. By this time illicit male brothels, or 'molly houses', were abundant in London, and in the public schools and universities the sin of Sodom was to become widely cultivated. W.T. Stead, writing in 1895, observed that 'should anyone found guilty of Oscar Wilde's crime be imprisoned, there would be a very surprising emigration from Eton, Harrow, Rugby and Winchester to the jails of Pentonville and Holloway.' The really unforgivable transgression, as Oscar Wilde discovered, was and remained homosexual miscegenation between classes.

Where in France the Code Napoléon had finally liberated homosexuals, established opinion in Britain became increasingly and ferociously homophobic. Davenport-Hines has unearthed a transfixing description by Beverly Nichols of what happened when as a boy he was discovered reading *The Picture of Dorian Gray*. In an ecstasy of incoherent rage, his father proceeded to spit repeatedly on the pages until his chin was covered with saliva; then he lifted the book to his mouth, and dismembered it with his teeth. When his innocent son bravely persisted in demanding what it was that Oscar Wilde had done, he received the answer written on a scrap of paper: *Illum crimen horribile*, Nichols *père* explained, *quod non nominandum est*.

Homosexuality then, like venereal disease, had become enmeshed in irrational terrors, but also in fears for the moral fibre of the nation, and of the threat to the virility that found its expression in military prowess. During the first world war it was put about that German homosexual agents were circulating in London, seeking to subvert and pervert the British soldiery – to infect the nation 'with Hunnish erotomania'. The Defence of the Realm Act was widened to make the transmission of venereal disease an offence. Nevertheless, a large proportion of the army (60 per cent, it was said, of soldiers in India had at some time been infected) had VD. Since they perceived this as a lesser evil than death in the trenches, it apparently became common for soldiers to infect themselves deliberately, and those with the disease got good returns by selling specimens of their discharges for the purpose.

The discovery of Salvarsan was by no means universally welcomed in Britain, and least of all by the medical establishment, for a cure meant escape from the consequences of sin in defiance of God's ordinance. Goodyear's rubber vulcanisation process posed an even greater menace. The misery and fear industry in the shape of commissions made up of gouty dinosaurs with permutable names, like Sir Weldon Dalrymple-Champneys, drawn from politics, the bench, the Church and the BMA, responded weightily. Virtue was equated by a curious perversion of logic with fear of ill-consequences. Without such restraint, promiscuity would reign and the family and hence society disintegrate.

These attitudes are with us still. A Lord Chancellor, only recently dead, opposed the Wolfenden recommendations on the grounds that a law which had held sway in England for 500 years could not be wrong. (The same argument could of course be better applied to the evergreen appeal of human vices.) Davenport-Hines has assembled a fine collection of piquant opinions, that echo like grunts from the primaeval swamp. Consider the following from a Roman Catholic priest: 'You can't be a homosexual if you're a civil engineer. Only actors and artists and people like that are homosexuals.'

Aids has woken sleeping demons; some of the least attractive facets of our society are once more on display. Davenport-Hines's research was inspired by his experience as a helper in an Aids hospice. He occasionally takes an uncomfortably lofty moral tone on such matters as the continuing inequality of women in our selectively permissive society; he takes for granted that homophobia can be nothing else than a reflection of Freudian self-loathing, refers without so much as a raised eyebrow to the 'revelations' of the fervid paediatricians of Cleveland, and his unremitting preference for Anglo Saxon monosyllables sometimes comes across like a shower of oaths. But he has assembled a treasure of fascinating material and writes with wit, style and insight, as well as bracing indignation. This book is a real corker; it will annoy all the right people, and, I vouch, give much pleasure to everyone else.

END OF THE PARTY DREAM

Simon Winchester
17 April 1990

It was a cold and cheerless spring afternoon in the gritty Shanghai tenement and Mr Li, a party cadre, was biting back the tears as his daughter interpreted the words he had just spoken.

'Though I hate to confess it,' she reported, unsteadily, 'I feel sure that after all I have seen, communism is now not an appropriate system for our country. But I must tell you frankly that it hurts to confess a failure, after so many years spent hoping for its success.'

For the past four decades, Li Jiangxie, a kindly-looking but prematurely stooped figure who recently became a grandfather, has laboured diligently for the good of the Communist Party of China.

He fought in the army, which he joined in 1938. He spent six years in indoctrination schools.

During the battle for the liberation of Nanjing, he soldiered alongside a man who was eventually promoted to the rank of marshal – and he thinks it was in part because of this that he has held, since shortly after joining the Party in 1948, the privileged position of a party cadre.

In his blue cloth cap and frayed blue suit, with the cadre's signature of a fake Parker pen in his breast pocket, he has been the imperturbable and unsmiling face of Communist orthodoxy in the most commonplace of surrounds, an East Shanghai cooking oil corporation. Five hundred workers have spent half a lifetime looking to him for guidance, listening to his teachings, and fearing his possible rebuke.

But now, speaking for the first time in his life to a Western visitor, he declares his disillusion and dismay with all that has gone before.

'I have been in the Party for too long to turn my back on it now,' he says. 'Great wrongs have been performed in its name. Three of my children are leaving China for ever – I wish my fourth was, too. I feel they cannot fulfil their potential here. There is no possibility of revolution in China – nothing like what happened in Romania could ever take place in this country. So I hope the youngsters will get out while they may.'

Mr Li – Jiangxie is the invented first name upon which he insisted for the interview – is about to turn 60, and will then retire from his cadre's post. His has not been, in material terms, a very rewarding position – though it was a comfortable sinecure during which he did little more than, as he put it, 'go in and read the *People's Daily* every morning' for the last 20 years.

He lives on the sixth floor of a crumbling block of flats, a building surrounded by piles of coal dust, broken bicycles, and, at this season, by mounds of rotting cabbages.

His own flat, just as clean as the perpetual whirlwind of coal dust allows, has two bedrooms, a living room and a kitchen. As a cadre he also has his own bathroom. He has a colour television, a washing machine and a large green refrigerator – the standard rewards of China's recent drive for modernisation. And over the years he has travelled on holiday – to Kunming, to Xian, to Suzhou.

On these trips he would occasionally see foreigners. This, however, was the first time he had met one. He shook my hand with an unusual firmness. 'I was a little afraid,' he said later. 'I was plucking up the courage.'

I first heard of him through his daughter, a friend of a friend. 'My father is very angry with the way matters have gone for China,' she said one day. 'He would like you to come to eat at our house. He wants to talk to you.'

Communist Party cadres, the supposedly intelligent elite from the Party's cells, essentially form the glue that holds the People's Republic together. Though they fall into many ranks, they can be described as performing four principal tasks: they are the low-level policy-makers, high priests of the Maoist religion, prescribers of doctrinal opiates, and spies. They rarely talk, except to each other. Even more rarely do they talk to outsiders. To do so would be regarded as the worst treachery.

But Mr Li, like many Shanghainese (or, as in his case, like many who have adopted Shanghai as home), is a feisty, dogged sort of man. 'I do not like being ordered around. I was brainwashed in those early days when I was young. I have sat back and watched for most of my life. Now I feel like speaking, telling you how disappointed I am.'

He was born in Shandong province, a little south of Beijing, the fifth son of a peasant family. His four brothers all died, starved to death as a result, he says, of the Kuomintang's policies of rapine and ruin. 'They stole all our crops. They burned our farm. It is not surprising, looking back on it, that I joined the Red Army. I was happy to oppose Chiang Kai-shek. He was an evil man.'

He admits he was no hero – his most senior post was as bodyguard to an officer who led the battle against Kuomintang forces in Nanjing. 'But I liked the army – the discipline, the dignity. I felt tremendously proud when I heard that Mao Zedong had declared the People's Republic.

'They told us the Party would do wonders for China. I believed it. It was an honest, proud belief. It was my dream too – that after all those years of war and infighting, here was an ideal that could change China for ever. My hero was Zhou Enlai – a good, sincere man. Not Mao – I never thought he was equipped to rule. He was too inflexible, too extreme. The Cultural Revolution proved that right.'

Mr Li, although a party cadre, was sent into the country during the Revolution. He worked on a farm, but was rehabilitated early, and resumed his work in Shanghai, relatively untroubled by the turmoil.

'It was afterwards that matters got so bad. Corruption was the terrible thing – everyone took money. I did not, I swear that to you. But my brother cadres did. And it was no good talking to the police here. They took money too. There was a standard price for a bribe – 2,000 yuan. That would buy you anything you wanted. Any problem could be solved.'

Corruption and nepotism were the spurs to the student rebellion that started in Shanghai three years ago. 'Frankly, I was in sympathy with them. Of course I could not say so. There was no point in arguing in the party meetings, because so many of my comrades wanted the system preserved. I kept quiet. Maybe I should not have done. But I couldn't have changed things. Tragedy was certain. We all knew that.'

The events of last June, the forceful suppression of the anti-corruption protests, did not surprise him. 'I was ashamed it was my own Red Army that did the work. I was saddened with the scale of it all. But most of all I was hurt, that all I had worked for, over so many years, was just thrown away.

'I used to have a dream for China – that one day this country that I love would be united, and happy, and free. Sometimes I cling on to this dream, and just say to myself that it will just take a little longer, or maybe even a lot longer. But mostly these days, and at the end of my career, I realise the dream has gone. That is when I know that everything for which I stood is wrong, that this system is not appropriate for China now. That is when I wish all my children to go away, to get out before they ruin their lives.

'What a dreadful disappointment it has been. What a waste.' He sat, his eyes downcast, staring at the table. His daughter did not speak. A siren wailed in the distance, and the wind rattled the shutters.

GETTING THE CREEPS

Maev Kennedy
23 April 1990

It paid to be boring in Suffolk at the weekend.

'Oh you're a pretty one,' enthused Dr Steve Hopkin,

'quite cute really, hold still.' And into the killing bottle went the millepede with the lovely orange stripe.

For anything with seven pairs of legs or more, it was a good time to be elsewhere. The massed forces of the Isopod and Mirapod Study Groups were scouring the countryside, no log unrolled, no stone unturned, no nettle patch unruffled. Within a stone's throw of the Thornham Field Study Centre they turned up 10 species of woodlice, several rare.

Their view of the world is singular.

At Sizewell the sun blazed, the nuclear power station hummed in the background, and Dr Hopkin, who co-ordinates the national woodlouse survey from Reading University, scowled at the clean sand and dry gravel, the green grass and the solitary bluebell cowering from the wind behind the boat huts.

'What we really need is for somebody to have dumped a lorry load of rubbish down the bank there. Ah, that's more hopeful!' He dived on an unsavoury newspaper anyone except a bluebottle would give a very wide berth. He turned up all seven common species of British woodlouse on the beach. *Halophiloscia*, only found in three places in the country, and not at all since 1977, got clean away once again.

'It is very exciting,' Charles Rawcliffe said firmly. 'It is the sublimation of the hunting instinct.'

Mr Rawcliffe, a retired customs officer from Edinburgh, is at 74 the acknowledged senior great white hunter. He scours a 723-square-mile patch of the Lothians, but made his great find in the glasshouse of the Royal Botanic Garden in Edinburgh. He posted two strange finds to Dr Hopkin, who sent them to Dr Ferraro in Florence, who said one had only been reported from Mauritius, and one appears to be new.

Dave Bilton, more of a water beetle man himself, returned to base camp disgusted over *Halophiloscia*, and planning to go back and dig traps. He had made the best find of the weekend, *Miktoniscus Patiencei*, but then he has form. His namesake scuttles through Asia: not, alas, called Dave, but *Armadilloniscus Biltoni*.

There were a few absent friends. The Isle of Wight woodlouse man was unavoidably detained at his work as a warder in Albany prison, and Dr Ionel Tabacaru was represented only by his magnificent prose.

As far as they know he is the only woodlouse man in Romania. Somehow, since 'la révolution du 22 décembre qui a renversé l'odieuse dictature communiste', as he put it, he received a copy of their newsletter, *Isopoda*.

He was appealing for more literature, but, as he delicately put it, 'malheuresement je n'ai pas une modalité de payer une contribution'.

The celebrated double act, Dr Paul Harding, director of the Biological Records Centre at Monkseaton, and Dr Steve Sutton of Leeds University, had explored the fauna of Hornbeam Wood.

'Very dull, actually,' said Dr Sutton.

'Brown, boring and hard to identify,' said Dr Harding.

There they met a man sitting on a treestump, worrying about the iridescent blue beetle which landed on him as he was doing the *Times* crossword.

Dr Sutton: 'He confused things by saying it walked on to him.' Dr Harding: 'But I asked the crucial question, did it jump off?'

Dr Sutton: 'It was a flea beetle.'

Dr Harding: 'You meet such interesting people woodlouse watching.'

Dr Sutton: 'But he wasn't one of them.'

Affection for their prey breaks through the scientific detachment of hardened hunters, except among the toughest, the centipede men. Wood-lice scuttle, millipedes release cyanide, but centipedes bite.

Of course, from the woodlouse point of view, the more they are admired the more likely they are to end up pickled in alcohol, but then that's so often true in life.

GALLIPOLI AND THE BLUE-RINSE TENDENCY

Ian Aitken
25 April 1990

When Thatcherite Conservatives celebrate British military victories there is always an underlying implication that the gallant participants were all card-carrying Tories.

The unspoken assumption is that Labourish sorts of people were skiving behind the lines, taking their orders from the TGWU or the NUM rather than the CIGS.

This slur has never had any foundation. The servicemen who beat Hitler were overwhelmingly pro-Labour, and astonished everyone by putting Clem Attlee into Downing Street. The soldiers who defeated the Kaiser later helped to create the very first Labour government.

Mind you, the regular army undeniably has a blue rinse, and its officers are probably Thatcherite to a man. But the idea that patriotism belongs exclusively to the Conservatives has always got up Labour noses.

Mrs Thatcher's tendency to wrap herself in the Union Jack, and to label trades unionists who don't share her view as 'the enemy within', has redoubled the feeling of insult.

Now Mrs Thatcher is on her way to the celebration, not of a British military victory, but of a thoroughgoing military fiasco created by her self-declared hero, Winston Churchill.

A lot of non-Tories died at Gallipoli, under the orders of upper-class ninnies. Yet unlike the annual ceremony at the Cenotaph, no one from the Opposition side of the Commons has been invited to participate.

One of Labour's two Old Etonians [and therefore a genuine gent] tried to rectify this yesterday. Tam Dalyell, one of whose ancestors founded the Royal Scots Greys while another was wounded at Gallipoli, raised the matter with the Speaker.

Mr Speaker Weatherill [late of the Bengal Lancers] sounded sympathetic to the idea that there should have been representation from Parliament as well as from HM Government. But as usual, he hadn't had any part in organising the ceremony.

So Mrs Thatcher, who wasn't even in the ATS during her war, will be Britain's sole representative at the Dardanelles today.

BRIDES

Simon Long
26 April 1990

She was nearly 30 when she was sold for the first time, last November. She was just widowed and had a baby daughter.

Like most Chinese brides, she had lived with her in-laws. But they had no use for her any more. For a struggling peasant household, she was another mouth to feed from not especially fertile land in China's north-central Hebei province.

So they decided to sell her. In a nearby village, they found a willing buyer. The parents of a 26-year-old despaired of his finding a wife by any other means. He was simple-minded, his speech slow, slurred and barely comprehensible, and he was treated as the village idiot.

She cost them 3,000 Renminbi (about £375). Her new husband was at least kind and gentle, but she missed her daughter, who had been retained by grandparents.

After two weeks, she ran away. All her husband's family – more than 100 of the 9,000 villagers – were mobilised to search for her. They failed. But a day later, she came back, unable to return to her home village without being detected and with nowhere else to go.

Her new parents ordered her to strip in their courtyard and prepared to beat her to teach her a lesson. Her husband stopped them, but they left her there, naked, for a whole wintry day.

The family decided to resell her. A local widower in his forties bought her for the same price. Again, after two weeks, she ran away, but this time, back to her first buyers. She promised she would never run away again, if they would only let her stay. But by this time, village mockery of the simpleton had become more remorseless because of his inability to keep his wife. His parents wanted no more of her. They gave the widower his money back and found a new buyer, taking a 500 Renminbi (£60) loss on the sale.

The trade in women is officially acknowledged as rampant in rural China. The abduction and sale of women and children figure in the list of 'Six Evils', the target of a nationwide campaign.

In December, the Communist Party's *People's Daily* reported that in one county in one province, Anhui, 25,000 women had been victims of abduction and sale. In January, police in the south-western province of Sichuan said they had freed 7,000 'slaves', mainly women bought as wives or servants.

Prices are often above 3,000 Renminbi. The woman I was told about was considered rather old. Many are in their teens, some 13 or 14.

Women have been seen and photographed in horse-box-like stalls at markets, dressed only in skimpy underwear, price tags round their necks. Some are kidnapped by organised gangs in the poorer western provinces.

For many men, it is cheaper to buy a bride than to pay a matchmaker and arrange a lavish wedding. For some parents, it makes economic sense to sell a daughter, rather than amass a dowry.

Farming in family plots has also intensified the traditional urge to produce sons, to carry on the family line and guarantee security in old age, which daughters, who go to their bridegroom's household, are not seen as providing.

Every week, the official media announce new arrests and executions in 'Six Evils' cases. But the problem is rooted deep in a society with a traditional disregard of women, and hard to eradicate when Communist Party control at the grass roots is weakened by corruption, unpopularity and a loss of ideological faith.

DUNKIRK SPIRITS

John Ezard
28 April 1990

As gently as if it was rescuing an exhausted man close to death, an RAF helicopter placed a wreath on the sea here yesterday in the middle of a circle formed by 72 of the little ships of Dunkirk.

The ships held a last watch as the flowers bobbed away. The 55-year-old London fire boat *Massey Shaw*, which saved 500 troops from the beaches, blew her water cannon in salute near two Thames barges, *Cabbie* and *Pudge*, which dominated the skyline. In file near them, a ceremonial escort of 86 modern yachts and warships stretched nearly two miles northwards along the horizon towards Belgium.

This epic ritual and pageant was followed by a fly-past and was watched in sunshine by tens of thousands of people on the one-time evacuation beaches. It was the climax of the biggest and most good-hearted commemoration and reunion held by the second world war generation since the conflict with Hitler ended 45 years ago.

The 50th anniversary of the Dunkirk evacuations, in which against all military predictions 700 little civilian ships helped save 338,000 troops, including the core of the British regular army, drew not only 5,000 Dunkirk veterans and their wives back to France for the Whit weekend, but many thousands of other second world war families.

Hotels for 30 miles around have been packed with grey-haired couples bringing Thermos flasks, English teabags and sometimes water purification tablets.

Churchill said that 'the legend of Dunkirk' would last

through all the annals of history. This weekend's turnout has shown that it is still at least vigorously alive in the heart.

It also demonstrated that the elderly British abroad are second only to German tourists in vigour of tongue and in the relentless speed with which they seize the last table in a café. 'Come and have a cup of tea,' a woman shouted to her husband as he mustered for a march-past and speeches in the town square yesterday morning. 'They'll only talk so you don't understand and go on talking for hours and hours.'

Also mustering to the music of cathedral carillons and tolling bells was David Milne, aged 75, after walking 262 miles from Lincoln for charity, and the oldest veteran, ex-RSM Alf Hunter, of Loughborough, aged 96, who fought in the 1914 – 18 war, too. 'No, I don't play football any more, but I box,' he said.

Nobody had trouble understanding the Dunkirk Veterans' Association's head, Lord Kaberry, when he gently broached the fact that the reunion would be one of the last of its kind; the veterans' average age is 75.

'Our time necessarily comes,' he said. But, he added, the events of the last year in Europe held out a real hope that the veterans' old dreams of brotherhood and peace might shine throughout the world. 'We shall hand on the torch we carry,' he said.

After marching past the town cenotaph and for a mile through its suburbs, the great throng moved by coach to reoccupy the beaches where – in the 7th century – St Eloi built a church among the sand grasses, calling it Dune-Kirk.

The order of service they used asked that during the singing of the last verse of 'Abide With Me' (*Shine through the gloom and point me to the skies*) the eyes of the congregation 'should be on the sea whence deliverance came'. At sea there was a splendour of little ships, in the sky a sudden flash of Spitfires and Red Arrows.

Then a group went to lay wreaths in Dunkirk Cemetery, where the gravestone of Pte D. R. Harris, of the Worcestershire Regiment, aged 21, killed 50 years ago yesterday, reads: '*Into the mosaic of victory, I lay a pattern piece, My only son, Into thy hands.*'

UNHAPPY OUTINGS

Christopher Reed
30 April 1990

The unlikely combination of America's most garish tabloids, the Establishment dailies, and militant homosexual activists are embroiled in a divisive debate over privacy. At issue is a campaign that could return homosexuals to the political offensive for the first time since the Aids outbreak.

The topic is 'outing', as in 'coming out of the closet'. In this case the clandestine homosexual does not emerge happily after finally relinquishing a guilty secret, but is dragged unwillingly into public scrutiny – by fellow homosexuals. Followed to a logical conclusion, supporters say public perception of who homosexuals are could be so altered by outing that homosexuality would lose its stigma.

So far results have been mixed. Homosexual secrecy has a long tradition, and the US gay press disagrees about forcing public figures into the open, while the tabloids gleefully exploit an unexpected bonus of gossip. The mainstream press tiptoes around naming names, while engaging in pompous and hypocritical ruminations about ethics and individual privacy.

Now the pace is quickening. The recent death of Malcolm Forbes, macho millionaire owner of *Forbes* magazine, led New York's gay periodical *OutWeek* to reveal, and mainstream papers to repeat, that the divorced father-of-five lived a gay lifestyle in his last years. His family declines to comment.

The most compelling case for enforced identification is the hypocrisy of a covert homosexual politician, judge, clergyman or other public figure, who opposes gays' interests while joining them off duty.

Hypocrisy in gay politics is counted as blocking funds for Aids, opposing recognition of gay domestic partners, obstructing reforms, or working in anti-gay environments. Allegedly gay hypocrites and the subjects of outing campaigns have been the married governor of an important industrial state; the former mayor of a major city; a Roman Catholic archbishop; a Wisconsin congressman; an influential, married north-western senator; a Washington leading conservative gay-basher; a multi-millionaire pop music entrepreneur; and a prominent showbusiness columnist.

In the cases of the governor and the senator, members of the activist gay group Act Up mounted public demonstrations outside their residences, naming them as closet homosexuals on placards or in shouted slogans. But the mainstream media self-censored this part of the proceedings in a country where libelling a public figure is almost impossible (unlike Britain, where lawsuits are only too probable). Also unlike Britain, US newspapers resist airing their squabbles. Much of the debate has therefore taken place in memos and office canteens rather than editorial pages. The *Washington Post*, *Chicago Tribune*, *New York Times*, *LA Times*, and *Time* magazine have all run news items on outing while avoiding specific names, often to reporters' resentment of what they feel is censorship of real events.

Time denounced outing's 'claims [to] an unjustifiable right to sacrifice the lives of others' yet mentioned the senator and the governor – obliquely, but closely enough for the cognoscenti to twig. This was a typical example of going both ways, for both names were revealed by reporter Rex Wockner, who runs a gay wire service from Chicago.

Now Mr Wockner has an ethical problem of his own. One of the most scurrilous tabloids, the *Globe*, has offered him $100 a week for a prior look for 'our info only' at his stories. As someone who believes in outing, but not for sensationalism, he is trying to decide what to do. Another hypocritical mainstream paper has been the *San Francisco Chronicle*, which assigned an openly gay reporter to an outing feature. Using his knowledge of gay media, the reporter brought the mainstream press a scoop on the on-off alleged lesbianism of Sonny and Cher's daughter Chastity Bono. Having enjoyed this titillation, the *Chronicle* then printed an anti-outing piece by Chicago's pungent columnist Mike Royko.

A *Chicago Tribune* news report on outing refused directly to name the governor, who is rather close to home. Reporters there ask how many demonstrators have to display his name on placards before the story is run: 200, 2,000 or 20,000? Management remains adamant.

While it is easy to understand the argument that clandestine gays attacking their own should forfeit their confidentiality, the case against apolitical celebrities is more difficult. Publicists who publicly deny their client's homosexuality argue privately that coming out would harm their career, particularly if a male romantic film actor was known as gay, for instance.

Others argue that Hollywood and the music business, for instance, are so inherently homophobic – though employing thousands of homosexuals – that it is a betrayal of the gay community to take their money while living a double life. US mainstream journalists, who take themselves very seriously, disagree. Now exclusively university-educated 'professionals', they reiterate journalism school's preoccupation with the ethics of the craft. But their weighty ponderings also enable them to maintain a double standard, say critics.

Michelangelo Signorile, a gossip columnist and leading outer on *OutWeek*, retorts: 'The people agonising about ethics and privacy are the same people who ran the Gary Hart and Donald Trump infidelity stories. They don't care about invading privacy. They just don't want to identify gays because it shows the strength of gay influence and enhances the movement towards acceptance.'

He adds that being dragged from the closet has not hurt those who experienced it, as gay congressman Barney Frank, tennis player Martina Navratilova and others demonstrate. In contrast, remaining closeted while widely suspected as gay can create a harmful vulnerability, as two US Olympic gold medallists discovered.

As the argument continues, the clearest point remains the least reported. If society were not so prejudiced against homosexuals, there would be no closets to be outed from, no resulting sensations – and no debate.

THE SALMAN FANTASY

Kathy Evans
7 May 1990

Salman Rushdie – or at least his cinematic death at the hands of the Almighty – is proving a box office success in Pakistan.

A new film portrays how a team of 'mojahedin' or holy warriors set out to kill him. *International Guerrillas*, as it is called, is packing them in, and promises to be the biggest success of its producers, Evernew Studios of Lahore.

The film crams in a lot of themes – corrupt policemen, Indian and Jewish conspiracies against Pakistan and the Muslim world, and the lascivious over-rich Arabs of the Gulf. But the big draw is the name Salman Rushdie.

The 3½-hour epic (a norm in the subcontinent) begins with the Holy Koran shrouded in reverent smoke and cuts to a scene of glasses laden with Chivas Regal whisky and the sound of champagne corks popping. A meeting of the worldwide Jewish conspiracy is in session. The head of the worldwide Jewish conspiracy, for some reason, sports, throughout the movie, a red plastic cowboy hat and a US cavalry jacket trimmed with epaulettes. He is constantly surrounded by over-plump Punjabi bimbos in tight red dresses.

According to the film, the British author is hidden on a lush island in the Philippines, protected by hundreds of security troops who look suspiciously like Israeli soldiers. He lives in a luxurious palace, drinking heavily and indulging in idle, anti-religious conversation.

But Mr Rushdie's other principal pastime is the torturing and execution of the numerous squads of Muslim guerrillas who turn up in vain attempts to kill the *Shatan*, or Devil of the written word.

Love interest is provided by the two great stars of Pakistani cinema – Barbara and Neeli. The latter plays an Islamic maiden who joins forces with the mojahedin to redeem her family's honour. Her fetching guerrilla outfits look anything but Islamic.

Divine intervention finally reaches Mr Rushdie in the form of lightning which strikes the author dead, blood running from his eyes and nose, and his body burning in flames; but not before his Jewish protectors convert to Islam, with a burst of song about the Beloved Prophet.

The producer of this Muslim blockbuster, Sajad Gul, says he aims to sell *International Guerrillas* round the Islamic world. Distribution rights are being negotiated with Britain, and he even hopes to get it shown on Channel Four, which is famous throughout the subcontinent for its Asian following.

'It will be very popular among Asians in Britain and the video version is about to be released in three months in both Urdu and Punjabi,' says Mr Gul.

He defends the film's anti-Jewish tone by saying the work is purely fiction. 'Mr Rushdie wrote a book about the Koran which is fiction. Why can't we make a film about him which is fiction?' he asks. He hedges the question as to whether he agrees Mr Rushdie should be killed. 'I think he should be killed spiritually because he played with our sentiments,' he says.

The more Islamic elements among the Pakistani press are now urging the Bhutto government not to tax the revenue made from the film.

But Afzal Ahmed, the actor who played Salman Rushdie, is worried. He says he sought guidance from the Almighty whilst on a pilgrimage to Mecca about whether he should take on the part and utter the curses against Islam the script required. He now finds that he, like Mr Rushdie, is receiving threats and is uneasy about leaving his house.

BLACK CHIC

Angella Johnson
9 May 1990

The white bus driver's eyes widened in astonishment as I boarded behind an elderly passenger and produced R1 (25p) for a five-minute journey into the centre of Pretoria. 'You can't ride on here,' he blustered. I asked why not. 'We don't carry your kind. You must get off,' he replied.

'I don't understand. Is this bus not going to the city centre?' I said, feigning ignorance of Pretoria's strict apartheid bylaw which prevents black and white people using the same buses.

He looked contemptuously at my fare on the till counter. 'This bus is for white people only. I can't carry you.' I held my ground. 'Do I have to *put* you off?' he said through clenched teeth, climbing out of his booth in a threatening manner.

My heart started pounding. It was the first of many occasions during my visit to South Africa when I was to experience blatant and aggressive racial prejudice for attempting to cross the barriers which still divide this colour-coded country.

'You can try,' I said, wrapping my arms around a metal handrail. The small group of mainly elderly and female passengers travelling at midday in South Africa's administrative capital shifted in their seats. Most looked embarrassed. No one spoke or met my eye, except a little girl who whispered excitedly to her mother and giggled.

It was if a time-warp had taken me back to America's deep South in the late '50s. So this was how Rosa Park must have felt when she refused to give up her seat to a white woman on that bus in Montgomery, Alabama, a small act of defiance that precipitated the Civil Rights Movement.

Apparently unsure of how to deal with the situation, the driver reluctantly took my fare. It was a modest victory. Last year a group of black men were arrested and beaten up when they boarded a similar bus during a campaign of defiance.

But my feeling of triumph was short-lived. On reaching the depot, surveyed by a statue of Paul Kruger, the first president of the Transvaal Republic, I was marched into the administrator's office. 'You know it is illegal to use these buses. They are not for your people. The law does not allow it,' said the fat, moustachioed Afrikaner sitting behind the desk, as if chiding a child. 'If you do it again you will be arrested. Use your own buses.'

About an hour later I found out how real his threat was when I boarded a double-decker bus packed with white office workers on their way to comfortable, segregated suburbs. The grey-haired driver refused to take my money, saying: 'You should know that your kind are not allowed on here.' He stormed off the bus in exasperation when I refused to leave, and within minutes the passengers had been transferred to another bus, leaving me as the sole occupant.

The police were called and I was prevented from getting off by a number of drivers who blocked the exit. One, his face twisted with hatred, threatened revenge: 'I know your face and we'll get you.' By this time a large, mainly white crowd had gathered to witness the spectacle of a black who had broken the rules.

'Welcome to South Africa,' said the policeman after he had charged me with illegally boarding a bus. A group of white youths cheered as I was bundled into the back of a yellow police van. At the police station I explained that I was a tourist and was unaware that South Africa had these laws. Again the system appeared unable to cope and I was released a couple of hours later.

Buses were desegregated only two months ago in Johannesburg, but Pretoria retains a law which maintains different vehicles for whites and non-whites. Such petty apartheid continues to thrive in conservative areas where local councils grimly cling to the crumbling relics of more than 40 years of white supremacy.

'Pretoria is the home of apartheid,' said Shadrack, a tall young black security guard who had begged me not to attempt my bus journey. 'Some things have opened up, but there are still places where we are not welcome.'

Most white South Africans agreed that Pretoria was the city where discrimination was still deeply embedded. Despite superficial changes, apartheid's fundamental social structures remain firmly intact. 'When you walk down the street, you still ask yourself whether you can walk into any restaurant,' said Sophia Masebo, a 27-year-old office worker who lives in Soweto with her parents, two sisters, and two brothers in three-room house.

It was surprisingly easy to lose sight of the various ways in which segregation is being unofficially maintained throughout the country. I soon accepted that some shop assistants would try to deal with white customers first, and that many restaurants would discreetly seat blacks in empty, dark corners so as not to spoil the ambience for the white clientele.

I learned to spot the bars, restaurants, and cafés where blacks were not welcome: invariably they had a little notice over the door, saying: 'Right of entrance reserved'. 'You can't sit there. All these tables are booked for a party at 2pm,' said the waitress as I and a friend entered the Krugersdorp branch of Mike's Kitchen, a national restaurant chain open to all races. The American-style, fast-food layout was only half full. Hurriedly we were ushered to a far corner. 'This is a much better place anyway. You can have a private conversation.'

I questioned whether in such a tiny town all the tables could be booked, and insisted on sitting near the centre with the other customers. She turned to my white male companion and said apologetically: 'Look, this is a CP [Conservative Party] town. If I put you with the other customers they will walk out. This is not personal, but I have to think about my business.' Our premature departure was greeted by applause.

Krugersdorp, 13 kilometres west of Johannesburg, is a small industrial town controlled by the CP. The poor black population from the nearby township of Munsieville shuffle along the drab streets, their heads bowed. 'There is an unofficial curfew for blacks here at nights,' said Anne, a white widow who runs a corner store. 'The CP wants to stop any integration. They are ruining my business because fewer black people seem to come into town these days, and they make sure they are out before dark.'

By the time I entered the estate agent's office, my outrage had dulled. 'I'm afraid I have nothing available for rent or sale,' said the little old lady. 'Why don't you try the Prudential?' I pointed to numerous property notices plastered on the wall and asked if they were unavailable because I was black. Her sun-wrinkled face took on a dull pinkish hue. 'Not at all. If we had anything, you could probably live there but you would have to get someone else to sign the papers.'

That is how many wealthy Asians, Coloureds, and blacks manage to live semi-illegally in whites-only suburbs. One Johannesburg agent offered to arrange for a white signatory if I was prepared to pay extra, but warned that the property would have to be in one of the few already mixed 'grey' areas. In trendy suburbs, like Hillbrow in Johannesburg, the colour bar has broken down over the years as whites moved out. Often the properties are overcrowded and badly maintained, but non-white tenants must pay extra for the privilege of living outside their settlements.

None of the subtle prejudices widespread in British society had prepared me for such insidiously entrenched racism. Even in liberal Johannesburg the sight of a black woman walking beside a white man is enough to make heads turn, and in most other towns it can cause consternation. When I complained to a white South African journalist that I had run a gauntlet of contemptuous stares by holding hands with a white man, he reminded me that just a few years ago that would have been tantamount to illegal sexual contact, punishable by a prison sentence. I almost welcomed the visual hostility.

There is no denying that South Africa has become a relatively freer country for many black people, at least in the cities. A black taxi driver told me: 'This is paradise compared to what was when we had to carry passes, and could only visit white areas to do domestic work.' He pays R250 a month – nearly twice as much as the average white person – for a studio flat in Hillbrow.

In Boksburg, a town notorious for banning black people from its lake and tennis courts, a silence fell over the bar of the Masonic Hotel as I entered. 'Your kind are not allowed in here,' said an outraged man big enough to play second row for the Springboks rugby team. When I retorted that I was a tourist, he got down from his stool and, towering over me, pointed his finger in my face: 'Don't get lippy with me, missy. We don't take kindly to kaffirs who answer back.' Tension rippled silently through the bar.

I waved my finger in his face, and demanded to see the manager. 'You better not fuck with him . . . he don't like kaffirs any more than I do,' he sneered. Eventually a portly pool player suggested, not unkindly, that I have my afternoon drink somewhere else.

When I related the incident to Beyers de Klerk, former mayor of Boksburg and leader of the local Conservative Party, he described the hotel as 'one of the white man's last drinking holes. The Supreme Court stopped us keeping blacks out of our lake and it's now being used by no one. Only three buildings in the town are now purely for whites.'

De Klerk, 48, believes in purity of the races. 'When you mix black and white blood you get nothing: just a brown no one, a Coloured with no culture and usually intellectually inferior. That's why I believe separatism is the only way forward.' He produced a well-thumbed Bible and read several passages from Deuteronomy and Matthew which, he said, bore out his claim that black people were inferior.

'I was a liberal until I began to study the scriptures and discovered that total segregation is holy in the eyes of the Lord. I'm not against the blacks, but they have a different set of standards. They are promiscuous, illiterate, and dirty. Democracy is not something they understand, and when this country gets black majority rule, as it is bound to within the next couple of years, we will lose our capitalist way of life.'

A bearded, florid-faced, pot-bellied millionaire property developer, de Klerk is proud of his Scottish, Irish, and Flemish ancestry. 'God basically made black and white people. Everyone else has bastardised through interbreeding. Even if my life depended on a blood transfusion from someone of a different race, I'd refuse it.'

It would be easy to dismiss this as the rambling of a mad man, but Beyers de Klerk claims to be representative of the 40 per cent of white South Africans who support the two right-wing parties, the CP and the paramilitary Afrikaner Weerstandsbeweging. The CP, the old National Party of the 1940s, believes in partition into industrialised, whites-only states linked to economically subservient black areas.

'Six months after this country gets a black president, I predict a white revolution which will be one hell of a bloodbath': de Klerk produced a handgun which, he said, he always carried.

At Utopia, a beautiful resort tucked between mountains at the end of a dirt road, Herman, the black gate attendant, refused to hand over the keys to my chalet. 'Have you made special arrangements?' So off we went to see the manager, who had accepted my booking the previous morning. 'You should have asked if we were multiracial,' she retorted when I insisted that she honour my booking. 'This is a private place . . . not even Indians are allowed in.'

Utopia, a popular get-away-from-it-all for white urban families, used to have a sign at its front gate which read, 'No dogs, no blacks, no motorcycles'. Herman said the words 'no blacks' were erased earlier this year but, while they now allowed dogs, black people were accepted only as domestic workers.

Most people accept that this kind of South Africa is dying and that black people are in the ascendant, and I came away optimistic that the tide of change is unstoppable. Large numbers of whites recognise that improvements for the blacks are the only way to maintain the country's first-world status.

Conditions were marginally better than I expected: in the cities especially, apartheid's demarcation lines have become less clearly defined. The different races can now use the same toilets, get married, and eat in the same places – even if it means sitting at opposite sites of a room – but they are still segregated by housing, education, and health care. It was difficult to accept that people of different colours continue to be prohibited from living in the same area. Some have circumvented the law, but only through the goodwill of white liberals.

That there is a growing Asian, Coloured, and black middle class is undeniable. Some of the homes in Soweto's affluent Diepcloof Extension would not look out of place in London suburbs like Hampstead and Highgate. But I found distressing levels of depression and deprivation among the majority of blacks. It is difficult to describe the choking stench from the sewage in the streets of the cramped squatter camps on the edge of many black townships.

So the country may be in a state of transition, but apartheid is alive and kicking and it will take time to push racism underground.

On my return to Britain, two English women were complaining about the toilet at Heathrow. 'It's like bleeding Bombay in there,' said one. 'You go in an' 'ave a look. A bloody little India.' I went to see for myself. Two Asian cleaning women, engrossed in conversation, were standing in a corner with their buckets and mops. The place was pristine.

IN GOD'S OWN KILLING FIELDS

Adam Sweeting
12 May 1990

It was dawn over the Australian outback, and the sun came up like a blood-orange bearing a grudge. Huge lizards twitched a nostril, anticipating breakfast. The trees resembled dinosaur bones jammed into the dust.

'We prefer the quiet life, just John and I,' opined Angela McShane. Meanwhile, her husband John – a slob in a bush hat and camouflage shirt – lumbered through the brush, busily assassinating horses with his hunting rifle. The animals left standing simply looked baffled, as well they might. Even the most paranoid equine could scarcely have foreseen sudden death at the hands of a couple of trigger-happy freaks, hundreds of miles from the nearest town.

This was the disturbing world of **Hunters** (Short Stories, C4). John and Angela, with their dog, crash around the neighbourhood in their battered truck, systematically denuding the landscape of horses, kangaroos and camels. I bet you didn't know they had camels in Australia. I bet they won't have soon.

The dead animals are immediately hacked into transportable portions before the heat gets to them, and auctioned off to a petfood company which boils, steams and minces them down into can-sized chunks. It's so hot out there that the raw meat soon starts to cook in the sun.

The sight of the McShanes' truck, fully loaded with wobbling hind- and forequarters with their dog perched nosily on top, was like one of Terry Gilliam's 'Monty Python' animations. John, disgruntled by the stinginess of the meat-processors, grumbled that to earn $150 a week each, he and Ange had to slaughter a ton and a half of horse, or the equivalent, daily (maybe eight animals).

Angela admitted she initially had some problems with the carving-up part, singling out the quivering of only-just-dead muscle as a source of particular difficulty (in the background, we saw her briskly slicing legs off at the knee while John cleaved backbones with his axe). But she's all right now. She and John can dismember a horse in 10 minutes. 'People eat, animals eat, it's life,' she warbled, in an accent like Meryl Streep's in the dingo-baby picture.

'What's the big problem? For goodness' sake, don't be a marshmallow.'

But there was more to Angela than met the eye. 'I have a lot of problems,' she confided at one point in her obsessive and rambling narrative. The problems were not specified (the layman might hazard a guess at psychological disintegration, brought on by isolation and marriage to a ruthless, sadistic maniac), but she thought the outback was the perfect place to, as it were, find oneself.

In a parallel dimension, she could have been a hippy frying her own brain-cells instead of committing 'roo-genocide, camel-carnage or horse-holocaust.

God's own earth is a source of continual wonder and target practice for Angela, as she explained. 'I *love* the earth and I see wonderful animals. They're lovely to eat, their meat is beautiful, easy to cook . . . '

The Flying Psychotherapist was long overdue.

GUMMER UNCOWED

Andrew Rawnsley
18 May 1990

In view of the beef scare and the growing public alarm about whether it is safe to consume anything produced by John Selwyn Gummer, this column's medical advisers have issued the following guidance about JSG, popularly known as Mad Gummer Disease.

1. An advanced symptom of Mad Gummer is force-feeding your four-year-old daughter with a hamburger in front of television cameras.

2. Watch also for eye-rolling, snorting, and stamping

when speaking from the despatch box, culminating in the breakdown of the nervous system.

3. Listen for the obsessive repetition of the phrases 'I keep nothing from the public. I tell the public the truth. British beef is entirely safe to eat.' The subject will appear foamy around the mouth.

4. Mad Gummer is accompanied with a fixation for quoting parts of the Bible and attacks on vegetarianism as 'wholly unnatural'. (In an attempt to make peace with the Commons' most senior vegetarian, Mr Speaker, yesterday, the Agriculture Secretary remarked: 'I eat vegetables myself with some pleasure' – which probably means, if John Gummer is eating them, that vegetables are now also quite unsafe.)

5. Other danger signs are the insistence that anybody who questions the Ministry's competence either 'invents conspiracies' (the Opposition), is 'alarmist' (the media), or 'seeks to spread scandal and fear' (any scientist who has the temerity to doubt the Ministry's view). These are all tell-tale signs of advanced spongy brain.

As far as one can tell, there is only a remote possibility of Mad Gummer being transmitted to humans. But there is worrying evidence that it can jump between different species on the Westminster food chain.

One of the junior agriculture ministers, David Maclean, is now thought to be badly infected. His aggressively supercilious rejection of any food safety fears as 'misleading and alarmist', and attacks on independent scientists as 'the so-called experts who pop up on the media', almost identically replicate the symptoms shown by the original carrier.

Most alarmingly, Mad Gummer now seems to be spreading to Tory backbenchers. MPs with farms or rural constituencies are particularly vulnerable. This backbench variant takes several forms.

In the relatively harmless Sir Hector Monro type, it manifests itself as offering thanks to the ministers for their 'outstanding efforts' in 'reassuring the British public that British beef is safe to eat'.

In the hideous Paul Marland form, it comes out in hectoring of any other view as 'outrageous and unsubstantiated claims' whipped up by 'a bogus professor and a dead cat'.

In the particularly tragic Roger King strain, it brings on outbursts like this: 'One of the things we are suffering from is an over-supply of experts on food quality peddling spurious science and inaccurate information.' (Another, far worse, thing is the over-supply of inexperts, like Mr King, peddling spurious and inaccurate rhetoric.)

There is worrying new evidence that Mad Backbencher can cross from the Tories into other political animals. For example, Geraint Howells – a previously normal Liberal Democrat – suddenly started foaming about scaremongerers.

Experts are now working on a test which will identify Mad MP at an early stage so that infected politicians can be put down with the minimum of suffering.

In the meantime, however tempting, do not take a single bite of John Selwyn Gummer. Too much bull.

WASP ATTACK

Alex Brummer
19 May 1990

There is a strong tendency within the liberal culture of the Anglo-Saxon nations to regard anti-Semitism as an alien phenomenon: a stain of Eastern Europe and even France but not of ourselves. Certainly, overt anti-Semitism of the cemetery desecration, goose-stepping and poster-daubing variety is comparatively rare and confined to those dubious minorities who inhabit the fringes of all societies. Yet there is abroad in Britain, the United States and, one is reliably informed, in Australia, an insidious manifestation of this disease closely associated with the stereotype of the Jewish financier.

In Britain, where we pride ourselves on tolerance, it is the white noise behind what the tabloids have dubbed the trial of the century: the case against the Guinness defendants. It was also an interesting and little-explored substratum in the House of Fraser affair, with the much-condemned Fayed brothers adopting an Egyptian phobia and an English upper-class snobbery against those disparagingly called the Israelites.

Across the Atlantic, a similar model has become common currency. The financiers at the core of the extravagant eighties are viewed as Jewish upstarts. The sons of delicatessen proprietors in Detroit, like Ivan Boesky, who were wrongly allowed to occupy territory traditionally available only to WASPS or descendants of the great German-Jewish banking dynasties: the Kuhns, Loebs, Schroders, Lazards and so on. These were Jews whose backgrounds have been so pasteurised by the reform strain of Judaism and long association with WASP houses that they became honorary members of the financial Establishment, if still excluded from the more rarefied golf and tennis clubs.

For much of the 1980s, being Jewish in Britain was highly fashionable. Mrs Thatcher's admiration for the virtues and skills of those with Semitic backgrounds is well known. Aside from her unusual alliance with the Chief Rabbi Lord Jakobovits, whose market views were more in keeping with her own than those of the Church of England, she blessed several Anglo-Jewish Conservatives with top office: Leon Brittan at the Home Office, Nigel Lawson at the Treasury and Lord Young at the Department of Trade. Many of these relationships were mixed blessings for all concerned. But few would dispute their profound contribution to the Thatcherite economic revolution – whatever its merits.

The openings to entrepreneurship offered by Thatcherism also provided new opportunities to Jewish financiers as doors in some boardrooms and City houses swung open. Many have thrived and are still there at the forefront of the free market – leading, for instance, the drive for privatisation from their seats in such pillars of the Establishment as auditors Price Waterhouse. Others, such as the Reichmann Brothers, developers of Canary Wharf, remain staunch in their ten-year conviction that Docklands, despite higher interest rates, can become the European business capital by the Thames. But, as with any large group of people with special skills in entrepreneurship, there will be those who overstep the bounds of propriety.

It has been noted in the Guinness affair that Ernest Saunders, the defendant at the centre of the alleged plot to rig the share price, is Jewish, as are many of those standing trial with him. But Mr Saunders personally has noted that his Jewish bloodlines were not imposed upon him until the scandal unravelled. Mr Saunders now finds himself in the dock with an array of Jewish businessmen, Gerald Ronson, Sir Jack Lyons and Anthony Parnes, and accepts that he must now consider himself Jewish because that is the way the Establishment views this trial. Never mind another group of defendants of differing ethnic background.

This is a transatlantic theme, too. Ivan Boesky and Michael Milken, the men who made and exploited the junk-bond, LBO, interest rate arbitrage and green mail detritus of the 1980s, have become the sacrificial lambs. But almost every house on Wall Street was willing to buy the debt they generated and willing to embrace the theories they espoused. It was corrupt Jewish influence in the heart of WASP financial territory which is to blame for the excesses. This theory has been put into hard covers and propagated across the US by the writer Michael M. Thomas, who perpetrates diatribes against a Jewish contagion in business under the cover of fiction.

Until recently Thomas had confined his views to the recherché columns of the *New York Observer*. But in his high-profile novel *Hanover Place* he brings them to a wider audience. Essentially, the novel is a fable of the 1980s. About half the 479 pages are devoted to extolling the virtues of the WASP lifestyle: the schools, the institutions, the clubs, the vacation homes in the Hamptons, the understated dress, the good taste and devotion to noble causes. This is the tale of Warringtons, a banking family more blue-blooded than Pierpont Morgan. Then, in the latter half of the 20th century, the Warringtons, in search of new talent, vision and profit opportunities, introduce a virus which plants the seeds of destruction. It is the dynasty of Morris Miles, Jewish son of the nether regions of New York.

The vehicle for exposing this evil is Miranda, first lady of the Crusade for Christian Capitalism and the estranged Warrington daughter. Her scatology is that of anti-semites through the ages. Miranda and her husband talking via Thomas's fiction: 'We'd be better off if Peter Stuyvesant had gone through with it and kicked the Jews out of New York . . . These Jewish guys have a chip on their shoulder as big as a baseball bat, so when they get an edge they like to whack the other guys around pretty good . . . If I point out that nine out of ten of those indicted of insider trading are Jewish, and that maybe there's a connection there, too, the world blows up in my face.'

There is no subtlety of language. It is the verbal equivalent of impaling fresh bodies in the graveyard. This is not happening in some remote corner of the Soviet Union in search of national identity, but in the heart of capitalism. It is an evil worthy of alert.

Hanover Place by Michael M. Thomas (Warner Books).

POLICE POWER

David Pallister
21 May 1990

On the night before he went public and dealt a crippling blow to the morale of the white-dominated South African police, Lieutenant Gregory Rockman struggled with a nightmare that had troubled him for years. Twice before he had nearly resigned. 'But I thought, no, better to do something constructive and to assist people against this brutal force,' he said.

The unrest last August in the townships around Cape Town, however, gave the Coloured police officer his first real experience of how ferocious his white colleagues could be.

' "What are you going to do?" I asked myself. "Are you going to leave it like this?" I said to myself: "If you want to call yourself a Christian you must speak out against injustice".'

And so it happened that the next day, when he was guarding a polling booth for the white elections, he collared a journalist and told him how a riot squad had laid into a group of black schoolchildren 'like a pack of wild dogs'.

The journalist could not believe his luck. 'Are you sure you want to say this?' he asked. 'You know you could lose your job.' Lieutenant Rockman replied: 'I don't care. This is my name, this is my number and this is where I am stationed. You say I gave you the story.'

Eight months later, the now plain Mr Rockman is the national president of the Police and Prisons Civil Rights Union, with a claimed membership of 5,000 black policemen and prison warders. More than 800 have been suspended and a further 60 dismissed for protests in support of the union.

He was suspended in November, shot at by another policeman in February, dismissed in March, several times arrested, and twice charged with attending an illegal gathering. 'But we shall not be intimidated,' he said in London during a three-week European tour to raise support for the union. 'We are serious in our demands and we want a peaceful solution.'

Mr Rockman calls himself a man of discipline, and with his wiry frame and soft, thoughtful voice, he exudes a sense of quiet authority.

He was born and brought up in a Coloured township in Port Elizabeth. His grandmother on his mother's side was white, the daughter of a train driver. 'Those were the real Afrikaners, and because of the Group Areas Act she had to make a decision. She became classified as Coloured and moved with her children to the township.'

In the anti-apartheid uprising of 1976, 17-year-old Gregory Rockman joined the school boycotts and dropped out of school early. It meant he was unable to fulfill his first choice of career as a teacher.

'One day, I saw an incident where a policeman went up

to six gangsters who were terrorising the neighbourhood. The policeman told them to leave, and I saw their politeness towards him. I said to myself, policemen have got power, and if I can be a policeman then I can be of use to society, to protect the people from these elements. A couple of months later I found myself applying to become a cop.

'When I made the application I realised that I was moving on to dangerous ground, wondering how the community was going to react. But I thought that we needed good policemen.

'When I got to [police] college, I found I was in a department full of racism. There was a standing order stating that any white policeman was superior to any black policeman, no matter what his rank. I found that strange. How can there be such a law? The lecturers could not explain.

'Nevertheless, I decided to continue and from the very beginning I was outspoken, protecting my colleagues' rights.'

Despite passing his three-year course in police administration with high marks, Mr Rockman had to press for promotion to sergeant and then warrant officer. In 1986, he became a lieutenant and moved with his wife into their first house. 'I went round the community and introduced myself. I said: "When I am off duty I am not a policeman. If you have a problem come to me. I want to be seen as a friend and neighbour," In that way I built up a very good relationship. If your attitude is correct towards other people you will get respect.'

His troubles started when he clashed with a number of insubordinate and rude white junior officers. When he reported them, he found himself the subject of an investigation.

'A brigadier from divisional headquarters came to see

me and said I was too politically inclined. "Are you still wanting to discipline white people?" he asked. I said: "To me discipline is discipline. It doesn't apply to colour." He didn't like what I said.'

Although the complaint against him was dismissed, Lieutenant Rockman was transferred to Mitchell Plains in Cape Town. There, under a Coloured colonel, he gained a reputation for effective community policing, defusing many clashes between rival gangs of youths.

His denunciation of his white colleagues caused a sensation, and amazingly, he was invited on to state television to repeat his allegations. Two white policemen were put on trial, but acquitted. Refusing to be silenced, Lieutenant Rockman was threatened in November with transfer to a remote posting.

By then he had become something of a black folk hero. 'One of the warders from Pollsmoor prison was sent to see me. They wanted to show I was not alone and that they felt the same as me. I invited some policemen working under me to my house and 13 of us, including eight prison warders, decided to form a union. The next day we launched it with 40 members in uniform at the meeting.' After the union's first protest meeting a week later in Mitchell Plains, he was arrested and suspended. The case comes up next month.

Since then, prison warders' strikes and union demonstrations in support of suspended members have continued in Johannesburg, Cape Town and East London. So far the union has attracted no white members, but Mr Rockman says he has had many sympathetic approaches from white former colleagues. 'The union has brought a split between those white policemen who want justice and those who want to collaborate with apartheid,' he says.

Last Tuesday, five prison warder members of the union, including three from the national executive, occupied part of the West German Embassy in Cape Town, in a protest timed to coincide with President F.W. de Klerk's tour of European countries including West Germany. The five were among 650 prison warders who were suspended without pay in March after they joined the union.

'That is a sign of our members' desperation,' Mr Rockman says. 'They are demanding that the government speak to us and recognise us. We want a non-racial police force based on merit and a non-racial democratic South Africa.'

Last night, on the eve of Mr de Klerk's visit to Bonn, the sit-in ended after it was reported that the Justice Minister, Kobie Coetzee, had agreed to reinstate the 650 suspended warders.

THE NICE MAN COMETH . . .

Jonathan Steele
28 May 1990

It was somewhere in a wheat field in the middle of Iowa that Nikita Khrushchev made his devastating promise. 'We will bury you,' he told his American hosts as they showed him the wonders of capital-intensive agriculture. The Soviet leader did not mean a military strike (although his remark, misunderstood by millions of televiewers, sparked off a boom in backyard nuclear shelters). He was talking about the imminent triumph of Soviet communism, which would sweep US capitalism aside by virtue of its superior performance.

President Gorbachev sets off today, 31 years later, on a tour of North America which could hardly be more different in tone and intention. He has been to the US twice before – for the 1987 Washington summit and his United Nations speech in December 1988 – but this will be the first time he will be able to see anything of how ordinary Americans live and work.

The contrast with the crises afflicting the Soviet consumer will be intense. Panic buying, crowds besieging shops, rationing by means of residence passports, tripling of prices – suddenly on the eve of his departure from Moscow everything has become worse. Soviet television coverage of his tour will be massive, and Gorbachev will use it to drum home to his people that things go better under market conditions. Nevertheless he cannot have wished for such an upsurge in the economic crisis just this week.

Add to that the Yeltsin problem, which will be nagging at him throughout the visit. If burly Boris manages to scrape into the Presidency of Russia with his programme of full sovereignty for the Soviet Union's largest republic, the challenge to Gorbachev will be immense. It is one thing for all other 14 republics to go independent or insist on turning the union into a confederation, but if Russia does the same Gorbachev will be isolated like some sort of Soviet Perez de Cuellar. The once mighty President will be reduced to a thankless conciliator without a national power base.

Even if these last-minute worries had not arisen, there would be no Khrushchevian bombast from Gorbachev. He comes as a man who has criticised the old Soviet system as fiercely as any Western Kremlinologist. He believes in interdependence, not international rivalry. He is trying to take ideology out of foreign relations. He has allowed his country's Eastern European empire to disappear more quickly and bloodlessly than the British, French or Americans disposed of theirs.

At home he seems to be taking his society towards a

market economy as fast as his conservative colleagues will allow him. He has the support of most of the Soviet media. Among the intelligentsia the fascination with the American Way is at a peak. Gorbachev is permitting the US a degree of intervention into his country's affairs which would have seemed inconceivable a few years ago, let alone in Khrushchev's time. During James Baker's visit to Moscow earlier this month US negotiators went over the draft of the new Soviet Emigration Bill literally line by line, to make sure it was liberal enough for the US Congress to give Moscow most-favoured-nation trade treatment. Washington, in essence, was writing Soviet law.

No wonder, then, that President Bush and other Western leaders have decided that Gorbachev's survival far outweighs the interests of Lithuania and the other Baltic republics. The only trouble is thought to be that he might go too far too fast and be overthrown by less radical forces. Here is where the Khrushchev parallel comes in. Unlike Khrushchev in almost every way, Gorbachev might suffer his ebullient predecessor's fate if he alienates too many of the constituencies which make up the traditional Soviet power structure. The debate among Western decision-makers is between those who want to pocket the stream of concessions and ask for more and those who feel it might be better to slow things down a wee bit, and even give something in return.

The key area is security policy, defence and the future of Europe. 'Giving' Gorbachev anything in the economic sphere would not help, since it is precisely here where conservatives' doubts lie. They already worry that he is moving too fast towards a market economy and taking advice and credit from the West. Security policy is another matter. The loss of Eastern Europe, the potential loss of the Baltics and the entry of a united Germany into Nato add up to a massive shift in the Soviet security posture.

Whatever his political views, any professional military man would need time to assess them. Add the logistical problem of relocating thousands of officers and men into new barracks inside the Soviet Union, and it is obvious why the high command wants to put a brake on the process.

Gorbachev can argue that the collapse of the Stalinist system in Eastern Europe is a benefit. It removes unreliable allies. It improves the Soviet Union's international image. It ends Moscow's subsidies to ailing economies, and provides a huge hard-currency dividend by allowing the Soviet Union to sell oil to Eastern Europe for dollars instead of roubles.

None of this is likely to be good enough for the military high command. They want evidence that the West is changing its own security policy to match or at least take account of the changes in the East. Some officers might be satisfied with a Nato review which produced a slimmer Western military machine in Central Europe: a reduced Bundeswehr, fewer US troops in Germany, a withdrawal of all tactical nuclear weapons. Others would prefer a more forward-looking shift towards a new European collective security system to replace Nato and the Warsaw Pact. At his joint press conference with President Mitterrand on Friday, Gorbachev made it clear that he is toughening his position against a united Germany joining Nato's military command.

Behind the Western debate over Gorbachev's survival, two new questions are emerging. Is Gorbachev such good news as he once seemed to be? Does anybody, whether it is Gorbachev or A.N. Othersky, any longer have the power to set the pattern in the ever-changing kaleidoscope which the Soviet Union has become? The good-news scenario has taken several knocks. Gorbachev's hardline reaction to the Baltic republics' striving for independence suddenly showed that he is not automatically a softie. Even at the risk of damaging his image in the West, he continues to reject conciliation, except on his own terms.

The reasons for his hard line are not hard to find. He is worried by the precedent which would be set if he allows republics to secede too easily. It is not that he is against independence on any terms, but he wants to be sure that negotiations with the various republics are done from a position of strength. He is worried about the dislocation which would come if Russian settlers were forced to return from all the outlying republics, particularly if they did so in a hurry as refugees. The flight of hundreds of Russians from Azerbaijan earlier this year was a disturbing omen.

Finally, there is genuine, humanitarian concern for what could happen in parts of the country if central rule is removed. All imperial powers like to see themselves as civilisers, bringing law, order and dispassionate justice. Russians are no different. The killing of Abkhazians in fiercely nationalistic Georgia last summer showed what can happen when the restraints of central rule are loosened. If Georgia became independent, and Soviet troops were withdrawn, how easy would it be to be an Abkhazian, or a South Ossetian?

However reasonable these arguments are, they do not justify Gorbachev's hard line with Lithuania. There are ways to control the process of the republic's departure from the Soviet Union other than by piling on the economic pressure. Gorbachev could have accepted Lithuania's wishes in principle and then opened negotiations to safeguard Soviet interests. The negotiations would take time, and they would be bound to be followed by a transition period during which the new economic relationships would take effect and Soviet forces would retain residual rights. Gorbachev chose otherwise.

His credentials as a progressive have also come under fire over his treatment of the Democratic Platform within the Communist Party. The Open Letter the Central Committee put out two months ago virtually forced many of the Platform's leaders to resign from the Party. In the Ukraine and Byelorussia it led to expulsions. If the Open Letter had been equally hard on conservative forces within the Party it would at least have had the merit of balance. Instead, it made Gorbachev seem anti-progressive. It also seemed political suicide.

If Gorbachev wants to diminish the conservatives' influence within the Party, he needs the Democratic Platform as allies. A strong contingent of delegates from the Democratic Platform at the party congress in July could be crucial in pushing through the reforms which Gorbachev says he wants. Why then alienate them? They agree with most of the goals he has set himself. As he put it recently: 'As political pluralism emerges, our Party must learn the art of parliamentary debates and election campaigns. It will have to form blocs with other parties, defend its views and do many other things. So there is nothing like a Berlin Wall between our platform and theirs. Anyway, the Berlin Wall has tumbled down.'

The Democratic Platform's main difference with Gorbachev is on its conception of the Party. It wants it to become a parliamentary Party, operating on an equal basis with other parties in a society where the civil service, the law-enforcement bodies and the army are 'de-ideologised' – i.e. removed from Communist political control. Gorbachev, by contrast, says he is still a Leninist. But can he really mean that if he believes in a multi-party system?

His reaction to the unprecedented May Day parade has not done him credit either. The fact that people carried slogans which are the everyday stuff of political marches in the West still seems to rankle. He has mentioned it several times in tones which suggest he has not yet realised what pluralism means. He called the marchers 'a rabble'. At a meeting with university rectors, he described the demonstration as 'political provocation, not a manifestation of dissent'. 'It was an attempt to infringe on Lenin, the Communist Party and on perestroika,' he went on. He called on the march's organisers to 'feel shame and responsibility in the face of their own people and dissociate themselves from the reactionary onslaught'.

Shortly after the march a group of deputies in the Supreme Soviet brought in a Bill giving harsh sentences to people who 'insult the President in public or slander him'. The punishment would be a fine of 3,000 roubles or two years in prison. Using the media for the same purpose would be dealt with more severely, a fine of 25,000 roubles or six years in prison. Fortunately, the Bill was substantially amended before being passed last week. The new version makes it clear that criticism of the President's policies is not an offence, and that insults are punishable only if expressed 'in an indecent way'. It is not certain that Gorbachev encouraged or supported the first version, although there must be a suspicion that he did. More is the pity.

Now Gorbachev has started on the most dangerous road yet. He is trying to move the country towards a 'regulated market economy' in which entrepreneurship and efficiency will be combined with social justice. Some Western nations may have got close to this ideal (although not by any means the entire undifferentiated 'West' which Russians in their ignorance go on about), but none has yet achieved perfection. Gorbachev is right to be cautious about rushing down the road too fast. Prime Minister Ryzhkov is right to try to cushion the blow of higher prices by means of income support. The worry is that his support system is not progressive. It will cushion the lowest-paid least. For a political group which says it wants to retain working-class support, this is an error.

It also looks unwise to keep so many large enterprises under central ministerial authority. To break the grip of the administrative apparatus and allow for grass-roots incentive, enterprises should be put under local control. A mixture of share-holding, with blocks of shares reserved for an enterprise's workers, for local soviets and for outsiders, would be a better solution than either keeping them under central control or opening them entirely to the free market. But Gorbachev has a real problem. Russia has no tradition of entrepreneurship. To give the green light to the market is no guarantee that efficiency will emerge overnight.

The evolving danger for Gorbachev is not that a palace coup with the support of the army will oust him from the Kremlin. It is that the country will gradually become ungovernable. The republics will move away. Rich regions, like the oilfields, will demand local sovereignty. Poor regions will call for hand-outs. Both groups will turn to strikes to get their way. Hunger marchers may converge on the warehouses, and consumers may become looters. Protesters may storm Communist Party buildings. The army may be involved in a series of increasingly brutal police actions to protect party authority in cities in the Russian heartland.

It sounds pessimistic, yet the increasing collapse of monolithic authority from the centre is not in itself a disaster. A functioning democracy is one with many power centres. Most Western societies manage to maintain a reasonable quality of life even when a high level of civil conflict continues in their midst, viz Ulster or the South Bronx. The Soviet Union is going to have to get used to a much greater degree of public disorder, riot and commotion than it has had for the last 30 years, but this does not spell doom. Perestroika has already gone too far for anyone in the Kremlin, whether an authoritarian or a progressive, to be able to stop the emergence of a multi-polar civil society.

The Great Facilitator has made all this possible, but those in the West who continue to place all their emphasis on Gorbachev's survival are misreading what is going on.

JOLLY GLOATING WEATHER

Joanna Coles
30 May 1990

It was a party for the privileged last night. The Queen, a fireworks display, and copious champagne from a veritable village of marquees across the famous playing fields.

Not bad for a school reunion. But then, this was Eton enjoying its 550th anniversary. Five thousand old boys, plus wives, had turned up.

The school, founded in 1440 by royal charter to teach the poor, has been immortalised by many former pupils, including Osbert Sitwell, who could never face going back, 'so much did it depress my spirits'.

For those who did return yesterday, it was a bit like an agricultural show without the animals and tractors. They found themselves herded into a selection of tents depending on the year they left, so that they could exchange after-school performances. If the car park was anything to go by, all were doing rather well.

So far, the school has educated 19 Prime Ministers and six Chancellors of the Exchequer. Its literary figures include Henry Fielding, Percy Bysshe Shelley, George Orwell, and Ian Fleming (expelled). Humphrey Lyttelton, the jazz musician, was also there and last night returned to provide entertainment.

In the supper tent, things were surprisingly subdued, perhaps because the champagne had run out by 8.15. 'There were hundreds of bottles,' the woman at the bar said. 'But this lot drink a lot.'

Supper, served in plastic boxes, might have been welcome on a flight from Gatwick to Marbella, but for those who had paid £62.50 for a ticket, it was no improvement on their school dinners.

Announcements over the public-address system urged people to leave as soon as they had finished eating. 'It's very important to leave the table so that things can be cleared up,' they boomed. With that the guests were herded to the river to await the Queen Mother and a procession of boats.

The braying began as the Queen Mother launched the new *Monarch*, the boat in which the most important boys row in the annual procession. As the boat wafted past, the cricket commentator Henry Blofeld (OE) reeled off statistics about the achievements of Etonians in the rowing world, accompanied by the school band.

A more laconic note had been struck earlier by the provost, Lord Charteris. Asked why the school was celebrating 550 years rather than 500, he said: 'Five hundred years of Eton came around during the war, when the fireworks were supplied by the opposition.'

Last nights fireworks were rather more spectacular than the rendering of the 'Eton Boating Song' which followed, because most of the old boys had forgotten the words.

And then it was back to the supper tent, converted into a dance floor, where an elderly Etonian remarked: 'There seem to be rather a lot of women here who look like Princess Michael.'

NO SEX PLEASE – WE'RE JUVENILE

James Wood
31 May 1990

A.A. Milne: His Life, by Ann Thwaite (Faber).

Four-fifths of this biography lies underwater, tempting but inaccessible, for this is a book in which the reader is invited only to paddle, not to dive. What is not said is far more interesting than what is, for Ann Thwaite offers just the top fifth of A.A. Milne's life, transparent and a little icy; the fifth which interests us least of course, because we can see through it, and because its iciness chills.

But Thwaite's approach may be the right one for a man similarly submerged, whose subaqueous secrecies rarely surfaced, a man who spent 70 years avoiding any kind of passionate involvement, let alone struggle, with love, sex, God or death. What we have here is a very English life, full of discretion and mildness, lived out at the close of a long summer of minor English art (1882–1956). A familiar life, with a familiar English dialectic: in which at an early age, passion is denied, and displaced into less threatening forms (sentimentality, adult childishness, nostalgia, lament) but emerges curiously strengthened by this displacement, ready to be put to new uses – in art (minor art), or in techniques of evasion, or in discreet living.

A.A. Milne's denial of passion (call it seriousness) appears to have come early in his life, for by the time he was reading maths at Cambridge in 1900, he already had what his biographer calls 'a dislike of being serious' that set him apart from his serious Cambridge acquaintances, men like Leonard Woolf and Lytton Strachey. However hard he strove to be a 'serious' writer (and the attraction of Thwaite's account is that the earnestness of this struggle is revealed) he would always be set apart from that Bloomsbury crowd. They went into the literary and philosophical thicket, and Milne went into Pooh's forest. Or as Pooh himself would say (someone Milne was fond of quoting): 'Some can and some can't, that's how it is.' Milne couldn't.

But he could write with delicacy, and sweet whimsy, and great charm, and *Punch* was publishing these effusions soon after he left Cambridge. The public loved his pieces, and he once said that he married his wife, Daphne, because when he first met her, she knew his writing and laughed at his jokes. It was the kind of marriage whose virtue lay in its permanence rather than in its passion. They shared little except emotional titbits. There were separate beds from the beginning (Daphne's suggestion), and in later years, small infidelities on both sides. One gathers this only by diving beneath the surface, for Ann Thwaite's commentary is discreet to the point of muteness.

Sentimentality really began for Milne in 1920, with the arrival of his son, Christopher Robin. Milne called him 'Billy Moon', and Christopher called his father 'Blue' (Daphne was 'Daff'). What was a weakness in his adult writing (he had written several plays by the time of Christopher's arrival) was a strength in his writing for children, and a strength in his fatherhood. He was a kind and loving father, who soon realised that paternity was inherently ridiculous, in that it called for an authority – or a pompousness – which he felt incapable of providing, without laughter and self-irony.

By the time the first Pooh book, *When We Were Very Young*, came out in 1924, Milne was already indulging in that familiar English retrospect, the elegiac lament – not merely in his poems for children, but in a remark that summarises an entire age. Looking back on Cambridge in that year, Milne wrote: 'Does any of that divine youth hang over us still? If it be so, let us thank Cambridge . . . for casting the spell on us.' An English retrospect: only a few years before, Rupert Brooke had lamented the end of his schooldays in similarly honeyed terms (not quoted by Thwaite): 'As I look back at five years there, I seem to see almost every hour golden and radiant . . . I could not, and cannot, hope for such divine happiness elsewhere.' Ah, divine youth! Honey still for tea, honey for the Bear – is there much to choose between them, except to say that if mere youth is 'divine', then childhood must be heavenly? And so it was for Milne, who once wrote that childhood is the only time when 'pure happiness' is possible.

The reader becomes weary of Milne for a variety of adult, no doubt foolishly adult, reasons. But they are worth listing anyway. Milne was painfully whimsical as a man. He sent letters declining lunch invitations in Pooh-verse ('I'd love to come to see you one day/ But cannot ever manage Sunday'); he had a foolish fondness for quoting Pooh's childish aphorisms in ordinary life, and referred to where he lived in Sussex as 'the Forest', a confusion of life and work which not only disturbed his son for many years, but reached its apotheosis in 1947, when Christopher's childhood toys (the originals for Pooh, Kanga and Piglet) went on a tour to America, and were mobbed – not so much a case of the man becoming his works, as of the man becoming his toys.

But all this is nothing beside the fraudulence of all

those who sentimentalise childhood (and this includes not only Milne, but all those determined to foist the Pooh stories on children who also find them whimsical and feeble). At the heart of this fraudulence is the notion of the lost Eden, the lost innocence of childhood. For there is, of course, no such thing as the innocence of childhood. Innocence, by definition, cannot be experienced, let alone enjoyed, while one is still innocent. It can only be relished after its expiry. So children cannot experience innocence – it is an adult construction, a retroactive projection. Hence the dishonesty of Milne's 'pure happiness'. To whom is this happiness 'pure'? Not to the child, of course, but to the jaded adult. And this nostalgia is not only a distortion of the real joys of childhood, but also a distortion of adulthood, because life's real unpleasantness (and Milne certainly experienced it, as a soldier in the first world war, and as an unhappily married man) is seen as not intrinsic to adult life, but always in relation to the bliss of childhood – not horrible in itself, but only as a diminishment from the earlier Eden. This is metaphysical dishonesty.

Milne's sentimentality is the kind that ruins lives, and one condemns it not for the pointless malice of pushing adult scalpels into childish flesh, but because this book shows the human penalties of such dishonesty. There is no joy for the reader, only the satisfaction that comes from inevitability, to witness Milne's sadness and emptiness as he gets older – a hollowness like Elgar's, another very English artist whose obsession with his lost childhood also crippled his adult life-impulses. Ann Thwaite's biography refuses to deal with these submerged dangers, and so becomes a cautionary tale in spite of itself. It deserves to be paddled in up to one's neck.

IN THE THICK OF IT

Stephen Cook
8 June 1990

Mick Agger pulls an orange life jacket over his head, climbs into one of the country's most unusual amphibious vehicles, and noses it down the ramp into a million gallons of soupy black sewage.

Waltzing and wallowing round the 100-yard-square lagoon, he flips the hydraulic levers of the 'sludge buggy' and the screw at the back churns the viscous mess into a bubbling maelstrom. The stench turns the stomach.

'I start in one corner and do about 12 circles,' shouts Mr Agger cheerfully above the roar of the engine. 'Then I move on and do another 12. Sometimes these great lumps come up from the bottom and float about.'

It's not everyone's idea of a rewarding job, but the matter-of-fact Mr Agger is used to it, even rather proud of it. 'We're contributing to the health of Leicester,' he says. 'What would the city do without a sewage works?'

The buggy, which evolved from vehicles used to cut reeds in canals and dykes, is designed to stir the sludge so that the thickest possible mixture goes off in tankers to be spread as fertiliser on farmers' fields.

Each of the four huge sludge lagoons needs stirring for 2½ hours four times a week, and Mr Agger is one of three men who take turns. He's a well-built man of 33, often mistaken for a farmer with his sun-bleached hair and nut-brown complexion.

He's worked for 13 years at Severn-Trent Water's huge Wanlip sewage plant by the river Soar just north of Leicester. 'Loads of people say, how can you do a job like that?' he says. 'But it doesn't bother me. Some of the lads keep it quiet, but I talk about it quite openly. You get people, especially contractors on the site, going around holding their nose, but there isn't much smell, really.

'I don't find stirring the lagoons too unpleasant, although sometimes there's a bit of gas comes up. When I first used the buggy the nose went right in and I thought, my God, it's not coming up.

'There are one or two jobs here, though, like cleaning the screens which take out the paper and plastic, where the smell sort of gets into your pores and seems to stick to your clothes. We have zip-up paper overalls, but the smell seems to go right through.

'I go into the kitchen at home and my wife Helen gets quite irate – I have to strip off outside and get straight into the bath. But the job's all right, you're out in the open, which is better than being stuck in some factory. It's a bit bleak in winter sometimes, that's all.'

Wanlip takes 25 million gallons of sewage a day, extracts five tons of paper, plastics and grit, pumps it into settlement tanks, then extracts methane to run its own electricity plant before the sludge goes into the lagoons. Eighteen hours after it arrives, the effluent flows into the Soar as clear water, heading for the river Trent.

Some of the more unusual arrivals at Wanlip have included ladders, 44-gallon barrels, road cones, wage packets, false teeth and eels. But on an ordinary day, the dark torrent in the 8ft-diameter main carries nothing exceptional, and the sight of it tends to stifle benign thoughts about humanity.

THE NIGHT THE WITCH-DOCTOR MADE ME MAGIC

Jocelyn Targett
25 June 1990

At the end of full time, with the score in the most important football match jammed at 0–0, a middle-aged man in a safari suit, whom I took to be quite mad, ran grinning and shouting into the bar where 30 or 40 of us were trying to watch Cameroon play Colombia.

He started jabbering nonsense at the top of his voice and the viewers joined in.

'Brrrrrrrr-Jah!' he bellowed. 'Oi!', the crowd replied. 'Brrrrrrrr-Jah!' he shouted, coiling up his body and springing out the sound. 'Oi!' the crowd replied, punching the air.

On noticing me, the madman threw his face into a contortion of amazement. He embraced me, closed his eyes and squeezed me, all the time flicking out odes in Ewondo, one of the 24 indigenous languages Cameroonians can swear and be sworn at in.

'You are a good omen,' he said. 'Wait here, I want to do something special with you.'

He ran out into the rain, his flip-flops flicking the dissolving red earth road up the back of his trousers. 'You have nothing to worry about,' I was told once he had gone and play in Naples resumed. 'He is only the witch-doctor.'

I had watched most of the first half in another little bar, but its down-valley transmitter packed up during the storm and we all had to run up the street to the nearest available television.

We didn't have to go far. In Cameroon there is on average only one television for every 500 people, but in

Nkondongo, a desperate slum of big-drinking football fanatics, every bar has to have one.

So far the game had passed with too little incident; we gasped at the Colombian near-misses, groaned at ours, and whenever he moved too much, snapped at the little boy sitting on a shelf holding the aerial.

Then, back came Apollinaire, the witch-doctor, brandishing a candle. Everything was about to change. 'To help break the deadlock,' he said, 'we need something out of the ordinary.'

I was it.

As instructed, I lit the candle with someone else's half-smoked cigarette. Apollinaire murmured a spell, then began grinning again. A cheer went up.

Then I had to follow him to the lorry park across the road and balance the candle on the rear of a defunct jalopy with go-faster rust down the side.

By the time we got back to the bar, Roger Milla, the hero centre forward, was just about to score a goal. When he did, we couldn't control our happiness; we jumped around all over the place, ran outside, inside, out and in again, yelled and hugged whoever came to hand. Even the aerial boy punched the air with his one redundant arm.

In my bar I was held solely responsible for the goal and was being mobbed as if I had actually scored it.

An eminent villa-dwelling lawyer had told me beforehand that I must watch the match with windows thrown open, so I could hear the roar of the city when Cameroon scored.

In Nkondongo, the advice was useless. First, no one who lives there owns any windows – they have just got the indoors and the outdoors. Besides, Nkondongo *was* the roar and we could hear nothing for the deafening sound of our own song.

When Milla robbed the Colombians for a second goal

minutes later, the witch-doctor came and grabbed my hand and took me back to where he was watching the match – with at least 60 others in the motor mechanics' pit of the Mobil garage across the road, a huge television balanced on top of a row of oil drums.

Here, fame of my magical properties preceded me. I was given a seat in pride of place, and several women gathered around for a chance to kiss me.

No one spent any energy worrying when Colombia pulled a goal back a little later. In fact, it went virtually unnoticed. In the pit, all manner of hollow metal objects were being bashed together. On the streets, cars blazed by, madly toot-toot-tooting. 'Brrrrrrrr-Jah!' shouted Apollinaire. 'Oi!' boomed the garage. No one even heard the final whistle. We just guessed, when the television started showing adverts, that it must have sounded.

We ran a few hundred yards to Nkondongo's favourite night out, the Radio Bar. The quick equatorial night started to fall and even before we could get the beers in it was disco-dark all over Yaoundé.

At the Radio, Cameroonian rhythms and trills were pumping out at hugest volume and families, lovers, friends, street sellers, policemen, taxi drivers and witch-doctors were jiving around getting very closely involved with each other.

A young woman I had never met before, her bottle of beer frothing on to me as she danced, gripped my left leg between hers and furiously jiggled her body up and down. I was beginning to feel quite flattered, when she broke off and danced the same way with an old lady, a child, and three other men. Meanwhile, I was getting shaken, rolled, pulsated, kneaded, beaten, primped and fricasséed by a never-ending supply of partners.

Apollinaire had been buying me pints of a mysterious green liquid he tried to pass off as the local Export 33 beer and it wasn't long before I was Brrrrrrrringing the house down with my ululations.

When Apollinaire, who turned out to be a prison officer, eventually insisted we go back to his place to 'struggle', I slipped away into the city centre. Here, as usual, an elderly woman was collecting discarded beer bottles in a bucket on her head so she could get the deposit back on them. She was doing good trade and, as she turned up the hill towards the distant beat of Nkondongo, she could expect to do even better.

GLAD TO BE GREY

Judy Rumbold
25 June 1990

Ivana Trump's hairdresser is the Stock, Aitken and Waterman of the Society Blonde set; he has perfected the art of producing large volumes of platinum from highly unpromising raw material.

For years her hair was teased into an intricate, lacquered sculpture of eked-out floss. But since being publicly humiliated by her husband and coming out of it smiling (as far as the chin tucks will allow) Ivana has seen to it that her hair cuts a less bimboid, more powerful silhouette.

Repackaged for her role as spurned wife-cum-media-darling, her hair pays homage to Donald's taste for thrusting high-risery and is piled up in a messy sort of beehive that says 'I may have surrendered half of my original features to the cosmetic surgeon's blade, but at least my hair stands proud.'

Trump and her contemporaries in what American *Vogue* has dubbed the Society Blonde Set – Lynn Wyatt, Pat Buckley, Nan Kempner – are women who have reached that certain age and status in life where Timotei-girl cornfield yellow or brassy-Ibiza blonde just won't do.

They have given up trying to compete with the hordes of significantly younger mistresses their husbands have acquired and instead surrender to the flattering effects of platinum – a cunningly contrived alchemist's cocktail of metallic tones that conveniently match their Am-Ex cards.

'Grey hair is nature's way of softening someone's hair to match their skin and eyes', says the John Frieda salon of London. But the social X-rays of Manhattan are not interested in nature. Accustomed as they are to artifice and fakery in all things, they wouldn't know natural if it sneaked up behind and administered colonic irrigation.

Instead, platinum is the thing. It adds softness to features, says Frieda, albeit features that look like they're wearing permanent peel-off face masks and have just walked headlong into a wall of Clingfilm.

Indeed, going platinum heralds a sort of arrival into the world of knee tucks, liposuction and divorce settlements. And let's face it, girls, when all a woman has to occupy her life is a mindless pastime such as arranging flowers or dabbling in interior decoration, she can either dream up some elaborate way of topping herself or decide to enter the social arena wholeheartedly and play the game.

The Society Blonde's hair must fly the flag of hope, even when all its natural instincts tell it to drop out, go grey or develop a weird streak of wiry white.

Gone are the days when a demure blue rinse or well-groomed shampoo and set symbolised dignified old age and moneyed elegance. In this country, coyly named shades like Green Envy, Tickled Pink and Saucy Beige have been exiled to gorblimey eel 'n pie land and people called Queenie.

But whereas the blue rinse was devised merely as a camouflage for the yellowing effects of gas cooking and nicotine, platinum is a deliberate statement. The brassy sculptured look in the US is, says Richard Burns at London's Michaeljohn salon, 'inbred. It's typical of tortured American fashion. Their hairdos always look too SOLID, too DONE.'

Since Mrs Thatcher underwent an image change: hung up the pussy bow, started having her press photographs shot through a pair of tights and lightened her hair, one would be forgiven for thinking she is considering a retirement as a Society Blonde. And Michael Heseltine too. But they haven't yet discovered the powerful allure of platinum.

Both fall into the trap of looking too pale. 'You have to be careful, when adding softness to the hair, of not getting into the beige syndrome,' says Richard Burns, 'otherwise you disappear – beige clothes, beige face and beige hair.'

Not much chance of Mrs Thatcher conveniently vanishing into the background. If it were possible to call a colour Dayglo Beige, she would epitomise it. Like the US Society Blondes, her hair isn't so much an intrinsic part of her body as a Tate Gallery installation-sized entity all on its own.

'Put it this way,' says Richard Burns, 'I couldn't imagine her with a neat little blow-dry. Her hair is solid, positive, immovable. It means business'.

So stubbornly inert is the Thatcher thatch that when she tripped up on a recent visit to China, the commentator's main concern was that she might 'break her hair'.

In this country there has been much talk about Silver Power lately, and by that I don't mean spurious New Agery or the market value of precious metal. Silver Power is an expression that highlights the uprising of women *d'un certain âge* against society's preoccupation with menstruation, contraception and childbirth.

Once free of the pressure to reproduce, women running on Silver Power experience a second wind: they go back to work, start a new career even, and generally get on with their own lives.

This seems an altogether more sensible arrangement than the lot of the Society Blonde. Anyone considering refuelling on Silver Power should avoid pulling up next to the wrong tank by mistake. Platinum Power can be both sociologically and environmentally hazardous.

NOTES ON THE CONTRIBUTORS

Ian Aitken
Born in Scotland in 1927, he specialised in logic and the philosophy of Kant during an MA at Oxford University. He joined the political staff of *The Guardian* in 1964 and was political editor from 1975 until recently, when he became political columnist.

Nancy Banks-Smith
She has been television critic of *The Guardian* since 1969.

Dennis Barker
After an interrupted education during wartime evacuation and 16 years' work on regional newspapers, he joined *The Guardian* in 1963 as Midlands correspondent. Since 1967 he has been the newspaper's people profilist. He is the author of three novels and six non-fiction books.

David Beresford
He was born in 1947 and joined *The Guardian* as home reporter after writing for several South African newspapers. He is now Johannesburg correspondent, and is the author of *Ten Men Dead* (1987), an account of the 1981 Irish hunger strike.

Ian Black
He joined *The Guardian* in 1980, with an MA from Cambridge University and a PhD from the London School of Economics. After sub-editing on the foreign desk, he became home news reporter and is now Jerusalem correspondent. He recently won the Lawrence Stern Award.

Owen Bowcott
Born in Bristol in 1957, he worked for BBC TV's current affairs and for the *Daily Telegraph* before becoming a general reporter for *The Guardian* in 1988. He is a co-author of *Beating the System* (1990).

Derek Brown
Born in 1947, he had a sparse education and a succession of jobs including: bus conductor, chip fryer and, briefly, assistant stage manager at a local theatre. He was a reporter for the *Southport Visiter* befor joining *The Guardian* in 1970, first as district reporter in Leeds and then as Norther Ireland correspondent, assistant news editor, general feature writer and Brussels correspondent. Since 1987 he has been Delhi correspondent.

Paul Brown
He trained as a journalist with a range of weekly and daily papers, and won the Investigative Reporter Award on the *Birmingham Post* in 1974. He moved from the *Sun* to *The Guardian* in 1982 and has been the newspaper's environment correspondent since 1989.

Angela Carter
She was born in 1940 and now lives in South London. A writer, her most recent novel is *Nights at the Circus*.

John Carvel
He was born in 1947 and holds a degree from Oxford University. He joined *The Guardian* in 1973, since when he has been business reporter, financial news editor, deputy features editor, chief political correspondent and home affairs editor. He is the author of *Citizen Ken*.

Helen Chappell
Born in 1955 and brought up in Singapore, she graduated from Cambridge University in 1980 with an MA in Social and Political Sciences. She became a staff writer at *New Society* and a book critic on *Company*, winning the Catherine Pakenham award in 1981. From 1987 until 1989 she was Third Person columnist on *The Guardian*. She is now a freelance journalist.

Desmond Christy
Born in Cardiff in 1953, he trained as a reporter on the *Chronicle and Echo* in Northampton. He later joined *The Guardian* as a

features sub-editor, was deputy arts editor for two years and now works for *Guardian Europe*.

Erlend Clouston
After an MA at Aberdeen University in 1970, he was a reporter with the *People's Journal*, the *Sunday Post* and the *Liverpool Daily Post*. He became a sub-editor on *The Guardian* in 1979 and since 1988 has contributed on Northern issues.

Joanna Coles
She studied at the University of East Anglia and wrote for the *Spectator* and the *Daily Telegraph* before joining *The Guardian*, where she is now a news and features writer.

Stephen Cook
Born in Leeds in 1949, he worked for the *Telegraph and Argus* in Bradford and BBC External Services before joining *The Guardian* in 1978. He wrote the Guardian Diary from 1985-88 and is the author of *Upperdown* (1984) and *Empire Born* (1986).

Nick Dallman
He was born in Hungary in 1924 and briefly studied economics at Budapest University. He left in 1945 as, in the battle between the advancing Russians and retreating Germans, the lecture halls lost their roof and students had to take their notes in cascading rain. Instead he joined a newspaper whose roof was intact. But for him the roof fell in all the same when he was arrested by the secret police in 1947, accused of conspiracy. He left Hungary the following year, leaving behind a half-completed film script which is probably still gathering dust in some police archive. He finished his studies at London University, worked for the *Sheffield Telegraph* and joined the then *Manchester Guardian* in 1959.

Matthew Engel
Born in 1951, he was a reporter with regional newspapers and then a Reuters correspondent. He joined *The Guardian* in 1979, was cricket correspondent from 1982-7 and is now feature writer and sports columnist. He is the editor of *The Guardian Book of Cricket* and of *Sportspages Almanac*.

James Erlichman
He was born in the US and was educated at Brown and Cambridge Universities. He worked as a Fleet Street reporter from 1976-79

when he joined the financial staff of *The Guardian*. Since 1986 he has been the consumer affairs correspondent. He is author of *Gluttons for Punishment* and won the Caroline Walker Trust Award in 1989.

Richard Eyre
He is director of the National Theatre.

John Ezard
Born in 1939, he was chief reporter with the *West Essex Gazette* and feature writer with the *Oxford Mail* before joining *The Guardian* in 1967, since which he has been an education writer and, since 1985, special writer.

Duncan Fallowell
He was born in 1948 and holds a degree from Oxford University. His books include *Drug Tales* (1979), *April Ashley's Odyssey* (1982) and *Satyrday* (1986).

Richard Gott
After gaining a degree in Modern History from Oxford he became a *Guardian* leader writer in 1965. In 1966 he fought the Hull North by-election as independent anti-Vietnam war candidate. He became *The Guardian's* Foreign News Editor in 1978 then Features Writer in 1979 untill 1989. He is currently Assistant Editor.

Walter Gratzer
He was born in Poland in 1932 and holds degrees from Oxford University and the National Institute for Medical Research. After a research fellowship at Harvard University he became lecturer in biophysics at London University. He is now on the staff of the Medical Research Council's Cell Biophysics Unit. He is a consulting editor and contributor to *Nature* and other scientific journals.

Angella Johnson
Born in Jamaica, she has also written for the *Bristol Evening Post*, the *Slough Observer*, the *Times* and the *London Evening News*.

Frank Keating
Born in Hereford in 1937, he became a local reporter for a succession of provincial newspapers. He jointed *The Guardian* as sub-editor in 1962. In 1964 he became a producer for ITV. He has written on sport for *The Guardian* since 1972, winning the 'Sports

Writer of the Year' award a number of times. He is the author of seven books.

Maev Kennedy
Born in Dublin in 1954, she studied at University College, Dublin. She reported for the Irish Times from 1975, was a parliamentary sketch writer from 1983-86 and has been a reporter for *The Guardian* since 1987.

Martin Kettle
He holds an MA from Oxford University and worked as a research officer for the National Council for Civil Liberties, *New Society* and the *Sunday Times* before joining *The Guardian* in 1984, as leader writer. He is now the editor of *Guardian Europe*. As well as being a regular columnist in *Marxism Today* and *New Statesman and Society*, he is author of *Policing the Police* (1980) and (with Lucy Hodges) *Uprising* (1982).

Christina Koning
Born in Borneo in 1954, she holds an MA in English from Cambridge University, studied fine art at Newcastle College of Art and worked for a PhD thesis on Wyndham Lewis at the University of Edinburgh. She has reviewed fiction for *The Guardian* since 1988 and is currently writing a novel.

Peter Lennon
He was born in Dublin and reported for the *Irish Times* before joining *The Guardian* in Paris in 1960. Between 1970-89 he wrote for the *Sunday Times* and then for *The Listener*. He is now a feature writer for *The Guardian* and has had short stories published in the *New Yorker* and *Atlantic Monthly*.

Simon Long
He was born in 1955 and was educated at Cambridge University (Oriental Studies) and Nanjing University. He worked for a merchant bank before joining the BBC World Service in 1986 as a commentator on the Far East, then moved to Beijing in 1989 as correspondent for *The Guardian*, the BBC World Service and the *Sunday Correspondent*. He is author of *Taiwan: China's Last Frontier* (1990).

John McVicar
He was born in 1940 and in 1969 was imprisoned for nine years.

Since his release he has worked as a writer and commentator, and has obtained a degree in sociology.

Seumas Milne
He holds a degree from Oxford University in PPE and an MSc in economics from London University. After working as an economist he joined *The Guardian* in 1984 and is now the labour correspondent. He is co-author of *Beyond the Casino Economy* (1989).

John Montague
He is professor of English Literature at the University of Cork.

Jeremy Morgan
He was born in 1950 and studied at London University. He entered journalism in 1973 and for ten years wrote mainly about industry, the oil industry and the Middle East. Since 1982 he has been a correspondent from Argentina for *The Guardian* and other publications.

Michael Morris
He was born in Lancashire and has been a reporter with the *Southport Visiter*, the *Southport Guardian*, the *Newcastle Evening Chronicle* and the *Manchester Evening Chronicle*. He joined *The Guardian* as a reporter in 1963.

Mike Oldfield
Born in 1950, he worked for the *Daily Mail* and *Melody Maker*, later becoming its editor. He is the author of *Dire Straits* (1984) and *Born in the UK* (1988) and since 1984 has been a freelance writer.

David Pallister
He was born in 1945 and trained with Thomson Newspapers. He has been a reporter with *The Guardian* since 1974 and is co-author of *South Africa Inc: the Oppenheimer Empire* (1987).

Melanie Phillips
With a BA from Oxford University, she joined *The Guardian* in 1977 as social services correspondent. She later was leader writer and news editor and is now policy editor and editor of Guardian Society and Environment Guardian. She is author of the play, *Traitors* (performed 1986).

Hella Pick

She was born in Vienna and studied economics at the London School of Economics. After being assistant editor of *West Africa*, she joined *The Guardian* in 1961, for which she has been correspondent for the UN, Europe, Washington DC and East Europe. She is now diplomatic editor.

Andrew Rawnsley

Born in the Virgin Islands in 1962, he holds an MA in history from Cambridge University. After working for the BBC he became a reporter on *The Guardian*, where he is now parliamentary sketch writer. He won the Young Journalist of the Year Award in 1988 and is presenter of Channel 4's *A Week in Politics*.

Christopher Reed

He was born in 1938 and trained in provincial journalism. He lived in Japan from 1969-73 where he wrote for newspapers including the *Sunday Times*. He joined *The Guardian* in 1974 as a stringer from Portugal and in 1977 moved to California, since when he has been California correspondent for *The Guardian* and other publications.

John Rettie

Ater a degree in modern languages from Cambridge University he worked for a range of publications and the BBC as correspondent from Moscow, Mexico and Latin America. He joined *The Guardian* in 1981 and is now Moscow correspondent.

Jan Rocha

After a degree in social studies from Edinburgh University, she worked as a volunteer in the Amazon, as a case worker for a spastics society, in work camps in Greece and on a kibbutz in Israel before becoming a freelance writer in South America. She has been Brazilian correspondent for *The Guardian* since 1984.

Judy Rumbold

Born in 1960, she holds a BA from St Martin's School of Art. She worked as fashion editor and writer for *Company* magazine and the *Sunday Times Magazine* beore she joined *The Guardian* in 1987 as style page editor.

Michael Simmons

With a degree in Russian and German from Manchester University, he wrote for the *Financial Times* before becoming the first editor of

The Guardian Third World Review and is now East Europe correspondent. He is author of *Berlin, the Dispossessed City* (1988) and *The Unloved Country: a profile of the GDR* (1989) and has just completed a biography of Vaclav Havel.

Helena Smith
After a BA from London University in modern Greek and philosophy, she became a reporter for Associated Press in Athens and contributor to various publications and radio networks. Since 1989 she has been Greece correspondent for *The Guardian*.

Jonathan Steele
He was educated at Cambridge and Yale Universities and joined *The Guardian* in 1965. He has been the newspaper's East Europe correspondent, Washington correspondent and chief foreign correspondent and is now Moscow correspondent.

Tom Sutcliffe
After a BA from Oxford he trained and sang as a countertenor for several years before joining *The Guardian* as a sub-editor. He was deputy arts editor from 1977-85.

Adam Sweeting
After two degrees from York University and various writing posts, including features editor at *Melody Maker*, he joined *The Guardian* where he is currently rock critic. He is the author of *Simple Minds* (1988).

Jocelyn Targett
Born in 1965, she won The Guardian Student Media Award in 1987. She graduated from Cambridge University in 1988 and joined *The Guardian* feature department. She was voted Journalist of the Year at the British Press Awards and is now deputy editor of *The Weekend Guardian*.

Simon Tisdall
After an education at Cambridge University and writing for regional newspapers, he joined *The Guardian* foreign desk in 1979. He was later deputy foreign editor and acting foreign editor and is now Washington correspondent.

John Vidal
He was born in Ghana and educated at Birmingham University. He

won the NUJ Design Awards in 1982 and 1983 and joined The Guardian as features sub-editor in 1984. He has been the deputy editor of the environment pages since 1989.

Ed Vulliamy
He was born in 1954 and holds a degree in philosophy from Oxford University. He was a researcher on World in Action from 1979 until 1986, winning the Royal TV Society prize for current affairs in 1985. He joined *The Guardian* in 1986 and is currently Rome correspondent.

Simon Winchester
Ater a geology degree from Oxford University he spent a year in Africa looking for copper before joining first the *Newcastle Journal* and, in 1970, *The Guardian*. He has been *The Guardian* correspondent in Northern Ireland, Washington DC and South East Asia and, after some years with other newspapers, rejoined *The Guardian* as Pacific Region correspondent, his current post. He is author of eight books, the latest of which are *Outposts* (1985), *Korea – A Walk through the Land of Miracles* (1988) and *Pacifica – The Emergence of a New World Culture* (1990).

James Wood
He holds a degree in English from Cambridge University and has been a book reviewer since 1988. He was winner of the Student Journalist of the Year Award in 1987 and also contributes to the *Times Literary Supplement*, the *London Review of Books* and the *Sunday Correspondent*.

Martin Woollacott
He was born in 1939 and after a degree from Oxford University and working for local papers he joined *The Guardian*. He was the newspaper's correspondent in Asia, covering the Vietnam war and the Indian emergency, and then from the Middle East covered the Iranian revolution and the Israeli invasion of Lebanon. He was the foreign editor from 1983-89 and is now an assistant editor while travelling.

Hugo Young
He was born in 1938 and holds degrees from Oxford and Princeton Universities. He worked for the *Sunday Times* from 1965-84 and since 1984 has been political columnist for *The Guardian*. He is chairman of the Scott Trust and author of *The Crossman Affair* (1974) and *One of Us* (1989), a biography of Margaret Thatcher.

INDEX

The Bookstall
in Ambleside
West Vancouver, B.C